KW-051-199

ALL HEAL

A Medical and Social
Miscellany

ALL HEAL

A Medical and Social Miscellany

A collection of Lectures
of interest to the general reader
given at
The Royal Society of Medicine

PUBLISHED FOR
The Royal Society of Medicine
BY
William Heinemann Medical Books Ltd

First Published 1971

© The Royal Society of Medicine 1971

ISBN 0 433 28500 1

Printed in Great Britain by
Alden & Mowbray Ltd at the Alden Press, Oxford

Contents

v

Foreword

This volume contains a selection of the articles of more general interest that have appeared in The Proceedings of the Royal Society of Medicine in recent years. In making the selection we the Honorary Editors of the Royal Society of Medicine have been guided by our wish to make as wide a choice as possible and one, moreover, of particular interest to the general rather than the specialist reader. We have confined ourselves to papers published since 1957 and have chosen no more than one paper from any individual author. As we made these choices it was clear that a number of other possible choices had to be excluded, either because of one of our criteria or for reasons of space. If, therefore, as we hope, this volume is well received, there is ample material available for it to be followed by a further similar selection.

September 1971

R. M. SHAW
R. A. BOWEN
G. E. PAGET

(*Honorary Editors of the Royal Society of Medicine*)

The Analysis of the Nervous System

THE RT HON. LORD ADRIAN

OM, FRS, MD, FRCP

27 November 1957

Charles Scott Sherrington was born one hundred years ago and we meet tonight to honour his achievements by a commemorative lecture—the first of an annual or biennial series. I shall not try to express both the pride and the apprehension which I feel as the first of the long line of Sherrington lecturers who will exhibit some aspect of him to posterity. The picture that will be drawn of him may become more stereotyped and legendary as one generation of lecturers succeeds another and in the end there may be no more than a faint outline in black and white. For many of us here the picture is still full of colour and lively detail. No doubt much of it would dissolve if we tried to set it down; and our pictures would not all agree, their colours and outlines have been distorted already by our own prejudices. But at least it is our good fortune to have more than a legend to turn to: we can speak of a friend, not merely of an eminent figure in the scientific Pantheon. We must do what we can therefore to ensure that the legend does not leave out what should be remembered. It must do justice to the inspiration which Sherrington gave to Neurology. We are entitled to speak of it, for we were the younger generation who should have sat at his feet, if he had ever been willing to admit his seniority. Though we cannot go back to the period when his work took shape we have warm memories of the scientist we commemorate and of the way he lived when his work was in full swing.

He lived so long that I for one can claim to have known him for thirty years and to have known of his work for forty, although he had become a professor fifteen years before I became a medical student. He aged so little and seemed so much our contemporary that he would startle us at times by describing some episode which called up a picture of Victorian London with horse-drawn traffic and portly gentlemen with beards and top hats. One such occasion will be remembered by those members of the Physiological Society who were at a wartime meeting in Cambridge in 1940, for after the dinner at Trinity we asked him to speak to us about the meetings he had attended as a young man in the 'eighties. It is a pity that we had no tape recorder handy to take down his talk, but we can console ourselves by reading the letter, published in *Nature*, in which he described an emergency journey with the first samples of Diphtheria Antitoxin prepared in England to the bedside of a small boy at Lewes. It was in 1893 or 1894 when he was Superintendent of The Brown Institution in London. There is no time to quote it all, though I should have liked to do so, for it is a good example of the vivid word painting which illuminates his prose and his verse.

Dr. Fawssett of Lewes was waiting in a dog-cart at the station. I joined him carrying my awkward package of flasks. &c. He said nothing as I packed them in, but when I had climbed up beside him, he looked down, and said 'You can do what you like with the boy. He will not be alive at tea time'. We drove out to the old house; a bright, frosty morning. Tragedy was over the place, the servants scared and silent. The boy was very weak: breathing with difficulty; he did not seem to know me. Fawssett and I injected the serum. The syringes were small and we emptied them time and again. The doctor left. I sat with the boy.

By the afternoon the boy was better and two days later Sherrington went back to London and he and his colleague Ruffer thought that Lister should be told. 'The great surgeon (not Lord Lister then) had visitors, some Continental surgeons to dinner. "You must tell my guests about it", he said, and insisted—and so we told them in the drawing-room at Park Crescent.'

The bare record of his career shows us a man who rose to scientific eminence by the accustomed route. He was at school at Ipswich, started medicine at St. Thomas's Hospital in 1876 and then went to Cambridge in 1879. He entered Caius in 1880, finished his medical course at St. Thomas's and began physiological research in the Cambridge laboratory with Langley. He was made Superintendent of The Brown Institution in 1891, Holt Professor of Physiology at Liverpool in 1895, and Waynflete Professor at Oxford in 1913. He was President of the Royal Society 1920–5, received the Order of Merit in 1924 and the Nobel Prize in 1932. He retired from Oxford in 1936, after the death of his wife and moved to a house at Ipswich. During the war, when he was homeless, he came back to Cambridge and stayed with the Master of Caius and Mrs. Cameron. He spent his final years in a nursing home at Eastbourne crippled to some extent with rheumatism but with no other serious infirmity. He died without warning in 1952.

The record of his scientific work runs parallel with that of his academic status. His earlier papers make valuable additions to the physiology and anatomy of the nervous system but do not reveal a general plan of attack. This became evident when he held the Chair at Liverpool and when he was 49 the publication of his Silliman Lectures at Yale established it as the key to a new outlook on nervous control. This book, *The Integrative Action of the Nervous System*, sums up the general methods and ideas which guided him in all his later work. It led to wider implications and more detailed analysis, but what he did afterwards at Liverpool and Oxford supplied fresh evidence but did not demand any revision of the original design.

The Simple Reflex

Reduced to essentials his plan of attack was to explore the central nervous system by devising the time-honoured form of experiment in which only one influence at a time is allowed to vary. The central nervous system might have been expressly designed to baffle such experiments, for it is there to be influenced by every circumstance which can matter to the organism. It is continually receiving messages from many sense organs and sending orders to many muscles. Sherrington's plan was to reduce this complexity by studying some very simple response which could be made to occur in isolation. By eliminating all the higher controlling regions of the brain and brainstem the spinal cord was left to carry out particular limb movements in response to particular sensory stimuli. These simple reflexes were still further simplified by isolating single muscles and nervous pathways and in the end the experimenter was left with a preparation in which the response would follow the stimulus with mechanical precision. Comparison of such a reflex response with the twitch of an isolated nerve-muscle preparation showed the differences introduced by the more elaborate pathway through the spinal cord.

He found that conduction across the junctional regions was more readily disturbed by adverse conditions, fatigue, oxygen lack, &c, and in reflex pathways in general there was a less exact correlation between the time of commencement and ending of the stimulus and of the response. These differences were shown to depend on the synaptic junctions in the spinal cord and not on the quality of the nerve fibres leading to or from them. In this way the characteristic properties of the reflex pathway could be established and it was then possible to build up from the simple reflex contraction of the muscle towards the whole pattern of behaviour in the intact animal.

Excitation and Inhibition

One of the most important differences which Sherrington found between conduction in the reflex arc and in the nerve-muscle preparation was that a volley of sensory impulses could arrest activity in some of the motor nerve cells of the cord besides arousing it in others. It could inhibit as well as excite and in general the reflex contraction of one muscle would always involve the relaxation of those opposing the movement. It was this 'Principle of Reciprocal Innervation' which opened the way to the further advance from the simple to the complex. It was the clue to the whole system of traffic control in the spinal cord and throughout the central pathways.

Sherrington's attack was bound to leave some strong points still holding out and the nature of the inhibitory effect had to be left until more was known about the properties of the synapse. There was then no clear evidence about the physical and chemical events which take place when the afferent impulses reach the end of their own pathway and cause the rise or fall in the activity of the pathways leading from it. Sherrington could safely leave these molecular problems to the younger generation who could use the latest techniques of biophysics and biochemistry. His own interests were more with the problems of integrated activity and he was content to leave excitation and inhibition where he found it.

It is encouraging, however, to know that the attack on the synapse has already reached a new position thanks to Sir Henry Dale and his colleagues and recently to one who was a pupil of Sherrington at Oxford. By the use of micro-electrodes Eccles has recorded the potential changes in the motor nerve cells of the cord. He finds that whereas excitation involves the expected decrease in the polarization of the cell membrane—the change which leads to activity—inhibition involves an increased polarization and so a higher threshold. How this change is brought about by the afferent neurones is still uncertain, but the chemistry of the junctional region may soon provide the answer.

The Control of Posture

When he passed from the simplest responses to the more elaborate, Sherrington was faced with a wide choice and had to select particular examples which would be favourable to analysis. Those which proved most illuminating were the scratch reflex of the spinal animal and the postural reactions of the decerebrate. The former was an example of a reaction which could be carried out by the spinal cord alone, but involved widespread excitations and inhibitions at many levels and great variety in the action of the limb muscles. But it was his investigation of decerebrate rigidity which led him farthest. It revealed the factors operating to give a smooth control of the muscular system and we are still finding fresh evidence of its importance.

His early work on neuro-anatomy had prepared the way and when he was established at Oxford the attack was concentrated on this theme. It was pressed home with improved techniques and enthusiastic pupils and it was a fitting sequel to the wider surveys he has made before. It showed that the ideas set out in his book retained their value for the details of reflex co-ordination as well as for the general plan.

The Stretch Reflex

This work at Oxford on the stretch reflex is so well known that I need not describe it at length. The decerebrate animal extends its legs rigidly and they resist efforts to bend them, although the degree of rigidity can be modified by the position of the head and trunk in space. The animal, in fact, maintains the steady contraction of the extensor muscles which would keep it standing if the brain-stem had not been divided. Magnus had shown how the general pattern of rigidity was modified by the signals reaching the vestibular nucleus from the otolith organs and he had been led from this to a masterly analysis of the control of posture and locomotion in the intact animal. Sherrington turned to the individual muscles and studied the effect of varying the pull on the extensors of the thigh. In the decerebrate animal these maintain a persistent steady activity which adapts itself to a varying load, so that the muscle changes its length much less than it would do if the nervous control had been cut off. The control was found to depend on the sense organs in the muscle which Sherrington had studied long before, the muscle spindles in particular. These signal the tension at each moment and their signals set up the answering reflex by which the muscle resists the change in length.

A remarkable feature of this reflex was its extreme simplicity: it was confined to the stretched muscle, the motor response copied the sensory stimulus, with no long delay, no after-discharge and no fatigue, almost as though there was no break in the pathway from the sense organs recording the tension to the muscle fibres maintaining it. The motor neurones must be open to influences from other routes, for the muscle must play its part in all the movements and postures of the limb, but it can work efficiently because the mechanism of the stretch reflex ensures that its contraction will be precisely adjusted to the changing demand.

The importance of this mechanism for adjusting the flow of impulses sent out to each muscle or to each motor unit in it has become even more clearly established by recent work. Sherrington emphasized its value in assisting the smooth transition from one motor activity to another and he was ready to compare it with the feed-back devices used by engineers for controlling the movement of heavy machinery. The engineer, like the brain and brain-stem, must decide what ought to be done but it can be left to the local monitoring instruments and their associated circuits to ensure that the movements do not overshoot their mark or overstrain the structure of the machine. In the same way the stretch reflex mechanism plays an essential part in the execution of each movement, though it has little to do with the decision responsible for it.

When Sherrington was examining the stretch reflex the general theory of feed-back circuits had not risen to its present mathematical dignity. His treatment of the subject was on a physiological level. But recent work has shown that the physiological circuits are more highly organized than he supposed. The muscle spindle, the main source of information about the forces within the muscle, does not act merely as a passive strain gauge. Its sensitivity is under constant adjustment by the spinal centres, for there are special motor nerve fibres to the muscular part of the organ: these can vary the tension of the sensitive region independently of the variations of tension in the whole muscle. The operation of this additional control has been worked out in the laboratories of Granit and Kuffler and it can be regarded as yet another example of a general principle of sensory physiology, the principle that the sense organs would be of much less value to us if they were not constantly focused and adjusted by the central nervous system. They control its activity but they are themselves controlled by it and made more or less sensitive to suit the circumstances. The control may involve widespread movement: shading the eyes against too strong a light, turning the head to catch a sound, or sniffing to identify a smell: it may depend on special accessory muscles attached to the organ, and in some cases there is evidence of efferent nerve fibres running directly to the receptor apparatus. Even the flexion reflex of the spinal animal might be regarded as an example, for its aim is the removal of the pain receptors from the stimulus which has set them in action.

Researches on the Brain

Sherrington set out to analyse the integrative action of the nervous system. His analysis of the spinal reflexes revealed a mechanism of neurones and synapses, operating by signals with inhibitory as well as excitatory effects and adjusted by information from the muscles to give a smoothly flowing pattern of movement. But his success at this basic level never encouraged him to feel that the same methods and ideas would do for every level of nervous activity. The simple reflex had been the key to the understanding of co-ordinated movement and posture but some other kind of key might well be needed for the understanding of what went on in the brain. At Oxford he had no time to look for it, there was still too much to be learnt about the reflex mechanism, the experiments which had to be done were always laborious and his eminence had given him other responsibilities which could not be set aside.

At an earlier period, however, he had made two excursions into the field of brain physiology. One was reported in his Silliman lectures and he referred to it again in his final summing up in *Man on his Nature*. It dealt with the highest level of all, for it was concerned with the visual sensations aroused by flickering light. By arranging the light source so that the bright and dark phases could occur simultaneously or alternately in the two eyes, he hoped to reach decisions about the site and the nature of the process which gives binocular fusion. The results were clear enough but their interpretation was, and remains, puzzling, for there is too wide a gap, too much unexplored territory, between the physical stimulus and the mental experience. The other research on the brain was done at Liverpool when he was working with Graham Brown and Layton. It was a careful mapping of the motor area of the chimpanzee and an analysis of the factors which caused the map to vary in detail from one animal to another. It was found that in any one animal it was rarely possible to elicit more than a fraction of the whole range of movement encountered in a series of experiments. Apart from its anatomical aspect this research may be considered the forerunner of many later investigations on the response of the cortex to electrical stimuli. It showed the much greater plasticity of the cortical than of the spinal neurones, the deviation of the response to a pathway opened by previous use, the progressive recruitment, the varied latency, &c., but in those days, forty years ago, the present range of electrophysiological technique was far below the horizon. Sherrington had to relate stimulus to movement, as in his work on flicker he had tried to relate stimulus to sensation. Some of the intervening events can now be recorded but then they could only be inferred and there were too few data to check the inference.

Thus at the end of his active work in the laboratory the brain and its control of behaviour remained a major field for experiment. Its control of or by the mind remained what it had always been, a theme for philosophers to debate. Sherrington never reconciled himself to Pavlov's whole-hearted acceptance of brain physiology as a sufficient explanation of the mind, though he was ready to await the results of new methods of brain research.

It cannot be said that our new methods have made it much easier to follow the operations of the brain in detail. They have added a great many data concerning the activities which take place inside it, but we are still waiting for more light on the basic problem of habit formation and the related one of attention. Yet the general scheme which was so effective for the spinal reflexes is still our best guide to the factors controlling the direction of behaviour as well as its detailed integration, for there is a gradual increase in complexity as we pass from the spinal to the cerebral level and the brain-stem gives us a transitional region where general behaviour begins to show itself.

The Brain-stem Level

When the cerebrum is destroyed, leaving the brain-stem in control, the animal can stand and walk and run and if it is placed on its back it will regain the standing position. Its behaviour has no survival value. It is that of an automaton which can do little else than stand and walk, but the standing and walking are both activities demanding a level of integration which involves the whole animal.

In fact Magnus and Rademaker were able to reduce most of these elaborate reactions to a sequence of simple reflexes. Each one is the immediate response to a particular sensory stimulus, though their combination shows an adaptation to circumstances which links them with cerebral rather than spinal reactions. Thus, in regaining the standing posture, if the normal sequence of actions cannot proceed, another sequence takes its place. An animal placed on its side will raise itself by a chain of reflexes starting by head movement controlled by the vestibular organs, but if the initial movement of the head is prevented, the body is righted by a different set of reflexes controlled by the receptors in the body wall.

The behaviour of the brain-stem animal certainly lacks all the variety and effectiveness of that of an animal with its central nervous system intact. This has survival value, for it is concerned with the activities by which the animal supports itself in its environment, the pursuit of food, the avoidance of danger, the adherence to the herd, &c. Sherrington spoke of the cerebrum as head ganglion of the distance receptors, signalling events beyond immediate contact with the body, and the difference is not merely in the sense organs which inform it. Operations carried out at this level differ not only in the kind of information which guides them but in the much greater plasticity of the structures which receive it. The cerebrum retains the mould of past activities, it can develop habitual patterns of action, so that skills can be acquired and the problem once solved can be solved again with less effort. Its reactions seem less like those of a machine because the relation between stimulus and response depends on the past as much as on the present.

Yet we can admit this great difference and still see an essential resemblance between the control of postural and of skilled behaviour. The animal without its cerebrum can rise to its feet and stand firmly on an unsteady platform. This requires a constant adjustment of the pattern of muscular contractions depending on the reflex linkage of afferent and efferent pathways with all the feed-back circuits for the individual muscles and the general control from the vestibular organs and the pressure and tension receptors. It could be imitated by an artificial controlling system working on the same principles: an elaborate design would be needed but once set up the machinery should work automatically. The setting up of the reflex system may well involve some gradual change in the synaptic pathways when the animal first acquires the power to stand, but once adjusted the nervous mechanism need not differ in essentials from that which gives the spinal animal the power to scratch itself.

The Cerebral Level

To ride a bicycle or drive a car involves the kind of skilled behaviour only possible at the cerebral level. It needs the distance receptors and the habits impressed on the cerebrum by previous activity. Some of it

B

depends, like human walking, on acquired habits of movement. We have learnt to keep our balance on the bicycle by turning the front wheel towards one side or the other. At first we turned it through many degrees and pursued a zig-zag course. Our manipulation of the handle-bars was not linked closely enough with the signals from the vestibular organs, with a result like the shunting of an engine with an insensitive governor. But with practice the linkage has been improved and the balancing can be done by movements of the body as well as of the arms. It needs no conscious effort and we are seldom aware of what we are doing.

In riding a bicycle or driving a car, or in walking for that matter, we must avoid pedestrians and oncoming traffic and, when we have acquired a proper road sense, this too can be done almost unconsciously. Yet for these adjustments there is a far less immediate connexion between the sensory signals and the end response. Our course is guided by the patterns of light and shade on the retina. It would not be difficult to design an artificial system to guide a car along a white line in the middle of the road, to stop it at the red light and start it again at the green, but with the brain to interpret the optical signals the control goes far beyond this. The car is steered to avoid a pedestrian, to give a wider berth to a child than to a grown-up, to pass another car before the oncoming traffic makes passing unsafe. These operations demand the power of recognizing the special features in the pattern of light and shade which indicate an adult rather than a child, a fast car rather than a tractor, and the recognition must be linked with an immediate estimate of speeds and even of the probable intentions of other drivers.

Although our driving would certainly be dangerous if we gave it no thought at all, the movements we make to control the steering wheel and the accelerator pedal are seldom based on conscious judgements. A small car near at hand will give the same sized retinal image as a large car farther off, but we judge its size and assess its distance and speed without more than general awareness, certainly without deliberate thinking. Once the brain has acquired this skill or indeed any skill, most of the operations required in it seem to be carried out almost as unconsciously as breathing or walking, although they demand most of the powers of recognition, generalization and judgement that are often considered as properties of the mind.

To give the cerebrum this great extension of its field of control it has the great expansion of the cortical sheet and the great plasticity of the nervous structures in it. These at least are important differences between it and the rest of the nervous system. No doubt we shall find other less obvious factors and they may compel us to adopt some new kind of analysis, but it is important to realize that for a great deal of skilled behaviour we have no real need to consider the intervention of conscious processes. Thought is not a necessary accompaniment of intelligent action.

The Mental Level

Liddell's admirable obituary notice of Sherrington quotes him as saying 'Some people think that thinking is all electric currents. Well!' He thought it something so different that it could not be fitted into the scheme of energy and matter which we use for the brain. 'Thoughts', he said, 'lie outside Natural Science'. In his Gifford Lectures, *Man on his Nature*, he is at pains to make it clear that this is a territory which neurophysiology cannot be supposed to reach.

The burden of these lectures, the final reflections of a scientist on what he had learnt, is that the reflex with all its elaborations is a conception to be used only for the material events which take place in the nervous system and that the neurologist has more than the material events to puzzle him. Yet the chapters in which he delivers this judgement are as inspiring as any in *The Integrative Action of the Nervous System*. They bring no sense of failure before a goal which can never be reached. He gives full weight to our mental experiences but his discussion is constantly reminding us of how little we know yet about the material activity of the brain, of how much nearer we might come to the mental level if we knew more of the physical events linking our sense organs and our behaviour.

Some of these events are already clearer. He deals with the changes in the electrical activity of the 'roof-brain' in sleeping and waking, attention and inattention. Since his book was written these have become one of the major fields of research in neurophysiology. There are new techniques which make it possible to study the activity of individual neurones in the brain during its normal working; their response to electrical stimulation has been followed with a new precision and there is a fair prospect of analysing the massive potential oscillations of the cortex in terms of dendrite and nerve cell activity. Some of this may turn out to be irrelevant, for we are still in the exploratory stage: there are a great many events in the brain which can now be recorded, beautiful instruments for doing it and a wealth of literature for reference. The difficulty is still that the conception of the reflex pathway loses its clarity when it has to be widened to include conditioned pathways; for one brain may look like another, but what it does in response to a given stimulus may be quite different because it depends on all the brain has done since it was first in action. Though we may be able to record them it will not be easy to disentangle the physical events in the brain, so that we can tell how the analysis should proceed.

Yet there should be no insuperable difficulty, no need to go outside the framework of natural science, in analysing the cerebral activity which accompanies skilled behaviour. It is worth insisting again that actions which would certainly pass as intelligent and purposive are often done without the intervention of conscious processes. We can try therefore to reduce them to the Sherringtonian scheme without feeling that the most important link has been left out: when this has been done we shall at least be able to consider how we think with a knowledge of how the brain achieves so much when our thoughts are elsewhere. The final puzzle will still be there, but without Sherrington's insistence on it we might deny its importance and get no farther.

It is time to recall the man who faced the final puzzle so squarely. All his life he had faced problems honestly without letting his wishes dictate the answer. His honesty was for himself, it was not the kind that is used to assert superiority and justify bad manners; it gave him no pleasure to be discourteous. But more than anything else it was his honest acceptance of what he found in the world and in himself that made us look up to him.

In his old age he had many visitors at Eastbourne and it was a delight to see him and to feel that he was glad to be seen. He would talk of friends, of the books he was reading, of physiologists of the past that he had known and of his admiration for what the younger generation were doing. No one who visited him then can have left Eastbourne without renewed strength and peace of mind. Sherrington found Nature often cruel and senseless and Man no better, but he was content to face his destiny in the universal plan. He helped us by his fortitude as well as by his science. For he was a great scientist but we who knew him are fortunate in having more than his science to recall this evening.

The Evolution of the Teaching-hospital Physician in our Time

SIR FRANCIS WALSHE

OBE, MD, FRS

29 *May* 1961

My first duty is to express to the President and Officers of the Society my deep appreciation of the honour they have done me in inviting me to give the second Nuffield Lecture.

By way of preliminary I may remind you that the Nuffield Lecture has something in common with another distinguished lectureship within the gift of this Society; namely the Hughlings Jackson Lecture, in that both were founded within the lives of the men they are intended to honour.

In different ways, both men have served medicine greatly and have laid us and our successors under a heavy debt of obligation to them, for while Jackson was one of the deepest thinkers in medicine of the nineteenth century, Lord Nuffield has by his unexampled generosity and humanity made it possible for other seekers after knowledge within the field of medicine and its related activities, not only to add to knowledge but also to apply its fruits for the benefit of humanity.

These two themes, discovery and the enlightened patronage and support of discovery, deal with means to an end, and are not ends in themselves.

As Newman in his famous discourses on the nature of university education reminded us a century ago, the profession of medicine is not a liberal, but a practical one: that is, it is not followed for its intrinsic interest but for an end beyond this.

Thus, what I am proposing to consider this afternoon is one of the means by which this end—the prevention and cure of disease—is sought, namely, the physician himself.

So diversified is the field of medicine and its associated activities—preventive and curative medicine, medicine in the ward and in the laboratory, administrative medicine and the rest—that this choice of a single agent is imposed upon me.

Today every kind of doctor, whether he admits it or not, is in some degree a specialist. At one extreme we have the general practitioner who is uniquely plunged in the tides of human lives, and at the other extreme, perhaps, the medical statistician who, by contrast, works in an almost Olympian remoteness from the human material of his studies. Indeed, in this respect his papers often remind me of the title of Thomas Gray's 'Ode on a distant prospect of Eton College'. For like the poet, in this if in nothing else, the statistician gazes from afar upon us and our weaknesses, genetic and acquired, perhaps even murmuring to himself as he does so, the well-known lines of the ode:

> Alas, regardless of their doom,
> The little victims play.
> No sense have they of ills to come,
> Nor care beyond today.

and then turns back to his graphs and his statistical significances.

Somewhere between these extremes we find the physician, and it is of his development in the past fifty years, as I have watched it, and in a small way participated in it, that I shall speak. Indeed, one can reflect only upon one's own experiences, and it has been said that 'a man who has never reflected upon the principles of his work has not achieved a grown-up attitude towards it. A scientist who has never philosophized about his science can never be more than an imitative journeyman scientist'.

To be more precise, the order of experience upon which I shall reflect is that of the physician attached to a teaching hospital. The topic may seem too narrow for such an occasion as this, but I remind you that amongst physicians he carries a great number of serious responsibilities: namely his part in the training of doctors and in setting an example of practice, in advancing knowledge, and in himself practising medicine, which still for the majority of his kind, involves private as well as hospital practice.

Those who were the clinical teachers of my youth, and later my senior colleagues, did fulfil these diverse roles and helped to form our traditions of practice, teaching and research. They gave us not only our vocational training, but also made major advances in knowledge. Their influence has been particularly lasting in the tradition of thorough clinical training which still lives and is a vital element in that insistence on first things first which has characterized British medicine. That first thing is the direct approach, the clinical assessment based upon history taking and physical examination. It was to this that Flexner in his well-known monograph on 'Medical Education' published in 1925, referred on his opening page as 'that kind of sagacious observation which is the stuff out of which science is ultimately made'.

Two Categories of Physician

I turn, then, to the changes which have marked the evolution of the physician in the last fifty years, and have given us today two categories of teaching hospital physician: the part-time consultant also engaged in private practice, and the professorial unit with its professor and assistants who work wholly within the hospital and its medical school.

We can agree, perhaps, more easily now than in 1920 when the units were first founded in this country, that the clinicopathological discipline which was the mainstay of my predecessors in medicine was becoming manifestly and progressively less adequate to cope with the problems of medicine, and that the methods and ideas of the physical and biological sciences were becoming increasingly essential to unravel the ætiology and the processes of diseases, so that today there is scarcely a single field of natural science that does not contribute to medicine, who, if I may personify her, was once the mother and the nurse of science.

Thus, it became clear that the structure of medicine and the demands of research could no longer be borne by the clinical staffs of the teaching hospitals as we had known them. Each increase in knowledge and in method complicated, not only clinical medicine as we practised it, but also the training of the doctors of the future. The formation of the professorial medical unit became an evident necessity, if a university standard of education was to be maintained, as the most far-seeing physicians have always desired it to be.

What was hoped for from this new element in the teaching hospital? It was accepted that in the final stages of preparing the medical student for the practice of medicine, the practising physician remained an essential teacher. His main work was not primarily to discover, but to inculcate established arts and techniques of medicine, and to humanize medicine: work which was of necessity largely repetitive, but required skill and ripe experience, though not altogether or even predominantly of a scientific nature. I speak now, be it remembered, of forty years ago.

On the other hand, it was intended that the professor and his assistants should be what James Paget, and following him, Thomas

Lewis, had called clinical scientists. That is, it was their role to advance medical knowledge and to bring to their work all the scientific disciplines that were relevant to this task. Necessarily, their work began with the patient and ended with him in so far as he provided the material of their labours.

The professor was designed to engage in research in some chosen field, to train assistants in clinical science, and in his undergraduate teaching to expound the principles of medicine, to arouse in his students an interest in its purely scientific aspects, and to lead them to the critical study of what they saw, what they read and what they were taught. In short, to fit them to reach the frontiers of the known, and even to extend these if later it was in them to do so.

All these designs and aspirations may be found expressed in Flexner's monograph to which I have referred, and also in the several lectures and addresses which Thomas Lewis gave during the 'twenties and 'thirties.

Time has indicated that Lewis's concept of clinical science must now be widened, and in one of his last papers the late James Spence of Newcastle amplified this concept in discerning fashion (1954).

After forty years of usually peaceful coexistence between these categories of physician, it is interesting to see how far the ideals of those who founded our professorial medical units have been realized, and what effect their being has had upon the part-time consultant.

The Wandering Symposiast

Of course, things rarely work out according to plan. In the main the part-time physician has continued his former role, but has perhaps of late years tended to drop out of the stream of active research, not wholly, but more than is favourable for his future prospects.

The clinical professor and his whole-time assistants have not developed quite uniformly. This is specially true of the professor himself, who has sometimes found himself expected to take the lion's share of organizing the teaching in his hospital, or who, being possessed by an administrative urge, has taken upon himself to do so.

This task has become progressively more exacting. It spawns committees and subcommittees with the fertility of a herring, and may take as much of the professor's time and energy as the private practice of the part-time consultant was sometimes said to do—though the professor's time-table is the more predictable.

Nor can we turn a blind eye to the growing fashion of international symposia and congresses, with their social accompaniments, which involve recurrent distractions in the life of the professor and may tempt him to the periodical desertion of his chair. The wandering symposiast, who, to be accurate, is as often the part-time hospital physician as the professor, is a new phenomenon in our time, and I sometimes wonder whether his journeys are really necessary. In strict moderation these functions have their value, but as a habit they are adverse to systematic work. Only the small carefully selected symposium evokes the flow of reason. The rest are, for the most part, reiterations of matters already published.

Thus, beset by conflicting claims and responsibilities, the clinical professor has not been invariably able to carry out what was to have been his primary role; that of engaging in and encouraging research.

It is true that the special research units which have been set up by the Medical Research Council do, when they are situated in the teaching hospital, keep alive the atmosphere of research, but they do not unburden the professor of his administrative and other activities.

A cynic has said that the part-time hospital physician is one who spends part of his time in his hospital, but I feel that this qualification does no longer always suffice to distinguish him from his academic colleague.

If, then, the clinical professor is not invariably in a scientific heaven, how remote is he from the solid earth which his part-time colleague so perseveringly treads?

I should like to elaborate this contrast for a few moments, for it is not without significance to my theme.

Physicians and Patients

The physician, of course, is not the court of first instance in the bringing of medical knowledge and care to the sick. This court is constituted by the general practitioner who rightly insists upon his prerogative in this respect, yielding it willingly only when he is himself the patient.

Yet the physician, when he meets his patient, does so alone. He has to listen to his story patiently and with evident interest. No satisfactory relationship is established between the private physician and the patient unless this requirement is met. It may involve listening to an authorized and to a revised version of the history, and my own experience is that wives are the most prolific authors of revised versions, for the really good wife is always sure that her husband does not really know what his symptoms are and what they are all about. I have to admit that not seldom she is the more reliable witness—but I refrain from any generalization.

Having accomplished this important business of history taking and completed his physical inquisition, the private physician is expected forthwith to announce some plan of action, and to commit himself to some opinion, however provisional it may be at this stage.

Moreover, if manifold investigations are called for, his patient expects to be given a glimpse of the programme, as it were, to be told something of the plot and of what denouement may be hoped for. No houseman or registrar stands between the physician and the need to meet directly and at once the emotional urgency of the situation as the patient and his family may see it.

In contrast, the approach of the clinical professor is more impersonal and is usually public, in the ward.

The patient's history has already been taken by the houseman and probably edited by a registrar, and has lost any spontaneity it may once have had. Like the patient himself, it has been tidied up, and none of those unpremeditated parentheses which occasionally illuminate and clarify the situation is likely to be uttered. The patient may then easily find himself already upon the diagnostic conveyer belt, moving from department to department, from expert to expert, with little or no clue as to what it is all about, and with no obviously designated person whom he can ask. In fact, no one is specially charged to tell him, and what is everybody's business may easily become nobody's business. At worst, if his professor is concentrating upon some special state of disease, the patient may drop back into the role of being the medium of some pathological process or syndrome, or a twig on a pedigree, with no identity as a human person.

Finally, our academic physician as he stands brooding by the ward bedside, has a subsidiary awareness that he is not going to be asked in a few minutes to descend to a family living room, to face the family group or clan, to give a firm decision, a plan of action, or a diagnosis, or, *horribile dictu!* to stand cross-examination by them. A houseman, or a registrar stands between him and the domestic and diplomatic aspects of the practice of medicine, important though these be.

Let me be clear that all this is not a criticism, but an endeavour to give a candid account of the contrasts between institutional and private clinical medicine as they are almost of necessity practised by the physician in these different circumstances, and—let us not forget it—as they are experienced by the patient.

How many of my professorial brethren will recognize themselves and their situation in this hasty thumbnail sketch, of course I cannot say. I must admit that even the most distinguished artist may paint a portrait in which the sitter cannot easily recognize himself, when for the first time—often an unnerving moment—he is allowed to see the canvas, but at least he knows how he has appeared to one earnest and unprejudiced observer.

You may well think that I have drawn too hard an antithesis between the academic and the practising physician. Perhaps it is too starkly drawn, for after all, the clinical scientist can find his problems only from the study and care of sick persons, and he must have the clinical experience to see these problems when they present. Moreover, it is in his hands to see that clinical science is not a dehumanized medicine, as indeed within my experience it usually is not.

Nevertheless my contrast is not without a significant reality.

Physicians and Research

Thus, if there is not an identity of experience between clinical scientist and practising clinician, there is at least an overlap, and it is to the other aspect of this overlap that I now turn, namely, the matter of original contributions.

Is it reasonable to expect the part-time hospital physician to engage in original research, and if so, of what order? Is it more difficult for him to do so than for his academic colleagues?

In the days before the coming of the National Health Service when the young teaching-hospital physician was wholly dependent upon private practice for his living and not largely independent of it, he had in many cases to take up appointments in small outlying hospitals which would bring him into relation with local general practitioners who, he hoped, would be a source of private patients for him. Thus at the naturally most productive period of his life he was often debarred or obstructed by too many routine activities to engage in any original work.

Nevertheless, as anyone familiar with the history of medicine in this country for the past hundred years will know, teaching-hospital physicians did undertake wholly unsubsidized research, in many instances with great distinction, After all, who else was there to do it?

I find it difficult to believe that a physician with consultant status on the staff of a teaching hospital can at this date plead these embarrassments which beset, but did not always defeat, his predecessors. He is surely free to devote some time to making at least some modest contribution to the advancement of medical knowledge if it is in him to do so, and he feels a responsibility in the matter.

At this point in any candid discussion of the subject we have to accept that many able and experienced physicians have no interest beyond the practice and teaching of medicine as they find it, and that some have never entertained an original idea in their professional lives, or noted a clinical phenomenon that was not already on record.

To force them to go through the motions of research would be absurd, and would distract them from the optimum use of the gifts they have, and these may be rich.

Nevertheless, in a university school of medicine the ideal is that every teacher is a learner, and every learner must in the nature of things be a seeker. Were medicine wholly scientific there would be no room for anyone who was not a seeker for the new and undiscovered, but where so much remains that is art rather than science, and insight into human beings rather than originality, the artist and the humanist in medicine still has his place, though the unceasing utilization of scientific means and ideas in medicine somewhat narrows his scope and makes his future not altogether clear.

I make this last comment, not because I wish to see the disappearance from our scene of the pure practising clinician, for his place is as important as ever, but by way of suggesting that the preservation in our educational scheme of a proportion of part-time physicians requires that some amongst them must do what their predecessors found it possible, under harder circumstances, to do; namely, to regard the advancement of knowledge as being amongst their responsibilities.

Perhaps, then, we should be reluctant too readily to absolve candidates for a place on the staff of a teaching hospital from some sense of responsibility to add to the store of new knowledge while they are still young enough to do so. It is possible to have too large a proportion of physicians and teachers who are content to move incuriously through life upon the permanent way of established knowledge and procedures, simply adding to their personal experience within these limits.

The Training of the Physician for Research

So far I have spoken as though nothing more were needed for the physician to undertake research in clinical science than a natural gift for this activity and a desire to engage in it. I have said nothing about his training to this end, and the moment has come to ask whether there is a role in research for the young graduate in medicine who has had no special training beyond that of the normal curriculum, and the often fortuitously chosen postgraduate clinical appointments he has to serve in before and after registration.

If medicine were a clearly defined and restricted scientific discipline, like chemistry or botany, we might expect this experience spread over seven years to be adequate enough, but we know the width and diversity of the subjects to be covered in a medical education, and the corresponding lack of depth which this range of subjects necessarily implies.

Therefore, it seems clear that something more, and something more clearly defined and restricted, must be as essential to the training of the clinical scientist, as to a would-be scientist in any discipline of physical or biological science. This seems to me to be a problem that we have never corporately faced, and to it I will later return.

In the meantime, I feel sure that there is a role in original observation for the graduate without this special training, even though it be restricted in scope. A century or so ago Claude Bernard assured his contemporaries that clinicopathological studies were played out as a source of knowledge, and that they should leave the wards for the laboratory where alone could fundamental knowledge be gained. Somewhat intimidated by this dictum, clinicians from time to time have been prone to repeat it.

I believe this obituary of the clinicopathological method to be as premature now as when Bernard first uttered it. New entities are continually being identified, and for those who will pick me up on the use of this word 'entity', I will remind them that an entity is anything we can think about, and that I am not hypostatizing the concept of disease.

To take but a single example within my own field of interest, recent clinical and pathological studies of cerebrovascular disease have profoundly altered our ideas on this subject. They have revealed that the arteries tributary to the brain that lie in the neck, the internal carotid and cerebral arteries, play as important a role in cerebrovascular

vertebral

accidents as do the vessels entering into and issuing from the circle of Willis. Hitherto, the neck had always been a no-man's-land for the morbid anatomist making autopsies on persons dead of cerebral vascular accidents, and atheromatous changes in these two large extra-cranial vessels were not looked for, or not attended to, until very recently.

We now know that the state of the cerebral circulation is as deter-mined by the state of these vessels as by that of the intracranial arteries. Comparably, in every field of medicine, new clinicopathological entities are being exposed, not because they are newly happening, but only because they are newly observed.

Therefore, for the trained senses of the alert clinical observert here remains, I believe, much·of importance yet to be discovered.

What we need is the retention into adult life of the eager natural curiosity of the child, perfected by training and by exercise, respected for the prime gift it is, and kept alive by a constant awareness of the great gaps in our knowledge of illnesses and the grave limitations in our power to prevent and to cure them.

Yet wider goals can be achieved by this trained alertness. It makes possible those planned studies of diseases which we have not adequately made in the past, and is the foundation of clinical trials.

Nevertheless, when we have said all that can be said in this regard, we have to admit that we cannot, in most instances, hope to carry our problems of the ætiology and pathogenesis of disease to a final con-clusion without the application of the physical and biological sciences. Therefore, we may not echo the call of Bernard to desert the ward for the laboratory. We must continue to retain the old lamps of clinicopathological study while getting what extra light we need from the new lamps of modern science.

Yet is the physician to cease to follow up his original observations at the point where these need to be carried to the laboratory for further analysis? Is he then to hand his problem over to the medically untrained scientist? If he has no special training in science he may have to do so, but ideally this should not have to happen. Too many medical problems have disappeared into the laboratory, finally emerg-ing in a guise unrelated to the realities of the disease being studied.

Thirty years ago Wilfred Trotter reminded us in these words that 'medicine more and more understanding the lost opportunities of the past will take to itself the methods of the experimental sciences and lead the direct attack upon its own problems'.

This, I submit, should be taken to apply as much to the part-time teaching-hospital physician as to his academic colleague, and in a rapidly changing profession, he will with difficulty, if at all, retain an equality with the professor and his assistants, or even his place in the scheme of medical education, unless he takes his part in this direct attack. There are forces at work favouring his ultimate elimination. He has to justify himself on both the vocational and the scientific fronts if he is to survive. I see no reason in the nature of things why he should not do so.

We have to accept, therefore, that when planned surveys of disease, epidemiological and statistical studies, genetics, and the classical clinico-pathological approach have told us all they can, there remains the necessary experimental method still to be pursued, and this involves the application of many physical and biological sciences.

Experimental Research

Over and above his purely medical experience, no one can achieve a true competence in more than one or two of these other disciplines: physics, chemistry, biochemistry, immunology and the rest. Since many unsolved riddles in neuropathology, for example, as in other aspects of pathology, require the knowledge and utilization of several disciplines for their solution, it is clear that small carefully chosen teams of different workers must often collaborate. One or more of these must be medically trained and of sufficient competence in scientific method to command the respect of his non-medical colleagues, and to keep the medical view and aims of the research in sight. It is unreasonable to expect non-medical scientists to be interested in and to undertake alone fragmentary aspects of a complex medical research programme, and to treat them as technicians without exposing the problem to them in its fullness, as far as this can be seen.

I will not repeat in any detail what I have said on a number of occasions in the past twenty-five years, that the history of research into the disease beri-beri is a typical example of how the advance of knowledge may be delayed when there is a lack of communication and of a common ground of knowledge between those who are attacking the problem from different points of approach.

The remarkable, but forgotten, clinical, pathological and experimental studies of this disease in the East Indies in the opening decade of the present century were, as we can now see if we know the literature, well conceived and rightly directed, but those engaged did not have the advantage of the biochemical knowledge that the second decade was to provide. The biochemists, when they took over the study of the deficiency diseases, were similarly handicapped by a complete ignorance of the clinical and pathological features of beri-beri as a human disease.

They misconceived these and produced an ætiological theory not compatible with the facts of the disease and ignoring some of the most significant of them, such, for example, as its cardiac manifestations.

It required several further years of research by Rudolph Peters to begin to identify and to reconcile the biochemical lesion with the clinical and pathological facts, and even now this has not been completely achieved.

This kind of situation must repeat itself until there are sufficient amongst us who are both medically trained and also fit to go into the laboratory and work beside non-medical scientists, both parties knowing what they are about, and neither, through ignorance, at the mercy of the other.

It is encouraging to see the increasing recognition of this necessity in medical research. The most complex chemical and metabolic studies are now successfully carried on by physicians who handle the diagnosis, care and treatment of their own patients. Nor is metabolic medicine alone in this enterprising and far-seeing approach to clinical science.

In neurological medicine and pathology, which have always had a close attachment to scientific methods of investigation, we have, I feel, been too long and too exclusively preoccupied with the normal and disturbed activities of the neuron, and have neglected the study of the neuroglia in health and disease, though disorders of this element in the nervous system can wreck neural function as disastrously as can primary disease of the neuron. This is largely because experimental methods adopted in neuronal study are wholly different from those needed for the study of the neuroglia, and we have been too slow in widening our outlook on research. The example of disseminated sclerosis is one painfully familiar to us all, revealing as it does the crying need for a reappraisal of our research methods and outlook.

Training for Research

If there be any substance and importance in the plea which I am making for a wider research activity amongst both academic and part-time teaching-hospital physicians, the question which arises concerns what is being done or planned to give the necessary supplementary training to the young men and women who are to be the teachers and the research workers in the medicine of the future.

I suggest that our academic and professional bodies and organizations are not doing anything, and that in the recently founded fellowships so presciently set up by the Medical Research Council for graduates who are to return to clinical medicine we see the first recognition of the necessity for concerted action in this matter.

All our students pass through the statutory curriculum and the subsequent year of house appointments, and then in the middle 20s we make it necessary for the ambitious and aspiring to spend yet more time in acquiring a purely vocational higher qualification, namely the MRCP.

Yet in essence the diploma is not a matter of further scientific training, but is primarily an endorsement of a status it is necessary to achieve before the young graduate is allowed to enter the ring and be viewed as a possible candidate for a place on the consultant staff of a teaching, or indeed of any hospital. In an increasingly hierarchical profession, everyone must jump this Beecher's Brook, no matter what his future work is to be.

This traditional ritual is peculiar to us amongst the English-speaking countries. It does nothing to advance scientific medicine.

After this final ordeal by examination, conducted on lines that have not changed since the nineteenth century, the graduate, now nearer his thirtieth birthday, is no nearer being trained to undertake experimental studies in medicine than he was before.

Is it reasonable now to expect him to do what is necessary to acquire competence in some scientific discipline to fit him to undertake them? After all, the fulfilment of his ambition to attain consultant status on the staff of a teaching hospital may often depend on quite other considerations than his fitness to add to knowledge by these means.

With the prospect of economic security growing nearer to him, can we expect of him the heroic virtue of submitting himself to further training outside the clinical ring fence, where he is likely to be forgotten by those upon whom his opportunities depend?

I need not elaborate this theme, but in the circumstances it is not surprising that we are not turning out enough adequately trained clinical scientists. We have taken no reasoned measures to do so, and

C

if in other fields of science the same haphazard attitude towards the higher education were the rule, we should have few scientists of the first rank.

Over twenty years ago, Thomas Lewis suggested means by which we might provide a foundation for this higher training for clinical science.

His idea was that the interested and promising student should, before he passes to the final and clinical stage of his medical education, be given or encouraged to take, a year's extra study of a science basic to medicine, such as physiology or biochemistry. Having achieved this he would return to the stream and complete his clinical training.

Such courses have long been available: at Oxford in the Final Honours School, at Cambridge in the second part of the Tripos, and in London in the Honours BSc course, which is perhaps, dare I say it, the most exacting of the three.

The student thus gains not only a fuller introduction to scientific method and thought, but also a year in mental and emotional maturity, and is at a great advantage if, subsequently, he feels moved to engage in research within the field of medicine.

It would be an interesting experiment, but one I do not expect to live to see, if one medical school were to decide to accept, for its final clinical course, no student who had not taken such a course.

Many interests would resist such a plan, many men would regard it as not likely to achieve its desired end since winners cannot always be picked in time, and probably the paralyzing combination of apathy, timidity, conservatism and indecisiveness would stifle such a project at its moment of conception. Certainly, there was no response to Lewis's simple suggestion, and a response to my more drastic remedy is even less probable.

It would require a band of real enthusiasts and idealists to achieve it, amongst whom a large quota of younger men would be essential.

Francis Bacon has said that young men are fitted for execution, old men for counsel. Certainly the first half of this aphorism is true, but I have never been persuaded that the second half is a reliable generalization. Thus, unless young men are interested in planning for the future, no such long-sighted planning as I have in mind is likely, for they must provide the impetus.

It was such a body of idealists, many of them young, that a few years ago gave birth to the College of General Practitioners, and no one can doubt what a powerful stimulus to higher standards of training and achievement in this branch of medicine this academically-minded body has already become.

Do no such fires burn in the young teaching hospital physicians of today?

I venture to submit, therefore, that unless we take systematic measures to train a proportion of medical students to be the clinical scientists of the future, we must fall behind those countries that have given thought to this problem. Whoever has travelled and has seen in some medical schools and hospitals overseas, the eagerness of the students in the best schools and the facilities and encouragement they receive in this respect will know the thoughts that must be in my mind.

I would urge my hospital colleagues to read once more, and to ponder the more detailed and reasoned statement of this case in Thomas Lewis's Huxley Lecture on 'Clinical Science within the University', published in the *British Medical Journal* in March 1935. He makes what I believe to be an unanswerable case for the plan of giving an extra year's scientific grounding to capable and ambitious students before they enter the final clinical stage of their hospital training, and against regarding what we now call the 'higher qualifications' as symbols of, or as necessary to, such a training; to which, indeed, as I have said, they bear no relation, useful as they may be as evidence of a higher level of competence in dealing with routine clinical problems.

Opportunity

Having said all this, a question yet remains to be asked. Of what use to train clinical scientists for our teaching hospitals unless we also go on to provide them with opportunities in their own country, and perhaps also in those of the Commonwealth overseas, to serve medicine through science?

Plans to increase the total number of hospital consultant physicians and to resolve the senior registrar problem are necessary and important, but they have nothing to do with the issue I am now considering. They simply increase the number and improve the status of trained men available to meet the routine demands of a National Health Service. Medicine is changing all the time, and the upgrading of physicians to consultant status is, of itself, not a contribution to the training or placing of clinical scientists. It is but a belated administrative device. Here I venture to remark in parenthesis that in what is becoming a status-obsessed profession, improving status is not to be confused with raising standards, which is quite another kettle of fish. Whatever the experience and ability of the physicians we upgrade, very many of them will work in small centres, or 'regions', which is the word I believe I should use, far removed from facilities for any kind of original work, and lucky in some instances if they have near at hand even the technical provision for all the diagnostic procedures now a part of practical medicine

The existence of the problem I am now considering is not something we can reasonably expect to be noted by the lay administration of a National Health Service. One has to be inside the profession of medicine to understand its long-term needs, and even inside it, foresight is always a commodity in short supply.

When I hear discussion arising from the familiar question, 'What is the future of medicine?' I feel inclined to reply that for us, the pregnant question is, 'Where is the future of medicine?'; that is, in what countries?

I have given voice this afternoon to some chastening thoughts. Of course, I do not expect them all to be received with enthusiastic approval. I have done this of set purpose, for to have given this lecture on a medical theme with which everyone could whole-heartedly agree would have been pointless, for it could have been no more than a sequence of glimpses of the obvious, and to offer this would not have been a compliment to this audience.

Therefore, I must leave you with my chastening thoughts, to accept, to select or to reject as you will, and thank you for the patience with which you have listened to me.

Cancer: The Patient's Viewpoint and the Clinician's Problems

SIR STANFORD CADE

KBE, CB, FRCS, FRCP

10 *October* 1962

The Eponymous Lecture to honour Viscount Nuffield was founded on his 80th birthday. It is a privilege to be invited to deliver this, the third Lecture.

I thank the President and Officers of the Society, who have thought me worthy of this honour but I appreciate that they have also laid upon me the duty to fulfil the dual purpose for which it was founded, firstly to pay a tribute, on behalf of the medical profession, to Lord Nuffield whose generosity and princely benefactions to the profession have never been surpassed or equalled and secondly to deliver a lecture devoted to the advancement of the science and art of medicine.

I have chosen 'Cancer' as my subject; not in the sense limited by pathology or therapy, but as an aberration of normal biology to which there is no complete answer as regards cause or cure.

I will spare you all statistics, not because I do not value their importance, but as my main concern it to paint a very broad picture of this disease, which in the Concise Oxford Dictionary is recorded as the figurative equivalent of 'Evil', and to draw attention to the implications as regards the patient's mind and the doctor's problems.

As a country, we have the unenviable distinction of the highest cancer mortality; this does not really mean that we have the highest cancer incidence, as there are so many fallacies in the collection of data in different countries. But the incidence in England and Wales is frighteningly great and I cannot express it better or more concisely than to quote Professor David Smithers (1960): 'In our community at present one person in every 4 or 5 born is likely to develop neoplastic disease at some period during life.' With his usual clarity of thought he adds: 'A country in which neoplastic disease is a frequent cause of death, is a country with cause to be proud of its medical service, since it is a lowered death-rate from other causes which permits a tumour death predominance.' In other words, cancer is a disease of the healthy.

The probability of acquiring cancer at the rate of one birth in four or five, the possibility of developing a malignant tumour in all tissues and every organ, the lack of immunity of any age group, the many histological types and the variability in their degree of virulence— when taken together make this a problem of formidable complexity. If in addition it is recollected that there is a latent period, often many years, between the inception of the neoplasm and its clinical manifestations it is clear that this is no single disease process, no solitary event but some abnormality in the sequence of normal physiological processes of embryology, growth, maturation, functional activity and senescence.

A useful classification of cancers is in two groups: 'Endogenous' and 'Exogenous'. Most human cancers are endogenous; all experimentally induced cancers in animals and the accidentally and involuntarily induced cancers in man are exogenous. The few exogenous human cancers are man-produced, the well-known industrial cancers, the cancers following exposure to radioactivity. Numerically these are insignificant, mostly preventable and in fact only pointers to the possible carcinogenic agencies in our environment, resulting in some aberration in the normal chemical and hormonal processes which determine the occurrence of endogenous growths.

The Patient's Viewpoint

Let us for a moment consider the average patient, be he a hospital patient in the out-patient department, or consulting his family doctor, or facing the specialist. What are the conflicting emotions which assail the man or woman, told or suspected of this, the most dreaded of mankind's afflictions? Having faced such a situation for nearly half a century, with patients of all ages, both sexes, of nearly every nationality, race, creed, colour, social status and education, and having with increasing experience as the years went by watched the patient's reactions, I can from my personal experience of meeting over 20,000 human beings suffering from cancer, summarize what I believe is the usual sequence of emotions.

The dominating emotion is obviously *fear*. With this fear as an immediate reaction is a sense of impending death, as most patients think or believe, quite erroneously, that cancer kills quickly, which of course is not necessarily true. Vaguely mixed with this feeling of being condemned to death is a sense of regret at the apparent brevity of life expectation, the regret that in the near future they will no longer be part of the pulsating rhythm of life around them, This feeling is quite distinct from the fear of death, it is the sadness at the loss of life.

Beyond this immediate and overwhelming, purely personal re-action there is, at a second emotional plane, the thought of those nearest to him or her, the effect of this illness on work and occupation and on the capacity of earning a living. This concern has no relation to the financial status of a patient; in fact the higher the social scale the greater the worry, usually from the greater commitments; and in the very highest income brackets the thought of death-duties and the panic measures to avoid or minimize them is a sobering reflection on the futility of amassing wealth

These thoughts and emotions follow each other in the patient's mind and lead to the necessity of facing a new situation, always unexpected and perplexing. Despair, however, is not as a rule a lasting state and subconsciously there obtrudes on the patient's mind the problem of facing the new situation. The normal human instinct of self-preservation reasserts itself. It is a natural reflex that the next wave of rational thought concerns itself with the battle to be fought with this personal foe and there is born some hope that treatment and faith in supernatural or divine powers will in the end win this battle for survival. In his subconscious mind the patient tries to equate treatment with cure.

Fear of cancer may be latent and precede both the disease and the diagnosis. Fear is undoubtedly the most potent cause of the delay in seeking treatment. It is a common observation, that doctors, doctors' wives, nurses and midwives frequently delay seeking advice and surround themselves by walls of illusions, often quite irrational. Doctors and dentists have been known to observe for months their own cancer of the tongue in a mirror and call it 'lichen planus', although they may have never seen a case, and probably have not even remembered this term since their student days.

Cancer of the breast is masquerading in the woman's mind as a 'sprained muscle', or the result of a blow, or associated with the menopause, in fact as anything and everything except the obvious. This 'pre-diagnostic' fear is often lost once the diagnosis is made clear to the patient. Fears may persist even after successful treatment; it is a fear of recurrence and according to the patient's personality is either hidden behind a veil of an ominous silence or revealed by a polysymptomatic exuberance. Fear of cancer occasionally leads to suicide even in the absence of the disease.

To try and alleviate or dispel fear is an important part of every form of treatment. A kindly sympathetic approach and an understanding of the patient's individual type of fear creates confidence in the patient's mind. This gift of inspiring confidence may not necessarily overcome the fear of the disease but helps the patient to overcome the fear of treatment. Fear of surgery, anæsthesia, radiotherapy or drugs is also not infrequently a cause of delay in seeking advice. The absence of pain in the early stages of most cancers also favours delay and creates illusions: 'It is painless—it cannot be cancer.'

In considering the patient's viewpoint it is necessary to take into account the emotions of the family. These can be graded from the most agonizing feelings of the parents in the case of young children who are victims of leukæmia, neuroblastoma, Wilms' tumour or osteogenic sarcoma, to the tragedies of husband and wife, often trying to conceal from each other the true nature of the disease. The wise management of the family can only be acquired in the very hard school of experience.

The Medico-legal Aspects of Cancer

Before leaving the patient's viewpoint, it may be of interest to refer to some of the medico-legal aspects arising in connexion with cancer. Sequence of events looms large in the patient's mind. 'Why, how and when did I get this awful disease?' And often retrospectively there is a recollection of some event, some injury perhaps trivial and vague. But the patient or his widow fastens on to this; hence the claims for industrial compensation or pension sometimes supported by medical opinions, although not supported by facts or by the known natural history of cancer. Most such claims are based on sequence of events: 'Post hoc, propter hoc', 'I was well when I joined the Army or Navy or Air Force—I got my cancer in the Service', or 'I fell whilst at work', 'I sustained a knock or a blow on duty'. Yet these incidents may have been so slight and trivial as not to require first-aid help or interruption of work. Such claims are sometimes supported by medical opinion based, perhaps subconsciously, on sympathy or pity. Often a statement is made that the cancer was or might have been aggravated by the incident. As the cause of cancer is unknown, it cannot be said with complete accuracy what effect an accident at work had on the course if the disease. But a just assessment can be arrived at in almost every case if the available evidence is scrutinized with impartiality in the light of our knowledge of the natural history of cancer and with the law of probability as applied to the population as a whole.

The Clinician's Problems

Before considering the technical management of cancer it may be of interest to refer briefly to the social aspects of the disease. Is the patient to be told? How much is he to be told? How to convey the news? It is my experience that the technical management of the patient is not only easier and simpler but more effective if the patient is made aware of the diagnosis. It is obvious that the attitude 'I never tell' is untenable, although in some cases there is no need to tell; either because the patient is already aware that he has cancer or because he or she accepts treatment: amputation of breast or arm or leg, colostomy, tracheostomy, &c., without asking the diagnosis. Neither is the attitude 'I always tell' wise or human. There are so many variables in the patient's 'mental make-up' according to race, education and character, that no rule is applicable to all. The truth can be made less unpalatable by a careful choice of words.

The Choice of the Method of Treatment

Fifty years ago, when I was a medical student, the problem of cancer treatment was simpler than it is to-day. There was in fact only one method of treatment, surgery. It was not a question of 'operability' in the enlightened sense of the word, but of 'removability' (if I may coin a word); a tumour could be 'cut out' or it could not. Inoperability in those days was synonymous with 'untreatability'. In my time, radiotherapy, hormone therapy and chemotherapy have been added to our weapons to deal with cancer. An inoperable tumour can be treated, often effectively, by means other than the knife, and in some patients a selective choice of a combination of two or more methods of treatment is available. A clinician confronted with the problem of how to treat a cancer patient, be he the family doctor, surgeon, radiotherapist or other specialist, should ask himself this fundamental question: 'What is the relative value of the various available methods of treatment *in this particular patient?*' Our duty is not only to follow the law of probability that this, that or other therapeutic measure is likely to achieve the greatest number of five- or ten-year survivals in the majority of patients. The clinician should divorce himself from his own specialty, he should for a moment cease to be 'surgeon', 'physician', 'radiotherapist', but a doctor in the clinical sense of the word. Each patient is an individual problem, each tumour is a biological enigma. Age, stage of disease, type of tumour, general state of health, should be taken into consideration and estimated not only as regards the chances of success to control the tumour but also in relation to the degree of disability inflicted by treatment and how such disabilities will affect the individual patient. Neither should it be forgotten that in no given case can it be predicted with accuracy if the treatment is likely to be curative or only palliative. Clinical assessment is difficult as the important factor of tumour-host relationship is not easily determined although it influences the course of the disease more than the more obvious factors of the stage of the disease, rate of growth, histological type and anatomical site.

Were it possible to lose sight of the side-effects of major therapeutic procedures, of the physical mutilations and functional disabilities, of the mental agonies and psychological disturbances, and consider treatment solely as a technical problem with object of achieving a certain end-result, the decision would be relatively easy.

But if preservation of life is to be gained at the price of social unacceptability, or a perpetual revolt of the patient against his physical state, victory against death is no victory for life, victory is a punishment.

The choice of treatment should therefore not be determined solely by statistical evaluation of a probability of cure in relation to various forms of treatment.

I would like to emphasize that the accuracy of statistical evaluation relates, strictly speaking, to cohorts and not to the individual. A devoted and distressed husband whose wife has cancer of the breast is not concerned with the percentage of five- or ten-year survivals in cohorts. He has no harem of a hundred wives of a certain age group all suffering from the same cancer. To him 100% success or 100% failure relates to the one and only wife he has.

This aspect should not be lost sight of in the management of cancer patients and it is this which makes me personally not in sympathy with the 'at random' selection, now somewhat in vogue.

Prognosis

Prognosis is not quite the simple matter of correlating age, histology, extent of disease and apparent adequacy of treatment. Although spontaneous regression of tumours does occur, albeit exceptionally, spontaneous remission is much more frequently seen. They are well known to occur in malignant melanoma and in Hodgkins' disease and often there is a periodicity of activity and remission in other tumours both primary and metastatic. What is not yet widely known or generally accepted is that the rate of growth and the spread of cancer can be actively promoted by the therapeutic measures used for its control. There is nevertheless very little doubt that surgery can precipitate local recurrence and hasten dissemination, that radiotherapy by local tissue damage can lower the local resistance and that hormonal or chemical changes can lower the general resistance or stimulate the rate of growth and enhance dissemination.

I will now review some of my thoughts, ideas, and beliefs on the limitations of surgery, the achievements of radiotherapy, the promise of chemotherapy and the fascination of hormone therapy. I will review this from my own personal experience and convictions—a kind of philosophical 'credo', not technical, statistical or didactic. Some of you may disagree, others disbelieve and some others may think me presumptuous to air my views so nakedly. But if my remarks are provocative, I hope they will provoke thought and criticism and not indifference or denial in anger.

The Achievement and the Limitation of Surgery

Adequate surgical excision in suitable cases eradicates the tumour in a proportion of patients. The prognosis, however, does not always depend on the length of history or even the stage of the disease; the histological variety is of a greater prognostic significance. Control of the disease may have been obtained for a number of years with an apparently complete arrest of the neoplastic process and yet there are cases where a local recurrence develops twenty and even fifty years after operation. In most cases, when surgical treatment is indicated, wide excision gives longer periods of remission and more often leads to permanent arrest of the disease, than less aggressive or conservative operations. Before submitting a patient to surgical treatment it is essential to define clearly the criteria of operability. Technical operability is not sufficient. Haagensen of the Presbyterian Hospital, New York, postulated such criteria in breast cancer and considered as 'categorically inoperable' all cases who did not comply with the assessment of these criteria although technically many of these patients were operable. Such criteria can of course be applied to many other sites, for instance, the neck in connexion with a radical block dissection. These criteria do vary with the individual surgeons, but should only do so within definite and somewhat narrow limits. This self-imposed discipline is of primary importance if the results of surgical excision for cancer are to be improved.

The limitations of surgery in the treatment of cancer are twofold: the limitations of surgery as a skill and the limitations of the surgeon as an individual.

The limitations of surgery are those imposed by the natural history of the tumour, its mode of spread and by the stage at which the patient seeks advice. Examples of such limitations are plentiful, such as the metastatic supraclavicular nodes in cancer of the lung or stomach, or the presence of œdema in breast cancer.

There is, however, in selected cases a place for extensive surgery even in the presence of visceral metastases; in such cases surgery is of palliative value but is none the less justifiable and may temporarily alter the course of the disease, prolong the survival period and limit the miseries of the terminal stages. It is not infrequently indicated in cancer of the stomach, the colon and the kidney.

To define the limitations of the surgeon as an individual needs a little more elaboration. Such limitations as a rule are not due to lack of technical ability. The surgical performance may be above all criticism, and yet the result will be an aggravation and not an amelioration of the patient's state. Such limitations may be due to a lack of long-term experience, but mostly they are due to confusion of thought and lack of a strict surgical discipline. A common example is surgery of breast cancer. Much has been made of the controversy between 'radical mastectomy' and 'simple mastectomy and radiotherapy', but this has only led to greater confusion and has certainly retarded progress. The figures put forward as evidence for the achievement of simple mastectomy and radiotherapy are not convincing, sometimes misleading and when looked at critically meaningless, as the material compared is in fact not comparable. On the other hand the large series of cases reported from reliable sources show that 80% of patients with a stage 1 and grade 1 breast cancer submitted to radical mastectomy survive at least five years and 65% may reach a ten-year survival period. No comparable reliable figures are available for simple mastectomy and radiotherapy. There is, however, abundant evidence that both methods fail to control the disease when applied to unsuitable cases. To operate by whatever method on late stage 2 or stage 3 cases of breast cancer not only fails to control the disease but definitely worsens the patient's state. In such patients mastectomy, simple or radical, promotes local spread of the disease as can be witnessed in any radiotherapy centre when patient after patient is seen with local recurrences, cancer *en cuirasse*, extensive nodules, ulceration, gross œdema of the arm, and fixed regional lymph nodes. These human wrecks are not merely the victims of cancer but equally the victims of misguided therapy. Strict criteria of operability would alter the picture and without surgery such patients would benefit from radiotherapy and hormone therapy to a much greater degree. There is considerable evidence that cancer can be seeded by the surgical act, not only in the case of the breast but in other sites, such as the urinary bladder, in laparotomy scars and in malignant melanoma; this is a local implantation of cancer cells. But there is also evidence that surgery, if ill-timed, can accelerate or promote the development of distant blood-borne metastases. The rapid appearance of multiple pulmonary metastases following a hasty amputation for an osteogenic sarcoma has been noted many years ago. Ferguson (1940), in an analysis of 400 cases of osteogenic sarcoma, separated them in two groups. Those where amputation was performed within the first six months from the onset of the disease ('early amputation') gave only 5% with five years' freedom from symptoms. In the case where the amputation was delayed for more than six months 34% were free from symptoms for five years. Amputation of a limb for osteogenic sarcoma should be done in a quiescent phase of the disease. Such a dormant state can be induced by local radiotherapy which influences the liability of metastatic spread; yet there are still a number of surgeons who practise ablation of limbs as the first and immediate and only measure with the same paucity of results now as fifty years ago.

The usual practice in the case of Wilms' tumours is to operate at once, almost as an emergency measure, and then refer the child for post-operative radiotherapy. That this common practice of immediate and urgent surgery is not effective is evidenced by the small number of children so treated who reach adult life or even adolescence. Yet Wilms' tumour is supremely radiosensitive and the response to radiation is enhanced by suitable concomitant chemotherapy, such as actinomycin D. Massive tumours, often filling a large part of the abdomen, regress rapidly and within a few weeks of such combined therapy nephrectomy becomes simple, easy and far less traumatizing; whereas attempts at the removal of large, tense, vascular tumours spread the disease by the blood stream and do so rapidly. Many other examples could be given of bad timing of the surgical act, of poor selection of patients, of lack of combined treatment.

The results of surgery in suitable cases have not been surpassed by other methods of treatment but there is no room for complacency and ample room for improvement. Fewer cancer patients would be submitted to operation, but to a better purpose if selection and timing were based on the life history of the tumour and not on the feasibility of its ablation. Another example of the surgeon failing, due to confusion of thought, is the so-called conservative or 'modified' operation, which is inevitably a compromise. Such is the conservative operation for *low* rectal cancer, when the primary aim of conserving the patient is lost sight of, by the obsession for conserving the anal sphincters. The attempt at a half-way house between a radical and simple mastectomy, when the pectoral muscles are not removed, is a further example; I believe that an adequate and accurate clearance of the axilla is more likely to be achieved when the pectoral muscles are removed than when they are preserved.

Such errors of commission or omission are not due to bad technique but to bad surgical judgement, which defeats the very object of submitting the patient to an ordeal so eloquently expressed by Lord Moynihan (1928) in an address to students: 'For us an operation is an incident in the day's work, but for our patients it may be, and no doubt often is, the sternest and most dreaded of all trials, for the mysteries of life and death surround it and it must be faced alone.' Of the surgeon's character, thoughts and burdens Sir Russell Brock (1962) with equal eloquence speaks as follows: '. . . he must, if he is to succeed, possess certain high qualities of feeling, and certainly he must possess a wholly intelligent approach to his subject and if possible a highly scientific one.'

To quote once again Professor Smithers (1960): 'It is no great tribute to the art of surgery to see a feeble old gentleman dragging out his life for a few months cured of an advanced pharyngeal carcinoma if deprived of many things which might have made these few months tolerable. It may, however, be of inestimable value to a young woman with a family to be alive following a total pelvic exenteration, if she has the staminal and the courage to sustain her greatly altered life.'

You may think that I am lacking in magnanimity, that I might be, or should be, a little more generous to surgeons at large, that good fortune gave me opportunities, denied to many, to spend my professional life in an ambiance of colleagues, facilities, equipment and opportunities somewhat more generous than the average, and that all this should make me more restrained in my criticisms. But such magnanimity would be based on lack of courage or even cowardice to speak the truth as it appears to me in the light of everyday experience. Such restraint would be illogical if the main purpose of therapy is to salvage a few more, perhaps many more, than are salvaged to-day from the inevitable destiny facing a cancer patient.

My critical observations on the practice of surgery in cancer are made without malice but in the hope that the contribution of this Nuffield Lecture, endowed for the specific purpose of the advancement of medicine, may be to translate what is still a cry in the wilderness into a policy of surgery founded not on the capability of a pair of hands to remove viscera, limbs, breasts but on an accurate critical faculty, based on the complementary knowledge of the disease and the limitations of any particular form of treatment.

Radiotherapy

The achievement of radiotherapy is great indeed and the speed of its development is equally remarkable. But it had its years of pioneering and exploration which have come to the 'end of the beginning', by the availability of megavoltage apparatus. In practice a much greater number of cancer patients can benefit from radiotherapy than from surgery. As a palliative weapon it has immense value, as a curative measure it can control some tumours when surgery is harmful, ineffective or impracticable. The selection of patients for radiotherapy requires the same accuracy and knowledge as the selection for surgery and equally great skill is needed in the detail of technique, in timing, dose, dose-rate, overall time, &c. But, like surgery, so radiotherapy can do harm by lowering the local resistance. Painful radionecrosis of the jaws, the shrunken fibrosed bladder euphemistically referred to as the 'systolic bladder', which renders the patient's life almost unbearable, the local skin recurrences exactly within the pigmented telangiectatic area following the so-called 'conventional' X-ray therapy; these unfortunately are not mere accidents but often the result of routine treatment.

Radiotherapy has an increasing potential of achievement with the availability of megavoltage and megacurie apparatus, with the nearly perfect precision of beam direction and the fractionation of dosage over longer overall periods of treatment. These advances have altered the meaning of the attribute 'radioresistant'. Bone and soft tissue sarcoma, irremovable adenocarcinoma of the bowel or ovaries are no longer resistant to the modern radiotherapy methods, either alone or in combination with chemotherapy.

The Promise of Chemotherapy

The great attraction of chemotherapy is that it is a systemic attack on cancer. It is still in its early stages of development, both as regards the compounds used and the techniques employed. But already it is recognized that certain cytotoxic agents have a selective action on certain tumours. To the original nitrogen mustard used in Hodgkin's disease and the reticuloses has been added a series of chemotherapeutic agents. Busulphan in chronic granulocytic leukæmia, chlorambucil in chronic lymphocytic leukæmia, 6-mercaptopurin in acute leukæmia in children, melphalan in multiple myeloma and malignant melanoma, methotrexate in chorioncarcinoma, teratoma of testes and squamous cell carcinoma of the mouth, and acute leukæmia in children. These and many other anti-neoplastic agents fall into two main groups—the alkylating agents and the antimetabolites. Their mode of action is somewhat different and hence a combination of both groups may prove of interest.

The screening of thousands of antibiotics for anticancer activity has added so far two compounds, actinomycin D and mitomycin C whose tumour-inhibitory action has been used clinically. Actinomycin D has proved of considerable value in Wilms' tumour, synovial sarcoma and rhabdomyosarcoma, especially in conjunction with radiotherapy, as, besides its direct effect, it increases the radiosensitivity of tumours.

A very large number of plant extracts have been examined for possible antitumour action. Of these, derivatives of natural or synthetic colchicine such as N-desacetyl-thiocolchicine, unlike most other agents, have a controlling effect on adenocarcinoma of the ovary and the bowel. More recently vinblastine, an alkaloid derived from the periwinkle, has proved of interest in the terminal stages of Hodgkin's disease and of melanoma.

The clinical use of chemotherapy requires specialized knowledge not only of the various available drugs but of methods of administration and dosage. Certain general principles must be observed in the practical application of the variety of drugs available. There is a narrow margin between the desirable effect on the tumour and the toxic effect on the patient. Bone-marrow depletion, hæmatopoietic depression, undesirable side-effects on mucous membranes, severe gastrointestinal upsets, are some of the side-effects which occur if the dosage used is to result in tumour regression. Many of the cytotoxic agents are chemically unstable and are excreted or detoxicated rapidly. To ensure an effective concentration of the active drug in the tumour and yet minimize the general undesirable effects, new techniques have been developed. The perfusion of limbs or organs permits the administration locally of doses which would be lethal if they were to reach the general circulation. Intra-arterial infusion at the nearest point to the tumour-bearing area permits the continuous or intermittent administration of the chosen cytotoxic agent over long periods of days or even weeks and an enhanced effect of the drug is obtained.

The advances in techniques of administration, the availability of an increasing number of drugs, the more effective and more rapid screening methods have resulted in a widening of the field of usefulness of chemotherapy in the treatment of cancer. It is no longer the last resort to be used only in the most advanced or otherwise untreatable cases. In some forms of neoplastic disease it is the remedy of choice: in the leukæmias, multiple myeloma, chorionepithelioma. In other varieties of cancer chemotherapy is part of a combined treatment by surgery or radiotherapy, or both, even in early cases. In patients with disseminated cancer it may be of considerable palliative value. The effectiveness of a given drug may also depend on the dosage programme and the time intervals between the administration of the drugs. Different tumours require not only different drugs but different schedules of treatment. The results of chemotherapy can also be improved or the period of effectiveness prolonged by the combination of several drugs. These should be chosen for their difference of mode of action and given either together to potentiate one another or in sequence to overcome drug resistance. The use of specific antidotes such as folinic acid and methotrexate, the preservation of autologous bone marrow with a view to marrow transfusion are refinements which permit a more radical chemotherapeutic attack.

The Fascination of Hormone Therapy

Hormonal control of cancer is the most exciting event in the realm of tumour biology. The concept that cancer is an irreversible state, independent and uncontrollable, is obviously no longer true. It can be controlled by physiological means; it is dependent on normal phenomena; it relies on its environment for survival. This concept of hormone dependence has led to an entirely new method of treatment. To the time-honoured methods of treatment—'cut it out', 'burn it out', 'poison it', methods which aimed at the direct attack on cancer with the object of destroying it—has been added an indirect attack, the weapon of physiological warfare against cancer. By altering the hormonal environment of the patient, the persistence or survival or rate of growth of cancer can be profoundly affected. In the history of medicine this is the first indirect attack on malignant tumours.

Admittedly it is applicable only to cancer of the breast and prostate and possibly in an indirect way to the lymphomas. Admittedly not all mammary cancers are dependent on the hormonal environment and, again admittedly, although the effect of such altered hormonal state on the control of cancer is not permanent but reversible, it still remains the greatest advance made so far.

A tribute should be paid to two men who contributed to this new knowledge: To Sir Charles Dodds, who by the synthesis of stilbœstrol put this new tool in the hands of research workers and clinicians, and to Charles Huggins, who by his designed, not accidental, discoveries proceeded from orchidectomy and œstrogens in the treatment of prostatic cancer to adrenalectomy in disseminated breast cancer.

The hormonal control of cancer of the breast and prostate can be achieved by several different ways: by the administration or by the withdrawal of sex hormones; by surgical or medical methods. Hormonal control of prostatic cancer is now the universally accepted method of treatment. Hormonal control of breast cancer is reserved for the late case, mostly disseminated, but could and will be extended to earlier stages of the disease. In the treatment of widely disseminated mammary cancer there is no other weapon which can be used with comparable effectiveness, to control the progress of the disease, to relieve pain and prolong life.

The Combined Treatment of Cancer

There are now at the disposal of the cancer patient four methods of treatment: surgery, radiotherapy, chemotherapy and hormone therapy. Each has an important place and each has its limitations. These methods are not competitive but complementary. They can be used separately, concomitantly or in sequence. The indications for such combinations and sequences are not always appreciated and their timing requires skill and knowledge.

A few examples will illustrate the possible varieties of combined treatment. In cancer of the tongue, the primary growth can be completely regressed by radiation and the lymph-node metastases by surgical excision. In malignant testicular tumours the reverse is practised, orchidectomy followed by radiotherapy to the regional lymph nodes. In malignant melanoma, chemotherapy is used as an adjunct to surgery or as the sole method of treatment according to the stage of the disease. In cancer of the breast, stage and grade of the disease are the main guides to the therapeutic attack by surgery or radiation or both, by surgery and hormones, or by hormones and radiotherapy. In advanced inoperable ovarian cancer, a simultaneous attack by radiotherapy and chemotherapy may lead to a degree of regression which permits surgery.

An unbiased assessment of the possible combinations of treatment shows clearly the need of a team of specialists. Such a team of varied skills, which must include not only general and specialist surgeons, radiotherapists and physicians but equally biochemists, organic chemists and physicists, should work in complete co-operation. Such teams exist and have existed for many years. Their success is recognized by the continued stream of patients such combined clinics attract. If a cancer patient has the good fortune to be referred to a hospital where such a team exists, he has a better chance of cure or palliation than the patient whose fate is in the hands of one individual and whose treatment is determined fortuitously by the specialty of the department he is sent to.

Cancer Education

Cancer education has its advocates and its opponents. It is still a controversial subject, although less so than a decade or two ago. The views on education vary from being just a part of health education and hygiene in general, to the sustained and specific object of telling all those who care to listen all sorts of things about cancer. But fundamentally the object of educating the population at large in matters of cancer is to achieve earlier diagnosis, in the belief that early diagnosis will lead to better control of the disease. This, of course, does not apply to all cancers but only to some of them. An aggressive policy has been pursued by the American Cancer Society: posters, films, pamphlets, lectures, broadcasts, television; man, woman and child have become familiar with slogans, the seven deadly signs, graphs, figures of mortality, these always climbing towards the sky-line. What has all this achieved? Something substantial no doubt, but not what it set out to achieve. It achieved the provision of vast sums of money for research, for the care of patients, special children's institutions, the popularization of the Papanicolaou's cytological diagnosis. It has achieved something else, more important, a familiarity with the word 'cancer', the acceptance of cancer as a common disease, a familiarity with the dreaded enemy—and hence perhaps less fear and less despondency, a lesser reluctance to submit to treatment. These are considerable achievements, but all this propaganda has failed in the major issue—which is to lessen mortality and morbidity and to prolong survival. I believe that education of the public is of value but far less value than the education of the medical student and doctor. Self-examination of the breast, the cherished hobby of some, is less likely to gather early cases than the inculcation of basic principles of diagnosis into the doctor. For every woman who by self-examination discovers a lump in her breast there are hundreds if not thousands who discover it accidentally, casually. What happens to these women? Some ignore it—this could be improved by lessening the element of fear; others go to their doctors, and may be told and not infrequently are told to keep it, the diagnosis being 'mastitis' or even more facile 'this is nothing'. Surely the first principle in cancer education is, to the doctor, that a 'lump' or an 'ulcer' is 'something' and not just 'nothing'; that being potentially lethal, its nature must be ascertained. To find a lesion and to be advised to do nothing about it, is as great a misfortune as to be unaware of the lesion. In brief, at this stage more could be gained by a greater 'cancer consciousness' of doctors than by any other means. Perhaps there is something missing in our medical education? Do we lack the logic to draw the right conclusions from the obvious physical signs, or the courage to interpret the patient's story and the abnormalities found on examination, till there is no longer any hope of avoiding the diagnosis of cancer? Is it not our duty to fear the worst, not to run away from it, but to face it? Is it still excusable to talk about 'change of life' in post menopausal bleeding, or of 'piles' in persistent rectal hæmorrhage without investigation or even examination of the patient? The average delay in diagnosis to-day is weeks and months, as it was years ago. The few patients who by public propaganda are induced to seek early advice are as nothing to the many who do so and are not given it.

As a surgeon I would like to conclude this third Nuffield Lecture by quoting the remarks of that great British surgeon, eloquent of speech, broad in mind, kind in nature, skilful in execution and courageous in his approach to cancer surgery—Gordon-Taylor:

. . . 'the vision splendid', which for us is that long-desired day, perhaps not too far distant, when in the cure of cancer gross mechanical destruction and cruel mutilation of human tissues shall no longer be required, nor the scorching methods and machinery of Hephaestus the blacksmith god, or Prometheus who stole fire from heaven! 'When the biologist shall know the laws that govern cell-growth with a knowledge akin in its sweep and accuracy to that of the astronomers', he will then have a power denied to those who scan the stars in the firmament, and that power will enable him to prevent, to control, and to cure cancer. (Gordon-Taylor 1948).

REFERENCES

Brock, R. (1962). *Canad. med. Ass. J.* **86,** 370

Ferguson, A. B. (1940). *J. Bone Jt. Surg.* **22,** 92, 916.

Gordon-Taylor, G. (1948). *Ann. R. Coll. Surg. Engl.* **2,** 60

Moynihan, B. (1928). *Addresses on Surgical Subjects*. Philadelphia & London, p. 215.

Smithers, D. W. (1960). *A Clinical Prospect of the Cancer Problem*. Edinburgh & London, p. 150

The Drift and Dissolution of Language

MACDONALD CRITCHLEY

CBE, MD

22 September 1964

Medicine owes to Hughlings Jackson the inceptive glimpses into the psychology of expressive disorders. His first reflections upon this subject appeared in print just a century ago (Jackson 1864). He looked upon aphasia, not so much as a focal cerebral deficit, as a 'taking apart' of a complex symbolic endowment, namely language. His dynamic thinking was decades ahead of his time, and we are still astonished at the exciting ideas he promulgated, and the way he anticipated many of our contemporary notions. I think that Jackson today would be intrigued with the opportunities opening up through the lessons of linguistics and information-theory, especially when linked with the technical refinements of speech-recording.

Edward Sapir—that most attractive exponent of philology—proclaimed that linguistics should concern itself with language in all its aspects: language in operation; language in drift; language in the nascent state; and language in dissolution. Although not entirely conforming with the Sapirean use of the terms, we might proceed to examine two of these aspects, namely, the drift and the dissolution of language. I borrow these expressions to indicate the opposite poles of disordered language, the mildest and the severest types of an aphasia respectively.

Drift: Minimal Dysphasia

Let us first examine what we might call 'minimal dysphasia', where the linguistic imperfections are often so slight and so fine as to elude routine testing. The shortcomings likewise in ordinary conversation pass unnoticed by both speaker and listener. These features may herald the slow encroachment of a space-occupying lesion upon the zone of language. We may therefore speak of a 'pre-aphasia', or of an 'incipient, inchoate, or ingravescent dysphasia' . . . the harbinger of an unequivocal speech-impairment. Or, these same minimal defects may be discerned in the final recovery-stages, as a 'residual dysphasia'.

Nothing less than an extended technique of testing will uncover these minimal signs. These may stand out against a background or setting of an adynamism, or lack of spontaneity, which also applies to language. This inertia may, however, be interrupted by activity which is impulsive and unrestrained, which again may extend to verbal behaviour.

The hallmarks of a pre-aphasia may be mentioned briefly. There will be a lessened facility in the choosing of words, the available vocabulary remaining intact. The number of 'types'—that is different words employed—is reduced. Less common terms are selected slowly, if at all, and with a notable inconsistency. Defect of word-finding is revealed when the patient tries to recite a catalogue of instances belonging to a particular generic class (animals, flowers); or sharing a common property (redness, sharpness).

Pari passu with the restriction of vocabulary in actual use is an over-employment of certain trite phrases and phrase-words, clichés, preformed speech-patterns, favoured word-linkages, verbal biases, and successive habits of connected speech.

An over-elaborate and unorthodox use of words may come to light during an interview. In naming articles before him, the patient may supply the correct term quite promptly, but then lapse into an odd spontaneous verbalism. Quite unasked for, he may proceed to indulge in verbose circumstantiality. Thus, shown a watch, the patient may name it but then go on to exclaim . . . 'and a very nice one too, if I may say so'. Or, '. . . my husband hasn't got one like that, and he's got everything'. This little *manie de parler* may be spoken of as 'gratuitous paralogia'. In some ways it recalls Petrie's *regressive metonymy* described in some leucotomized patients (Petrie, 1949).

An inadequate performance of sequential tasks as opposed to isolated ones, may prove revealing. Both interpretation and recapitulation of verbally presented material may be poor, particularly when interlocking or consecutive themes are concerned, and when references are allusive or ambiguous. The patient may fail to paraphrase such commonplace slogans as 'Players please', or wise saws like 'easy come, easy go', 'still waters run deep', or 'a bird in the hand'. This failure may be due to a defect either in comprehension or in explanation (Zangwill, 1964), or in both.

In attempting to repeat a couple of consecutive jokes or fables, the patient may confuse the two propositions, and contaminate his narrative with inappropriate ideas and words. The patient may likewise fail to solve arithmetical problems when posed verbally, in speech or in print. Spontaneous letter-writing, or the production of an essay upon a set theme, may also betray a minimal dysphasia, whether inchoate or residual. Such a text will in addition lend itself to linguistic analysis, and disclose aberrations in the token-type ratio, or in sentence-length, or in the verb-adjective fraction. Inadequacy may be observed in what Luria (1958, 1959) has called the regulating function of speech. For example, the patient may fail at such a consequential task as 'when I tap the table once, lift your right hand; raise your left hand when I tap twice; and if I tap three times, do nothing'. Or, directed to squeeze a rubber bulb with the right hand in response to the flashing of a red light, and with the left hand when a blue light appears, the patient may soon become confused and make stereotyped actions (Mescheryakov, 1953, Ivanova, 1953). Likewise the pre-aphasiac fails when given some such instruction as . . . 'when I count as far as 12, raise your hand' (Luria, 1958). A pre-aphasiac may be unable to supply an analogy when given a series of three items, e.g. 'lion, teeth; eagle, . . . ? . . .'. He will remain perplexed even when the missing word is included among others and put to him in a multiple choice type of question.

Behind all these minor defects one may also observe a raised duration threshold, or a slowness in both the execution and reception of verbal material in the case of very mild aphasiacs. Botez's term 'inattention' in this connexion is not a happy one, as the author himself realized (Botez, 1961).

Dissolution: Maximal Speech-loss

Let us turn from these minimal cases to a consideration of massive defects of communication—Sapir's dissolution of language—for the 'method of extreme cases' is one which is often of unexpected value in studying a problem. *Aphasia totalis* is rare save as a transient phenomenon. Ordinarily the maximal speech-impairment is met with in cases of 'monophasia'. This term refers to those cases where spontaneous speech is restricted to a kind of *hapax legomenon*, that is, a solitary 'word' or holophrastic word-cluster, which is reiterated in a stereotyped fashion. Russian neurologists refer to this phenomenon as a 'word embolus'. Other terms like 'formula-speech', 'word-rests', (*Wortreste*), or 'speech automatism' have also been used at times, but in this country we usually follow Jackson and speak of 'recurring utterance'. Originally described in the eighteenth century, this phenomenon was first specifically investigated by Hughlings Jackson, inspired, I believe, by the memory of a boyhood acquaintance who was so afflicted.

Jackson's four-fold classification of these recurring decimals of speech is a little artificial. By far the commonest state of affairs is for the patient to give vent to the stereotype 'yes'—or 'no'—or sometimes both of them. Analysis of 100 cases of recurrent utterance (compiled from Henschen, 1922) where a solitary comprehensible word was concerned has shown that in 63 it was a matter of *yes* and *no*, the remaining 37 being made up of a great diversity of utterances. It was possible to break down these figures. Of 65 such cases out of 134 patients, 36 were males and 29 females. Negative particles (*no*, *nein*, &c.) alone were used by 6 (2 males and 4 females); affirmative particles (*yes*, *oui*, *ja*, &c.) by 23 (11 males, 12 females); and both negative and affirmative by 36 (23 males, 13 females).

The survival of these two particles is not surprising for they constitute important as well as common units of spoken speech, as I have stressed at length elsewhere (Critchley, 1961). Their rank in written speech is far less exalted. However, the mere frequency of *yes* and *no* in normal diction cannot be the whole explanation of their important role as a recurring utterance. Though *yes* and *no* rank high in the Lorge-Thorndike tables of frequency of usage, they stand lower than many other words (articles, prepositions, conjunctions) which rarely if ever appear as stereotypes. Table 1 shows their place in the Lorge-Thorndike word-lists, as compared with other terms, common in normal parlance, rare in aphasia (Thorndike & Lorge, 1944).

When a recurring utterance comprises some term other than yes or no, it is often a most unusual and unexpected one. Likewise, when entailing more than a single 'word' it may show itself as a phrase, and a seemingly significative one at that. Frequently, speech automatism is duplicated—'yes, yes'; 'no, no'; 'come, come'. According to Sapir (1921), reduplication in speech indicates distribution, plurality, repetition, customary activity, increase of size, added intensity, continuance. In the context of our present problem it suggests a primitive method of enhancing meaning with verbal economy. This striving towards communication on the part of the patient may be all-important.

A stereotyped phrase may be either banal in context (like 'Good morning', or 'je ne peux pas parler' or 'Ich kann nichts'), or else a wholly unexpected one ('Ace of Spades', 'Boulevard de Grenelle,

Table 1. Some of the most commonly occurring
words in the English language

Word	Lorge magazine count	Lorge-Thorndike semantic count
THE	236,472	Not known
AND	138,672	Not known
A, AN	131,119	Not known
I	89,489	24,250
IN	75,253	96,674
IS	33,404	43,816
WITH	32,903	38,041
ON	30,224	28,382
BUT	23,704	21,380
ME	23,364	5,818
ONE	17,569	14,860
NO	11,742	9,492
YES	2,202	593

131'). However plausible in content, the phrase is incongruous in its setting. Each 'word' wears the garment of a semanteme but in reality it is quite devoid of reference-function. Perhaps we should speak of 'displaced semantemes' or 'pseudo-semantemes'. Terminology obviously raises difficult problems. The fact that the so-called 'word' appears on all occasions means that it actually ceases to be a word. Its method of employment precludes its habitual reference-function. When, for example, the aphasiac proclaims nothing but the syllable 'come' he is admittedly employing a dictionary word with a conventional connotation. But as the patient uses it there is no such attached significance; it might just as well be any other word, or a piece of nonsense, or even a grunt. The recurrent utterance 'come' does not therefore qualify as a word in the strict sense, for it is a linguistic counter that has been filched, to be used out of context in an inconsistent and highly individual manner. Since the stereotypy is not, strictly speaking, a word at all, the patient cannot pronounce a part only of it, any more than he can say any other word. To a particular aphasiac, his recurrent 'Battersea' meant nothing, and consequently he could emit neither 'Batter' alone, nor 'sea'. The same remarks apply to clusters of 'words' occurring as stereotypes. As Jackson (1879–80) said '. . . these phrases, which have propositional structure, have in the mouths of speechless patients no propositional value. They are

not speech, being never used as speech; they are for use only compound jargon'. Often the phrase is interjectional, with profane or
obscene overtones ('My God!' 'Jesus'), sometimes curtailed or deformed ('Cré nom', 'Mede (=merde)'; 'é nom é ieu'; 'sacon').[1]

Impressed no doubt by his juvenile experience, Jackson drew attention to the frequency with which a fragment of jargon forms a
stereotypy. Here again, reduplication is common, if not the rule
('Tan Tan', 'zu zu', 'watty watty', 'taratata').

Modification of the Recurrent Utterance

Whether the recurrent utterance be a 'word', phrase or piece of
gibberish, certain modifications may develop over the course of time.
The stereotyped formula-speech is at first produced on every possible
occasion, however unlikely. Hence, to begin with, it possesses the
attributes of a compulsion, emitted at times when silence would be
more fitting. Thus during a three-corner interview between doctor,
patient and relative, the aphasiac may butt in with his inappropriate
verbal automatism, like Epimarchus, incapable of speech, but unable
to hold his tongue. In its role as a compulsion the stereotyped sound
may be uttered in an explosive, almost violent fashion, 'released like
a vigorous trumpet-blast' (*wie kräftige Trompetenstösse*, von Monakow
1914).

The positive side of this problem deserves mention. It is unnecessary
to discuss at length the various hypotheses which seek to explain why
a particular expression should appear as a recurring utterance in an
individual patient. We can be sure, however, that it is no haphazard
event. Though we may not understand, meaning is certainly there.
The role of an overpowering emotion immediately prior to the stroke
has been widely accepted, as suggested by Freud (1891). Whether
Jackson's theory of a 'stillborn proposition' is credible, or Gowers'
modification thereof (1885), depends upon one's knowledge of the
immediate pre-morbid circumstances of each case. Certainly I have
observed patients where Jackson's theory could well apply, but also
others where that of Gowers would seem more reasonable. Again
there have been many other cases where none of these hypotheses
would fit. The common iteration of jargon, as well as of 'yes' and

---

[1] Another compulsive manifestation sometimes observed in aphasiacs, bears
a distinct relationship with our subject. The patient interjects at regular intervals
a tic-like phrase into the stream of talk. Moutier's (1908) patient could not speak
four words on end without the exclamation 'Ah merde! cré catin de casaque!'

'no', though not flatly contradicting the views of Freud, Jackson and Gowers, is rather more difficult to explain.

While remaining the sole item of communication, the recurrent utterance later loses much of its tic-like nature. The patient now becomes able to inhibit the upsurge of stereotypy, and he may remain silent for longer periods. At this stage additional speech automatisms may develop so that the vocabulary will now comprise a handful of recurrent utterances. But this does not indicate the existence of a code. That is to say one particular stereotype does not 'stand for' any specific object or idea, with another stereotype linked with another. It bears no analogy, for example, with the binary principle of the drum languages of Africa. An apparent exception was Broca's patient Lelong who had several recurring utterances (Broca, 1861). One of them, 'tois'—a corruption of 'trois' no doubt—was used solely in the context of number. Another important advance will by now have come about, leading to some measure of communicative play, despite the attenuated vocabulary. This results from the patient learning to utilize to the full the suprasegmental phonemic factors. By altering the prosodics of the recurrent utterance the aphasiac now makes his solitary 'word'—'no', for example—refer in an idiosyncratic way to a variety of concepts: greeting, dismissal, acknowledgment, affirmation, denial. The melody of speech is restored, even enhanced. The patient 'sings' his recurrent utterance, as Jackson put it. Thus the patient has learned to endow his involuntary stereotyped 'word' with his own idiosignificance. In this way the sound emitted takes on a meaning for the occasion like a disguise—a meaning which is not fixed or consistent, but which is elastic, expedient, and dependent upon the setting. This same meaning may or may not be shared by others, for communication depends upon the skill with which his attempts can be decoded.

This property whereby a solitary word can constitute not only a sentence-word, but can also relate to a great diversity of ideas, is well known to linguists aside from the problem of aphasia. According to Dostoievsky (1876–81) 'it is possible to express all thoughts, feelings, and even reflections, in one word', and he gave an account of a ridiculous argument between six topers, comprising merely one unmentionable word.

Such adaptability precludes any grouping of the recurrent pseudo-sememantemes into syntactical classes, e.g. declarative, interrogative, interjectional, hortatory. One and the same stereotype can serve now as an exclamation, now as a question, later as a proposition.

Non-verbal aids to communication, such as kinesics, soon become pressed into service. With his intact limb and facial musculature the patient will employ a rich pantomime in order to eke out the meaning he seeks to attach to his solitary utterance. At a later date, if and when the stereotypy becomes established as the sole articuleme, the patient may make an extraordinary adjustment. The ability of such patients to transmit information of a complicated sort is astonishing. Superficially this would appear to represent a fantastic antinomy between intellectual integrity and failure to verbalize. It would be unwise, however, to accept the clinical dissociation at its face value, for searching test-procedures will almost certainly uncover other defects.

At this stage in recovery the patient may respond to re-educational measures (Kuttner, 1928, Alajouanine, 1956). Half the patients with recurrent utterance improved while in the other half the stereotypy is perpetuated. In favourable cases the patient can often be made to emit a pre-formed speech pattern. Thus he may be coaxed to articulate, albeit haltingly, the days of the week, numerals, letters of the alphabet, if put into an appropriate frame of endeavour. By accurate imitation of the therapist's lip-movements, he may be prevailed upon to repeat phonemes, then words. He may be encouraged to complete a familiar verbal automatism started by the examiner: 'Bull and [Bush]'; 'black and [white]'; 'sausage and [mash]'.

However, such accomplishments may get no further than amounting to a mere trick, or *jeu des mots*. In an ordinary setting the spontaneous utterances stay chained to the original stereotypy, with the verbal acquisitions appearing merely at the bidding of the neurological ringmaster. An all-important factor in retarding recovery is the persistence of an oral apraxia, an epiphenomenon which is often overlooked. During the stage of rehabilitation new words are as a rule articulated slowly, hesitatingly, on a staccato monotone. Such newly acquired diction is quite unlike the fluent melodious evocation of the recurring utterance.

Apart from his attempts at talking, the monophasiac is seriously handicapped when he tries to write. Rarely if ever can he do more than scribble, or laboriously copy a text. The recurrent utterance, be it noted, does not obtrude itself as a recurrent grapheme, a point which contradicts Jackson's view that stereotypy of speech is due to the automatic action of the opposite hemisphere. It may well be that an oral apraxia plays a part in perpetuating the initial efforts at spoken communication, a mechanism which does not affect the act of writing.

Other means of expression are at times less difficult for these patients with recurrent utterance. For example a monophasic secretary may find it possible to communicate better by recourse to a typewriter than by relying on speech, writing or gesture. Thus a young woman rendered aphasic after carotid ligation, could say nothing whatsoever except 'no'. Put before a typewriter she slowly and unassisted executed the following note: 'Dear Doctor Critchley. Where are the speech therapists? I am getting fed up. Love, V. . . . H. . . .'

Attention is rarely directed towards the perceptual defects in cases of recurrent utterance. In greater or lesser degree they are usually present, a point which detracts from the conventional ascription of this type of speech disorder to an extreme Broca's aphasia.

Nowadays morbid anatomy attracts less attention among aphasiologists than it did and it is unnecessary to pursue here this matter of localization of lesions in recurrent utterance. It is more tempting to turn one's back upon pathology, and to regard recurrent utterance as the clinical manifestation of severe speech-loss, brought about by a conjunction of various factors, including *inter alia* a necessary volume of brain-damage; a sufficient magnitude of speech-defect; abruptness of onset; potent emotional and intellectual circumstances operating just before the stroke; and an associated bucco-labio-lingual apraxia. More appropriately we should focus attention upon a dynamic type of ætiology rather than on a static location of a mere brain-defect. 'An insignificant spar remaining from the shipwreck of speech' is how Alajouanine (1956) vividly described the phenomenon of recurrent utterance. Perhaps, by a close and imaginative examination of such verbal flotsam, we may learn to reconstruct some of the circumstances of the disaster.

Mental Status of Patients with Recurring Utterance

Those neurologists who have carefully observed over a long period of time patients with an established recurrent utterance can hardly refrain from trying to assess the state of mentation. How striking the contrast between the crippling failure to communicate, and the relative integrity of alertness, social behaviour, and adjustment. To what extent is the patient handicapped in his conceptual thinking? What is the nature of his silent rumination? Can he still utilize a verbal type of imagery even though he is incapable of verbal exteriorization?

Such questions naturally tie up not only with disputes as to the intellectual status of aphasiacs, but also with a still older problem, the normal relationship between Thought and Speech. For centuries, philosophers have locked horns in an uncompromising contest over this latter point. Opinionated pronouncements have been made, characterized as much by disaccord as by dogmatism. To some it would seem that no problem exists, and that the answer is obvious to all save the obtuse or the prejudiced. Unfortunately, however, philosophers answer this question now one way, now the other, but always with the utmost assurance.

In reviewing the age-old arguments, it seems astonishing to find how rarely the schoolmen have resorted to the lessons which might be learned from observing those who are speechless but still vigilant. Inter-disciplinary sectarianism has rarely been broken down, and the promising co-partnership of philosophers and aphasiologists has scarcely been broached.

Although the victim of recurrent utterance is virtually bereft of words as a tool in communication, he is not necessarily deprived of the service of words. Jackson used to say that he is speechless but not wordless. But whatever alliance exists in such a case between speech and thought it must be indeed remarkable. He can identify words when he hears them, even though complete verbal comprehension is impaired. To some extent he can 'manipulate' words at a silent level, as when he picks out and assembles letters to form a word, or when he points to an appropriate word from a list of alternatives before him. His performance may be hesitant, even halting, but the very fact that some attempt is made is important.

A patient whose speech is restricted to a stereotyped 'no', may be shown an article and asked to name it, for example a pair of scissors. Obviously its identity is recognized. Pressed for an answer, the patient may painfully emit a post-dental fricative sound but no more. With a pencil he may scrawl an S and then give up. On a typewriter, or with cut-out letters, he fares better and selects an 's' and a 'c'. Shown a list of possible alternatives the patient may point to the word 'scissors' but even so fails to verbalize. Or, given a dictionary, the patient may thumb the pages until he arrives at 's' and then he may narrow his search to 'sc' and even 'sci'. Further than this he may not be able to go. Again the patient may succeed in giving some inkling that he has a knowledge of the word which he cannot exteriorize. By tapping, or by squeezing the examiner's hand, he can indicate the number of syllables in the elusive term (Proust–Lichtheim manœuvre). All these procedures serve to show that the patient still possesses an engram of the word 'scissors', vague and intangible though it be.

In the context of the Thought-Speech controversy, such experiments can only mean either that in ordinary circumstances thought remains possible in the absence of words; or else that to the monophasiac words are still available despite a powerlessness to exteriorize them. Both these conclusions are compatible with those of Whitehead (1938) who said '. . . language is not the essence of thought. But this conclusion must be carefully limited. Apart from language, the retention of thought, the easy recall of thought, the interweaving of thought into higher complexity, the communication of thought, are all gravely limited'.

Some measure of conceptual thinking lies therefore within the capacity of a patient with recurrent utterance. In this exercise he utilizes to some extent words at a silent level. This is one problem: the question as to the nature of his silent browsing is another. At such times, he is not in contact with an interlocutor; he is neither decoding information, nor trying to act upon it. He is merely caught up in silent reverie. Is this day-dreaming a type of imageless thinking? This is unlikely, though the images involved may not be of a verbal sort. In such circumstances this type of aphasiac may well be simply a passive agent for a series of images which are mainly of a visual character. These images will be loosely connected, being linked one with another by the freest of associations. Consistency is not there; nor is profundity.

In many ways the phenomena of recurring utterance differs from the malperformance of most other aphasiacs. From all the clinical evidence it would seem that the patient possesses at least some measure of inner speech and conceptual thinking. Faced with a situation like putting a name to an object he appears to have some idea of what he wishes to say. So far there is little difference from other aphasiacs. But as soon as the preverbitum ends by the patient with recurrent utterance breaking silence, a fantastic travesty of verbal behaviour takes place. Irrespective of what he wants to say or tries to say, his articulatory muscles take charge and involuntarily shape themselves according to a rigid pre-determined pattern, so that one audible complex and one only becomes exteriorized. This resulting sound bears no relationship whatsoever with the idea within the preverbitum. As Alajouanine & Lhermitte wrote (1963): 'Thought is squeezed into a mould so as to produce the same copy or similacrum each time.'

E

The physiological mechanism appears to be twofold. First there is an imperfect selection of the necessary sound-symbol, a defective ecphoria in fact. Secondly an uncontrolled, uninhibited activity of the muscles of articulation takes place, like a severe action tremor which appears as soon as a deliberate attempt is made to execute a skilled movement.

Speech-recording in Aphasiacs

Modern instrumental methods of recording constitute a considerable advance over the guesswork descriptions of the past. Furthermore such records lend themselves to unhurried and repeated analysis. Certain new points come to light with an important bearing upon the theory of speech in aphasia, the research now becoming nomothetic as well as idiographic (Allport, 1942). Some of the problems of recurrent utterance may in this way become clarified.

An up-to-date mode of transcribing an aphasiac's performance can be devised by extending and elaborating the technique of recording a psychiatric interview, practised by Pittenger, Hockett & Danehy (1960). It is really a logical development of what Hughlings Jackson taught, namely that one should set down a faithful record of exactly what a patient says and does, and not a personal interpretation.

An extended transcript of a structural interview is illustrated in Fig. 1. On the bottom line one reads the examiner's question and the patient's reply set out in conventional typology. Silent pauses are marked by a symbol and registered in tenths of a second. Just above, the patient's speech is translated into the broad or international phonemic script, to which have been added the approved supra-segmental notations, indicating stress, pitch levels, and terminal contours. At the top of the record is a description of the patient's gestural and mimetic behaviour as agreed by a panel of observers at the interview. Between the last two transcripts are placed the various expressive features, or 'emphatics' of speech—as Laziczius called them (Sebeok, 1959)—according to the symbol-system of Smith (1952) and Trager (1958). Here we find a note as to such paralinguistic features as volume and tempo of utterance, register effects, audible overtones, drawling or clipped modes of delivery, as well as the interpolated glottal closures, breaks, nasalization, spirantization, exhalations, and so on.

Such a graphic record of the patient's behaviour consequently entails a detailed account of a communicative 'package', that is to say

Smiling, and rubbing right hand with left.
Then points vaguely towards the microphone
with the left hand.

>   《◆》>   >   《《

^   ^^   ⌄   ⌄

S: S:

Q   Q   Q   Q   Q
(30)   (11)   (14)   (10)   34

/ ²k̂əm + (p)ensil + ²kəm + ²kəm + ¹kəm + ²k̂əm: /

What is this article?   Q
(a toothbrush)   (6)   Come   (p)encil   come   come   come   come

Lifts left hand and smiles in a worried
fashion.

⌐²   ⌐

>   >   S: S:

^   ^   ⌄   ⌄

Q   Q   Q
(19)   (6)   (20) ×

/ k̂əmll + k̂əm + sɑɔɔt: + s'l /

Do you know what it really is?   Q
(20)   Come   come   ss   ss

Fig. 1. *Extended transcript of an interview with an aphasiac whose recurrent utterance comprised the monosyllable 'come'. The top of the record contains a description of the patient's gestural behaviour. The middle part comprises the symbols indicating the various 'emphatics' or emotional overtones. Below that is an international phonemic transcript of the text, to which are added symbols indicative of stress, pitch levels, terminal contours, and silent gaps. On the lowest line there is set the examiner's question and the patient's reply, in conventional typology.*

(Reproduced with permission from Aphasiology and other Aspects of Language: Macdonald Critchley, Edward Arnold (Publishers) Ltd.)

a complex set made up of mutually reinforcing signals. Though demanding much time, close attention, and experience, a record like this is invaluable, demonstrating amongst other things that throughout the interview the aphasiac is striving to communicate by one means or another, the difficulties of the task being evidenced by the delays and indecisions, and the manner in which the words appear. Every interpolated sound, every mutilated phoneme, indeed every silent period is an eloquent signal, just as it is in a psychiatric interview. The introduction of a sigh, or laugh, or yawn must not be regarded as linguistic 'noise' but rather as an integral part of the information—

in aphasiacs just as in normals. The transcripts demonstrate very clearly the Smith-Trager aphorism that in speech 'nothing, never happens'. 'Communicative behaviour is continual; and motionless silence is a special kind of communicative act.' Within every utterance, however imperfect, there lies a meaning which can be neither disguised nor concealed. This is implied in the 'law of immanent reference' which means that no matter what else human beings may be communicating about, they are always communicating about themselves, about one another, and about the immediate context of the communication (Pittenger *et al.* 1960). This law—which includes Ruesch & Bateson's notion of 'metacommunion' (1951)—is obeyed by all speakers, however aphasic they may be.

A study of aphasia by way of 'visible speech', i.e. sonography or spectrography, is new. The drawback of audible recordings lies in the difficulties of translation into accurate printed symbols. Visible speech surmounts this problem. As Herodotus said: ὦτα τυγχάνει ἀνθρώποιοι ἐόντα ἀπιστότερα ὀφθαλμῶν ('The ear is a less trustworthy witness than the eye'. Herodotus i, 8). Comparison of the broad band spectrograms of normal and aphasic speakers emitting the same word, shows obvious differences. The normal records are briefer, crisper and tidier (*see* Fig. 2). Aphasic records are longer, blurred, less defined. We can also observe the intromission within the breath-stops of foreign elements like subvocal spirantization—the hallmark of doubt or distress—or a nasalized prolongation of a consonantal phoneme. Hence it can be said that even at a purely phonemic level, the utterance of an aphasiac differs from that of a normal subject, though the difference may escape the ears of the untutored observer. The possible importance of these spectrographic findings is great, for they suggest that aphasia embraces a physiological disorder of lower as well as higher nervous activity, just as in the case of agnosia.

This line of research into aphasia obviously promises to prove most informative. The linguistic philosopher Whatmough (1956) has emphasized that up to now no one has attempted to match or compare the findings of speech spectrography with those of electroencephalography. 'If ever this could be done,' he said, 'it may point to an answer to the old poser of whether "thought" is sub-vocal language.'

Indeed we can take up this last point and direct our specific attention to the silent pauses which occur during an aphasiac's efforts to talk. This is specially profitable in the case of recurrent utterance, where the victim strives in vain to emit one term and produces quite another,

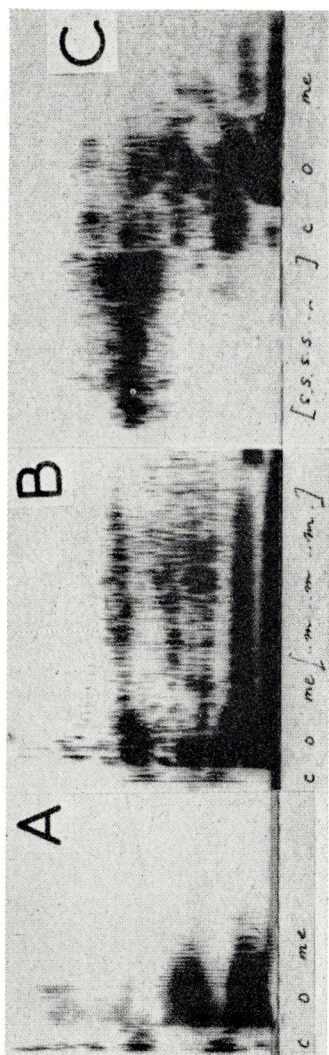

Fig. 2 A. Spectrogram of a normal subject saying the word 'come'. B and C, 'come' spoken by an aphasic patient with this particular recurring utterance. Note in B the excessive nasalization as an excessive terminal glide. In C there is an initial sibilant glide made up of a non-vocalic 'noise'. In B and C the formant is less distinctive than in A (Reproduced by courtesy of Professor D. B. Fry, Department of Phonetics, University of London).

A.D.
aet 49
L. frontal
(a)   tumour

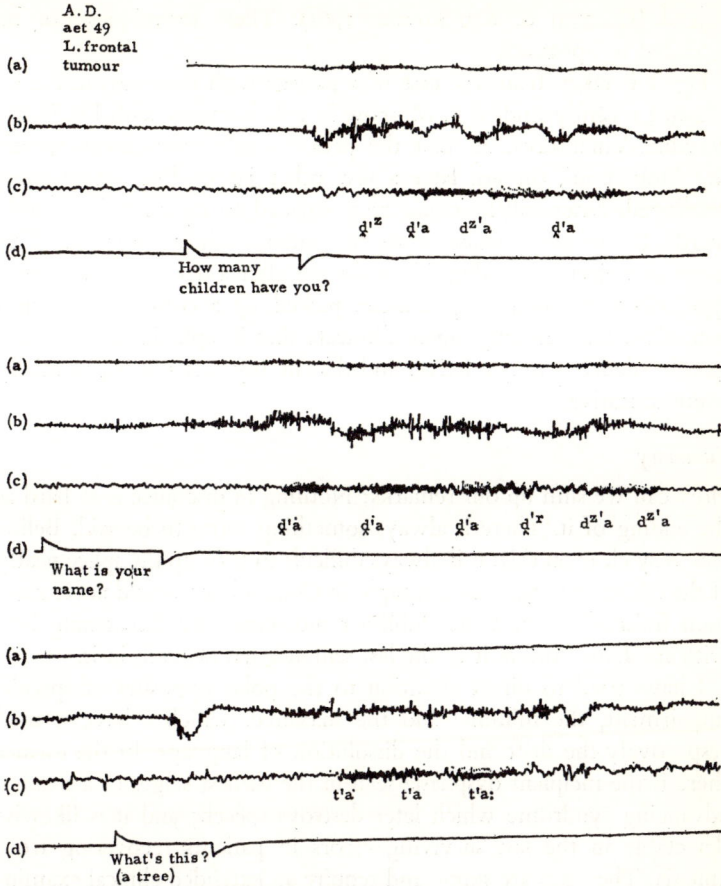

Fig. 3. *Electromyogram taken from (a) orbicularis oris right, and (b) orbicularis oris left, of an aphasic patient with recurrent utterance, (d) indicates the request put to the patient. His audible response is recorded microphonically in line (c).*

(Reproduced with permission from Aphasiology and other Aspects of Language: Macdonald Critchley, Edward Arnold (Publishers) Ltd.)

It has long been known that the silent preverbitum may be the seat of subvocal movements of the articulatory organs. Behaviourists have paid particular attention to this phenomenon, which they often quote in support of the identity of Thought and Language. In recent times, electromyographic studies of the tongue and lips during silent thinking have been popular in the USSR (I. S. Iucevitch Novikova 1955, Bassin & Bein 1955, A. M. Fonarev, N. A. Kryshova) and also in

Poland (Herman & Krolikovska 1961). These techniques can be extended to aphasiacs.

Fig. 3 is taken from the case of a patient with recurrent utterance whom I recently studied in Moscow in collaboration with Dr. H. N. Pravdina-Vinarskaya. At first the patient's sole spontaneous speech was 'nou, nou', though later a few other jargon-like automatisms developed. Later still he could be persuaded to repeat a few simple words. In the silent phase while the patient vainly endeavoured to name an object, succeeding in producing after a delay only a stereotype, electrodes in the lip muscles picked up a complex of action potentials. Such findings again illustrate that in aphasia as in normal speech, silence is only relative, and that in any event, it is potentially communicative.

Summary

How can we sum up our remarks? Nothing in discourse is so hard as the ending of it. There is always something more to be said. Belloc was very clear on this: it is always difficult to turn up the splice neatly at the edges. Panurge's monograph on Conchology would never have been finished had not the Publisher intervened by threatening him with the Law. And as it is, the last sentence has no verb in it.

I have tried to direct attention to the polar opposites of speech-impairment, the minimal and the maximal, which I have termed respectively the drift and the dissolution of language. In the former there is the incipient dysphasia seen in the earliest stages of a steadily advancing syndrome which later destroys speech; and it is likewise detectable in the last surviving errors in patients recovering from aphasia. The signs are subtle and require an extended clinical examination for their discernment.

The contrasting and severest type of speech-loss is found in aphasiacs with recurrent utterance. In such cases there exists an extraordinary mésalliance between the content of the will to speak, and the resulting sounds. As propositions these are meaningless, and it matters little whether they take the form of lexicon words or of gibberish. There is no reason to doubt that some sort of inner speech operates, in which verbal symbols are involved. The ritual strangulation which takes place at the end of the preverbitum may well be due to the unrestrained activity of a compelling buccal apraxia. What determines the pattern of the ritual in a given case is conjectural.

Newer techniques throw light upon the speech-mechanisms in

aphasia, and suggest the simultaneous involvement of lower as well as higher speech centres.

'The real life of a thought only lasts until it reaches the frontier of the words. There it petrifies, is dead from then on.' This dictum of Schopenhauer's is surely a caricature of the normal physiology of speech. But it certainly applies to cases of recurrent utterance, especially when he went on to say: . . . 'thereafter it is imperishable, comparable to the fossils of prehistoric animals and plant. . . .'.

REFERENCES

Alajouanine, T. (1956). *Brain*, **79**, 1.

Alajouanine, T. & Lhermitte, F. (1963). In: *Halpern's Problems in Dynamic Neurology*, p. 201. Jerusalem.

Allport, G. W. (1942). *The Use of Personal Documents in Psychological Science.* New York.

Bassin, F. V. & Bein, E. S. (1955). *Conference on Psychology*, 1–6 July, p. 315.

Botez, M. I. (1961). *Acta. neurol. scand.* **37**, 111.

Broca, P. (1861). *Bull. Soc. Anat. Paris*, **6**, 330, 398.

Critchley, M. (1961). *Perspect. Biol. Med.* **5**, 101.

Dostoievsky, F. (1876–81). *Diary of a Writer.*

Freud, S. (1891). *On Aphasia* (trans. 1953). London.

Gowers, W. R. (1885). Lectures on the Diagnosis of Diseases of the Brain. New York.

Henschen, H. E. (1922). *Klinische und anatomische Beiträge zur Pathologie des Gehirns. Part 7. Über motorische Aphasie und Agraphie.* Stockholm.

Herman, E. & Krolikovska (1961). *World Neurol.* **2**, 991.

Ivanova, M. P. (1953). *Dissertation*, Moscow St. Univ.

Jackson, J. H. (1864). *Med. Pr.* **1**, 19, 41, 63.

Jackson, J. H. (1879–80) *Brain*, **2**, 203, 323.

Kuttner, H. (1928). *Mschr. Psychiat. Neurol.* **70**, 287.

Luria, A. R. (1958). *Lang. and Speech*, **1**, 14.

Luria, A. R. (1959) *Word*, **15**, 341, 453.

Mescheryakov, A. I. (1953). *Dissertation.* Moscow St. Univ.

Monakow, C. von (1914). Die Lokalisation im Grosshirn. Wiesbaden.

Moutier, F. (1908). *L'Aphasie de Broca.* Paris.

Novikova, L. A. (1955). *Conference on Psychology*, 1–6 July, p. 337.

Petrie, A. (1949). *J. ment. Sci.* **95**, 449.

Pittenger, R. E., Hockett, C. E. & Danehy, J. J. (1960). *The First Five Minutes.* Ithaca, NY.

Ruesch, J. & Bateson, G. (1951). *Communication: The Social Matrix of Psychiatry.* New York.

Sapir, E. (1921). *Language: An Introduction to the Study of Speech.* New York.
Sebeok, T. A. (1959), *Word,* **15,** 175.
Smith, H. L. jr (1952). *An Outline of Metalinguistic Analysis.* Washington.
Thorndike, E. L. & Lorge, I. (1944). *The Teachers Wordbook of 30,000 Words.* New York.
Trager, G. L. (1958). *Stud. Linguistics,* **13,** 1.
Whatmough, J. (1956). *Language: A Modern Synthesis.* London.
Whitehead, A. N. (1938). *Modes of Thought.* Cambridge.
Zangwill, O. L. (1964). In: *Disorders of Language.* Ed. A. V. S. de Reuck & M. O'Connor. London.

Postscript (August 1971)

This lecture contains a pioneer description of what might be called 'pre-aphasia', or, to avoid an etymological hybrid, 'proto-aphasia'. Later papers have since elaborated this conception, and in particular have described various techniques for the elucidation of minimal degrees of dysphasia. Two other novel ideas were promulgated in this address, neither of which has been adequately followed up by subsequent workers in the field of aphasiology. The first of these concerns an account of a method for the detailed recording of the nuances of a clinical interview with an aphasic patient. This manœuvre is a logical development of the technique propounded eleven years ago by Pittenger, Hockett and Daneby for the transcription of a psychiatric conversation piece. The second point emphasized in this Hughlings Jackson lecture was a promising means of analysing the verbal performance of an aphasiac through the medium of spectrography ('visible speech'). Its possible utility was emphasized in that it might bring to the fore disorders of expression at peripheral as well as central levels, after brain disease.

Moorfields and British Ophthalmology

SIR STEWART DUKE-ELDER

GCVO, FRCP, FRCS, FRS

11 *September* 1965

To give the inaugural lecture in a series is a task both difficult and responsible, and I am deeply conscious of the honour your Committee has conferred upon me by selecting me to fulfil it. For this I thank them. But the responsibility weighs on me; for in a sense it might well be held that the first should set the tone for future lectures. In this case, however, that is to be impossible; for I suppose in most cases you will doubtless select someone who is contributing actively and lavishly to our specialty and this platform will become the forum for the announcement of fresh advances and new discoveries with all the thrill and excitement that these bring.

Alas, for me these days are past. I think it is true to say that real originality in scientific thought tends to fade away—if not before—at least in the decade between 45 and 55 when the cycle of life changes and biologically we ought to die. Most research bodies are indeed wise in dispensing with their research workers at the age of 60; and, although many complain vociferously, it is on the whole good that before this, as a general rule in academic life, the chores of administration tend to replace original work in the laboratory. The most that one can thereafter do is to sit back and think; to try to keep pace with the frightening mass of new ideas that multiply in geometric progression as each year succeeds the last, not only in your own but in allied disciplines; perhaps to integrate some of them into a coherent philosophy; and, most important of all, to ensure that more opportunities and facilities are given to the next generation than were available to the previous one, so that anything you may have done does not die with you and the march of progress may be sustained when you have left the stage.

I therefore have my limitations—for I have nothing original to say. I must, of course, speak of William Lang. I met him but did not know him well, for in his time I was very small, I knew Basil, and when he died in 1928 I was appointed to the staff of Moorfields; so in a sense I blended into the tradition of them both. Fortunately, Maurice Whiting, who is even older than I, knew them both well and it is good that he is able to speak personally about them.

Instead, your President has asked me to talk in this first lecture about their place—and the place of men like them—in the history and development of British ophthalmology; and as my text I propose to talk of the influence of a school of thought in the evolution of a subject, and in particular on the influence of the Moorfields school on the development of British ophthalmology, and the place occupied by Lang in its story.

I think it is true to say that not only in ophthalmology, not only in medicine, but in most of the constructive aspects of life, the quality which matters most is not individual brilliance but the ability to attract and inspire others. It is true that in the founding of a school an individual of brilliance is an asset; indeed, often a necessity. By and large, Emerson was right when he said that an institution is but the shadow of one man. But unless the one man holds as one of his primary objectives the attraction to himself of pupils of ability, and unless he has the capacity to enthuse them and fuse them into a corporate team, anything he may achieve is limited to a short life-span, and when he disappears so does the shadow.

And so in medicine. It was essentially his extraordinary attraction for the young and his power to inspire them, rather than his intellectual gifts and his unusual clinical flair, that enabled Sir William Osler to establish the tradition of the scientific teaching of internal medicine in the hospital wards of three successive medical schools—McGill, Johns Hopkins and Oxford.

No one would call William Holland Wilmer a great ophthalmologist for he contributed nothing original of note to our specialty; but I think that his influence in the modern development of American ophthalmology exceeded that of any other man; for on his personality, his ability to attract and inspire others, and, incidentally, his flair for collecting money—on these qualities depended the founding of the Wilmer Institute, just recently rebuilt, the first scientific centre of ophthalmology in America, the first in time and probably still the first in influence. On this depended the revolution of American ophthalmology which, within three decades, has become transformed from a clinical discipline wherein research was practically non-existent to an exuberantly prolific growth of scientific achievement which in its mass and excellence is now unequalled anywhere in the world.

In the history of the development of ophthalmology as a specialty and as a science, the primary school without any question was that of Vienna, established at the end of the eighteenth century. There, and at that time, ophthalmology, then an uncoordinated offshoot of surgery, largely peddled by illegitimate practitioners and quacks, was for the first time given the dignity of an academic science in its own right. For in 1773 Guiseppe Barth was appointed by the Empress, Maria Theresa, as Professor of Anatomy and Ophthalmology in Vienna; and for the first time ophthalmology was given half-a-chair value.

In the eighteenth century, of course, the corpus of knowledge was relatively small; and half-a-chair was good value. In the previous century a Descartes knew everything there was to know from the structure of the human brain to the achitecture of the universe. In the early eighteenth century, Boerhaave, the greatest physician of his time, was Professor of Medicine, Botany and Chemistry in Harderwick in Holland. In the later eighteenth century Albrecht von Haller, who created the science of physiology, was Professor of Anatomy, Surgery and Botany at Göttingen. So at the time half-a-chair was indeed high status. How different from today when we can well have a department of virology within the department of microbiology, within the department of pathology, within the department of medicine, each subsection hardly understanding the language the other is talking, let alone what they are talking about.

Barth was more of an anatomist than an ophthalmologist, but fortunately for us he took on an apprentice, Josef Beer, and kept him working primarily as a draughtsman of anatomical specimens. But Beer liked the practice of ophthalmology better than drawing, and after seven years' tutelage with Barth he broke out on his own into ophthalmology. And in 1812 the Emperor of Austria created a Chair of Ophthalmology and appointed Beer the first sole Professor of Ophthalmology in the world. He was given three rooms which are still extant, two equipped with eight beds and the third serving as operating theatre, library and classroom. Here academic ophthalmology was born.

Beer did not revolutionize ophthalmology, although some of us still occasionally use his knife; although his professional life was short, for he had a stroke in 1819, seven years after his appointment, he attracted others to this new discipline and enthused them with its potentialities—a succession of men such as von Ammon and Frederick

Jaeger, visitors from distant lands such as William Mackenzie from Glasgow and Frick from Baltimore. Above all there was Ferdinand von Arlt, the son of a humble blacksmith in Bohemia, who was the great consolidator of the school and who occupied the Chair in Vienna from 1856 to 1883; he stabilized ophthalmological practice for two generations by his great textbook, *Die Krankheiten des Auges*, and ophthalmic surgery for half a century by writing the surgical section of the *Graefe-Saemisch Handbuch*; he attracted the ablest and the best into the emergent specialty and numbered among his pupils Albrecht von Graefe, Stellwag von Carion, Eduard Jaeger and Ernst Fuchs, a succession of men who maintained the world-wide reputation of the Vienna school until the catastrophe of the First World War.

In England the development of ophthalmology depended essentially on the school of Moorfields. It was slower from the start than the Vienna school; it took half a century for it to achieve real world fame; but although it occasionally experienced decades of the doldrums, it still flourishes after 150 years, perhaps today more vigorously than ever before. And the main reason was that in addition to flashes of brilliance, it always succeeded in attracting to it surgeons like William Lang.

Essentially because of the ravages of the Egyptian ophthalmia that swept the country when the soldiers of the armies that fought Napoleon in Egypt in 1798–9 were disbanded to spread trachoma thoughout the population, it was founded in 1805 by John Cunningham Saunders. It was an act of courage at that time to adopt as a specialty a branch of medicine practised largely by illegitimate practitioners, and it would not have been practical without the support of the immense professional weight of Sir Astley Cooper.

The early surgeons were good: Saunders, Benjamin Travers, Sir William Lawrence, and Frederick Tyrrell were as capable as any in the world, and their names will always be remembered in the story of ophthalmology. In brilliance they did not equal the galaxy in Vienna; but from the historical point of view the most important thing they did was to train students in the new specialty. The school was started by Farre, Travers and Lawrence in 1811, six years after the hospital had been founded. In the first seven years 412 students had been enrolled; a quarter of a century later 1,320 had passed through its doors. And from it a sound and eminently practical ophthalmology was spread, not only throughout England but throughout the English-speaking world. Delafield and Rodgers returned to America to follow the inspiration of Saunders and found the New York Eye and Ear Infirmary, Edward Reynolds to found the Massachusetts Eye and Ear Infirmary, William Buller, famous for his shield, to Montreal to become the first to specialize in ophthalmology in Canada, and Richardson to open the Madras Eye Infirmary. So impressed were the East India Company of the value of the last emigration that shortly thereafter from Moorfields were sent Jeafferson to found the Eye Hospital in Bombay and Egerton that in Calcutta.

But it was not until the middle of the century that Moorfields became translated from English-speaking to world fame. The decade at the middle of the century was indeed an extraordinary epoch when Europe emerged from mediævalism into modernity—politically, as the old empires of the Continent were carved up to give place to new powers; industrially, as machines, electricity and railways began to replace men and horses; and in the whole of medicine as a new and questioning spirit of observation and experiment replaced the doc-trinal authority of Galen and Paracelsus, when Charles Darwin was creating the biology we now know, Rudolf Virchow the cellular pathology and Claude Bernard the physiology we still expand, when Louis Pasteur was creating bacteriology, when Richard Bright and Thomas Addison were practising true clinical medicine, when anaes-thesia was being introduced and aseptic surgery was dawning with Lister, when the ophthalmoscope of von Helmholtz was making the study of ocular disease a science instead of a competition in guess-work.

It was indeed fortunate that at that time of flux when scientific ophthalmology was born, there emerged men at Moorfields who could not only swim with the tide but ride on the crest of the wave. Of these I must choose four: initially Sir George Critchett, the star surgeon, and Sir William Bowman, the great scientist—the first appointed to the staff in 1843, the second in 1846—to be followed by John Whitaker Hulke, the pathologist, and Sir Jonathan Hutchinson, the consummate physician.

Three of these are household words wherever ophthalmology is practised; the least known is Hulke; and I think unfairly, for he founded the tradition of pathology at Moorfields, a tradition ably maintained by his successors such as Treacher Collins, John Parsons and George Coats, and today more vitally alive than ever. In addition to being a general surgeon, first at King's and then at the Middlesex, an ophthalmologist and a pathologist, he was a geologist and a palæontologist of international repute. Learning the use of the recently introduced ophthalmoscope with Bowman at King's, and enthused by his master's studies of the new microscopic anatomy, he wrote: 'We can read the appearances in the fundus during life as if portrayed in the pages of a book, but our knowledge of them must remain imperfect without the explanation offered by dissection and the microscope.'

In 1859 he was awarded the Jacksonian Prize by the Royal College of Surgeons for his essay on 'The Morbid Changes in the Retina as seen in the Eye of the Living Person after Removal from the Body'. In 1867 he was made a Fellow of the Royal Society for his researches on the retinæ of man and animals, particularly reptiles; for his palæontological work he was given the Wollaston Gold Medal of the Geological Society in 1887, and shortly before he died he became President of the Royal College of Surgeons.

Of the four great consolidators of the Moorfields school the greatest, of course, was Bowman. But it is an interesting confirmation of my remarks at the beginning of this lecture that his original contributions to ophthalmology were negligible—nothing in comparison with the lavish gifts of his great contemporaries, von Graefe in Berlin and Donders in Holland. His unique brilliance as an original observer faded out at the age of 26, by which time, however, with the aid of the recently evolved microscope, he had revolutionized the minute anatomy of the kidney and striped muscle and had become a Fellow of the Royal Society. In ophthalmology, apart from minute anatomy, his name lingers only around the lacrimal passages. But by the charm and strength of his personality, his transparent integrity as a man and his eminence as a scientist, and his strange power of enthusing and stimulating others, he did more than any one to consolidate the traditions of the school of Moorfields and to establish British ophthalmology as a world power.

From that time Moorfields dominated and moulded British ophthalmology, sometimes for good, sometimes for ill. For good because it served as a central source of inspiration with a tradition sufficiently established and consolidated to continue to attract a succession of the ablest men, the only place where systematic teaching was persistently pursued, so that its influence continued to be disseminated, the place above all others where there was sufficient material to train the resident in the craftsmanship of surgery, and the only place where the tradition of pathology was kept alive.

For ill, for, like an automated factory, it tended to train people in the art of appeasing the multitude rather than in the intensive study of individual patients as is the habit in the clinics of Europe. Ever since its inception in 1805, even until today, the unending horde of patients has been the constant but ineffectual plaint of the staff. Thus it was with Saunders. In its first year the hospital saw 600 patients; in its fourth year 2,357; in its fifth year Saunders died at the age of 36. Several of his successors were similarly murdered—Tyrrell at the age of 49, Dalrymple at 49, Scott at 48; and today, seeing over a quarter of a million patients annually, the originality of those of its staff who survive tends to be drowned in the ocean of humanity in need.

During the century following its consolidation the tradition thus established has remained so strong that Moorfields has survived until its second revolution—this time in the academic sense—in the middle of the present century. There were on its staff, of course, many able ophthalmologists whose names have failed to survive the winnowing of time; there were a few stars of singular brightness, men perhaps of genius or near-genius, such as Nettleship, Parsons, Coats and possibly Treacher Collins; but the tradition was maintained essentially by a succession of exceptional clinicians and surgeons of ability above the ordinary, whose names will always be remembered. There were: Warren Tay, who followed Critchett; Sir John Tweedy, who followed Hutchinson, perhaps more of a medical politician than an ophthalmologist; Marcus Gunn, one of the first to elucidate arterial disease in the fundus; J. B. Lawford, the early bacteriologist, the first to see the newly discovered tubercle bacillus of Koch in the eye; Stamford Morton, who designed the ophthalmoscope we use today; Holmes Spicer, the great clinical observer who developed the school into its modern form and whose work therein was continued by Goulden and Davenport; Herbert Fisher who used to quench my youthful enthusiasm when it became too exuberant; William Lister, whose name should always be associated with holes in a retinal detachment; Claude Worth, who pioneered modern conceptions of the significance of squint; Cyril Hudson, who taught me how clinical observation should be done; Foster Moore who introduced a new era in medical ophthalmology.

Among this eminently respectable upper middle class belonged William Lang who was on the staff from 1884 to 1912. In the larger scale of things he was no genius whose name will live forever; but he was typically Moorfields, and he imprinted his name firmly on the development of ophthalmology during his lifetime. This concerned the theory claiming that uveitis was due to focal infection, a study which occupied the whole of his professional lifetime, of which he was the main architect and the stoutest upholder. Hitherto the teaching of von Arlt was widely accepted: that the causes of uveitis were scrofula (30%), rheumatism (21%), syphilis (17%) and the remaining 32% indeterminate. Lang was first attracted to the new doctrine in 1896 when he observed that a case of rosacea keratitis cleared up on the radical treatment of dental sepsis. His last great contribution was in opening the major discussion in the Ophthalmological Society of the United Kingdom in 1923, when he arraigned not only the teeth but the tonsils, the remains of adenoids, the nasal sinuses, all the mucosæ, respiratory, alimentary and genito-urinary, as well as sepsis of the skin, as the cause not only of 50% of cases of uveitis but also of glaucoma, acute and chronic, zoster, retinal detachment, weakness of accommodation and convergence and asthenopia.

We all know what occurred in the second and third decades of this century. To eliminate the recurrent bacteriæmias that were the cause of so many ills, uncritically and indiscriminately hosts of patients were rendered edentulous, and if the ocular inflammation did not clear up, an alveolectomy was done; there were holocausts of tonsils and adenoids, every nasal sinus was opened and sometimes the entire mucosa stripped away, gall-bladders and appendices followed each other into the scrap-heap, and sometimes colons were removed, prostates were massaged and uteri scraped; and if the patient survived all this mutilation, and the iridocyclitis still recurred, a streptococcus was reclaimed from some unremovable recess and a vacine given.

The doctrine did not spread to Europe where the classical view was retained, largely owing to the influence of the Vienna school championed by Löwenstein and Meller, that the most common cause of iridocyclitis and choroiditis was tuberculosis; but with their mouths still heavily furnished with gold-capped teeth and elaborate bridges, the Europeans suffered iridocyclitis no more and no less frequently, no more and no less severely than the edentulous English. But the doctrine spread like wild-fire to America where Billings played the role of Lang, and it seemed to receive experimental confirmation in the somewhat poorly controlled animal experiments of Irons, Brown and Rosenow about the time of the First World War.

Nor were ophthalmologists the only enthusiasts for the doctrine spread over the whole of medicine and physicians and particularly rheumatologists held the same views. But the interesting thing is that long after physicians, bacteriologists and pathologists had demonstrated that bacterial metastases did not commonly occur in this type of case and that the cultured uvea in cases of exudative uveitis was invariably sterile, the ophthalmologists of this country continued to be fascinated and hypnotized by the doctrine, largely because of the authority of William Lang.

And today no one can say that he was wholly wrong, for there was and still is a basis of truth in his views. And if we in our modern wisdom speak of allergy or hypersensitivity, if we dream of unknown and possibly nonexistent viruses and possibly innocuous pleuro-pneumonia-like organisms, and if we talk learnedly of collagenous disease and the cannibalization of tissues by autoimmunity, we have really gone little further in solving the enigma of exudative uveitis than had William Lang.

Indeed, throughout its long history medicine has been dominated by the uncritical worship of a constant succession of unproven hypotheses. These have been accepted wholeheartedly with no scientific basis, no objective analysis of the phenomena they were assumed to explain, and no proof of their efficacy by observation and experiment. To a large extent this is pardonable for, unlike the scientist who seeks objective truth for its own sake, the doctor must accept something tangible, must believe in something for the simple practical reason that he must do something for his individual patient. In my youth the fashion of the day was focal infection; it was followed by the craze of allergy, then of psychosomatic illness, and today we similarly magnify the role of autoimmunity to the influence of which many things we do not understand are being ascribed.

And the tendency is not confined to ophthalmology, or even medicine. You may remember that the great Kepler, when he took over Tycho Brahe's post as Imperial Mathematician in Prague in 1601, while mapping out the stars in their courses in the Heavens to prove that the Copernican universe was correct, and accumulating the mass of observations that allowed Newton to synthesize his vast conception a century later, still had to employ much of his time casting horoscopes for his patron and his clients, the value of which he could not credit.

The purpose of this lecture was to assess the influence of the Moorfields school in the evolution of British ophthalmology and the place therein of William Lang. He was typical of the immensely competent

F

clinicians, the careful observers, the devoted and enthusiastic workers who, by great good fortune, have always formed the backbone of the staff of Moorfields and have succeeded in maintaining a steady standard of excellence in British ophthalmology for a century and a half. The appearance of genius is rare; and it is rarer still for its emergence to coincide with a revolutionary leap forward in the progress of medicine so that a new tradition can be established as occurred in the middle of the last century. Such a combination may occur again; but in the intervals, during the ordinary times, we need men like Lang to maintain, to keep alive and to improve the established traditions, to serve as the stepping-stones from the basis of which someone, some day, when the opportunity arises, will be able again to take a great leap forward.

The Status of Doctors

THE RT HON. LORD SNOW

18 *May* 1966

The reason I presume to talk to you is that for a long time I had to think about the status of engineering. This was something I had to do in my civil service career and, later on, in my spell in Government. In this country far too few people are becoming engineers and the few who do are not honoured, rewarded or esteemed very much by society. This is a real weakness on our part, as against other comparable countries; it is a great problem which none of us knows how to solve. But until we do solve it we are at a major economic disadvantage. During the course of my thoughts on engineers I have compared the engineering profession with the medical profession. Some of the facts about the two are not dissimilar: some of the education is not dissimilar, and one or two of the criticisms I am going to make of medical education may be applied equally to engineering education; and we are as short of doctors as we are of engineers.

Status is a very odd concept; it is a very subjective concept. None of us knows quite what it means, but it means something important. Although it is important in drawing people into a profession, it appears not to be by any means the most important single factor. For instance, in this country the Bar has traditionally had a very high status. The rewards are extremely high; even a moderately successful junior at the Bar makes more money than any but a handful of doctors or engineers. Yet at the present time there is a really chronic shortage of persons wanting to become barristers.

The status of both doctors and engineers in this country leaves much to be desired—more so for engineers than for doctors. Like engineers, doctors have a really serious professional training, and they have a much longer history. There were professional doctors in ancient Egypt. At Salerno, one of the oldest universities in the world, instruction was confined to medicine; this was the first of the universities of Europe, before Paris or Oxford.

It occurred to me to think about status in the three countries in which I have lived for any length of time—this country, the United States and the Soviet Union. There is the status accorded by general opinion—what the whole community thinks of these professions; and there is the status of what might be called informed or academic opinion. These may be somewhat different.

I will start with a very objective fact: there are still marriage brokers in New York. A marriage broker charges $300 if your daughter marries a doctor, $400 if she marries an attorney, $300 if she marries an engineer. These figures come from the Jewish marriage market in New York, and they seem to me to indicate roughly the relative status of these professions.

Not long ago the National Science Foundation in the United States did an opinion poll among the general population on the status of occupations, and the order was: first, doctors; second, scientists; third, politicians and academics who, oddly enough, got mixed up together; and then engineers a long way behind. I think we can take for granted that in the United States the status of doctors, so far as they have any status at all, is very high; it is not quite so high among academic opinion, for reasons I will come to, the main one being that doctors make far too much money.

In the Soviet Union the position is reversed: engineers have by far the highest social prestige, scientists are some way down the scale, doctors very much further down. In January 1966 the greatest of contemporary Soviet engineers, a man called Korolev, died of cancer at the age of 60. He had a state funeral and 40,000 people were reported to have attended. Would any doctor have a funeral of that size? This was the man behind the whole Russian space programme; he was a genuine and serious engineer.

In this country I think the order is somewhat different. Here the prestige order is, probably: first, scientists, largely owing to the traditional English respect for the high academics, the repute of the Royal Society, and so forth; second, doctors; third, engineers. I think most people in this country would accept that scientists are widely respected; doctors, although my friends tell me their prestige is going down, I think still come second; engineers, unfortunately for our economic future, are very low down.

Why is this? The answers, I suspect, are very complicated. We are all prudish about this, we find it hard to be honest, we do not even know what is the truth. But assuming we are not going to have complete egalitarianism (for which, as Bernard Shaw used to say, there is something to be said, in fact a good deal to be said), then I suspect that we leave to chance more than with other things the rewards for people in arduous, responsible professions that require long training.

When the Review Committee issued its report a friend of mine in the House of Commons criticized the awards for doctors on the ground that the industrial working class would take this very hard. On many things I agree with him, but not on this: I believe that society is perfectly prepared, in a country like ours, to accept at least modest differentials without much trouble, and we have to think what these differentials should be. Obviously, putting it harshly and crudely, we cannot afford to lose 300 doctors a year any more than we can lose a rather smaller number of good engineers.

Doctors' pay in the United States is very good. In the midwest I have seen suburbs inhabited by rich doctors and nobody else, which means that they are not terribly popular with the academic community, and this has probably separated them from the rest of society in a way which I think undesirable. I do not want to go into American medical politics but it is certainly true that doctors there are not regarded with unqualified enthusiasm by the society which they purport to serve.

In Russia, doctors' pay is genuinely poor, much less than that of engineers or scientists. In this country, I would say the pay of scientists, doctors and engineers is very close together, they are in the same professional belt. I do not believe you can distinguish within 10% at any level. Granted equality of training and equality of talent, then so far as I know the rate of pay on all sides should be the same. But an apparently highly paid profession like the Bar is not attracting candidates either quantitatively or qualitatively.

In this country, although there is a parallel between doctors and engineers, there is no doubt that doctors are more esteemed than engineers; doctors have a higher place in the popular imagination and I think also in the more esoteric imagination. A novelist can bring a doctor into a novel without any trouble at all, people know who he is; but try bringing an engineer into a novel and it is terribly difficult—they have not got recognition symbols in the way the medical profession has.

It is, I think, true that neither the engineering profession nor the medical profession plays its part in public life in the way that I certainly would like them to. Clearly it is to be expected that most people who have the professional training will in fact become doctors and engineers and nothing else; but it is true of many other professions, such as the law and science, that some members filter out great virtue and value to the community in other areas of activity. This does not happen in this country with engineers, and only to a limited extent with doctors.

Let me give an example: this is not a political speech in any sense, but I congratulate the Conservative Party on trying to get on good terms with the academic community. They are trying to set up committees, drawn of course from dons, which can give them academic advice, which will reach the universities of the country. The Labour Party did this in 1945 and many of the ideas which are now coming from the Labour Party sprang from this kind of academic advice. No one has thought of bringing in engineers, and certainly not doctors, to this kind of relation with politics. Why? Both professions have extremely intelligent, very widely experienced people, of sober judgement and so on, and yet the idea is effectively unthinkable. Dons are one thing and engineers and doctors are clearly another. We shall not get these great professions into their right perspective until it is automatic that they give advice on all kinds of things outside their ordinary workaday life, as we think of dons or economists giving advice.

In the same way I should like to see a tiny sprinkle of people leaving the medical profession and taking their part in public life, and far more engineers than now doing exactly the same thing. Again, it does not happen: there are a few doctors in the House of Commons, there are one or two in administration, but surprisingly few. This is not so in the Soviet Union: Kosygin is an engineer, Brezhnev is an engineer, Gromyko is an engineer; it seems that there is a level of professional infiltration into government which we completely lack, and I think this may become a serious weakness in the western world. I want not only engineers in the layer of government, but doctors also. I think they have a great deal of human wisdom to contribute, without which we shall be genuinely impoverished in any process of decision-making which we can foresee.

I am surprised that medical education has turned out to be a less good humane education than might have been expected. It has obviously become, for some reason, entirely professional, and that applies equally to some of the deficiencies of engineering education.

Engineering education in this country is all right, it has produced relatively good engineers, but nothing beyond. Medical education, to an extent, suffers from the same faults.

Doctors, in my experience, are better citizens than most of us; despite their temptations, they are relatively honest and upright and make relatively good husbands. They are pillars of society and yet there is a weakness; I believe the weakness to an extent springs from the temperament of those who elect to be doctors, but much more from the way they are trained. Doctors, like engineers, appear to be remarkably conformist, conformist in their young manhood, conformist in their professional life. The more I have thought of medical education the more I think that speculative and rebellious intelligence is surprisingly neglected—that part of the intelligence which makes people question, often foolishly, often nihilistically, often unrewardingly, but makes them question the whole of the axioms of the life which they lead. I believe this part is as deficient in medical education and in the medical profession as it is in the engineering profession. This is entirely contrary to what happens in pure science. Pure scientists are an awful nuisance—they are so as young men, and they are not much less of a nuisance until they are very old indeed; and yet they are intensely valuable because their speculative and rebellious intelligence is never quenched, it is encouraged by the process, it is there all the time; and that is why any government at any time is going to have scientists probably playing a really active part within it.

I was once a tutor at Cambridge and I loved my medical students for whom I was responsible. But compared with the rest of the students in the college they were, together with the engineers, by far the most conservative part of the whole body of students. These were people who would never do anything which was intellectually rebellious. Some of them made nuisances of themselves on Boat Race night and May Week nights, drank hard, chased girls; that was fun, they were hearty, cheerful characters who would make good citizens; but they did not, as I dearly should have liked them to do, question the assumptions in the way my scientific students did.

It is not that I want all medical students immediately to belong to the left wing organizations of our universities. What I want is a scatter. It is bad for any profession if all its entrants are automatically more conformist and more conservative than their contemporaries. This is happening now to medical students and engineering students.

Statistically there is no doubt about it, these are the people who by the standards of modern student society are on the conservative side, and they never budge. It seems to me that the medical profession should think a little about this education. What is lacking? These people are no different from others. Of my pupils some had a sense of genuine dedication, a vocation, some came in because their fathers were doctors, a surprisingly large number, I remember. They were good human material, but they were never given much chance to think. I would have thought that preclinical education was extremely dull. Medical education wants some re-thinking, it wants some adjuncts probably entirely outside medical subjects, and to give these people something to make their imagination work, or it will never work again in their lives.

Engineers likewise start with a highly disciplined course, highly professional from the outset, and never have a chance to stretch their speculative intelligence until they become old men. I would like to see both disciplines have something like social history, economics, as a compulsory part of the pre-professional stage. This would mean they would have to think, be exposed to argument and know what it means, know that in fact traditional instruction is not the only thing in the world.

I do not think doctors suffer from the other great weakness of engineers, that is, their complete lack of verbalism. Engineers can often be extremely clever but they cannot spell and they cannot speak. The doctors I have known are extremely articulate. I suspect the descriptive processes they have to go through, both themselves and presumably with their patients, are extremely good verbal training, and I do not think it is an accident that the one thing the medical profession has done, apart from producing doctors, is to produce writers. I do not think it is an accident that there are almost no engineering writers, and very few from the scientific professions. On the other hand, the medical profession has produced some really good writers in the last hundred years.

I will not reproach doctors for lack of verbiage, which is one of the defects of the engineering profession, but I do reproach them for the lack of speculative intelligence in medical education.

This situation is not helped by the extreme specialization from which we are all suffering. We try to squeeze into a qualifying graduate course a content which thirty years ago would have been thought impossible. (Sir J. Chadwick once told me he thought the practical content of a physics Part II at Cambridge was about twice what it was in his time). This is true not only in medicine and engineering but in academic life generally. There must be qualifying examinations, possibly less factual but more scientific than at present; and then postgraduate courses should be added. We cannot possibly, when there is an accumulation of knowledge which is going to increase exponentially for a long time, expect our bright children to go into medicine and qualify between 21 and 24 without strain and without loss. The brightest ones will not do it: if given the choice they will prefer something like economics.

That brings me to what is really the core of what I want to say. If we get the education right, I believe we shall get some part of the status of the medical profession right. Here I am thinking very largely of general practitioners, since the real problem is the function of the general practitioner in society. Here we have two things, one is the esteem in which society holds doctors, and the other is the part which the doctor gives to society. I am not going to be hypocritical; I believe it is a one-sided contract, more one-sided than most of us realize. Any possible system that I can imagine is going to require a doctor to give more to society than society can give him, of that I am quite sure; in other places I have been I have known this is true. The work is always there, intolerably arduous, intolerably responsible, much more so than in most professions and whatever the rewards, they will not be sufficient. This will always be true. If I were a doctor I should not think this entirely to my disadvantage: I should feel my conscience was pretty clear because of it. But, that being said, our general practitioners do seem to have a unique function in society, through the possibility that they may be nuclei which can to some extent help avoid or help minimize the fractionization which is going on in the whole of advanced life, in the whole of advanced society, and in particular in the whole of advanced England. I believe that some kind of foci are going to be desperately significant.

None of us knows what is happening to our society; in many material ways people are living more comfortably than they have ever lived in the whole of human history. That is obvious, and yet there are great dangers. I doubt if we have the social insight to see how deep these dangers are, but we can see their efflorescence in the increase of crime and juvenile delinquency and so on. The kind of forces which bind society together are getting very weak. This is a thing which my Russian friends are constantly worried about, and some of their activities which puzzle us are explained by this reason. In this country and in America, modern life is becoming entirely deprived of any sense of community. There is no wise man, the religion which was preached is no longer listened to. We have to find people who are respected, who are on the spot, who are sensible and who can perform some kind of function of religion. I believe that general practitioners have always understood this, and certainly in the suburb where I was born, the one person I knew when I was a child, who was educated and relatively humane and wanted the children of the parish to get on, was the local GP. I do not think he was a very clever GP, though he kept us all alive, but he was a nice and good man, in one of the early suburbs of a provincial town. How are we going to continue and possibly develop this particular spiritual and social function of general practitioners? I do not know, but I know it is desperately important. I know also that there are organizational reasons which make it very difficult. I cannot go into that, except to say that obviously people with thousands and thousands of patients cannot possibly practice, in the sense I mean, very effectively.

I want to go on with something else, not the organizational problem, but the conflict between this social function of the general practitioner as I conceive it, and the claims of scientific medicine. It seems to me that if we think only of scientific medicine, only of how people's bodies are actually working and how they are to be made to work, it is possible to imagine a system from which the human and social leadership might easily be eliminated within a generation. You would have an immense computer service, with very large groups of general paractitioners working comparatively anonymously and, in cases where the computer showed any sign of doubt, at once rushing patients off to the nearest specialist. To an extent this happens in America and in other societies. I believe it is a perfectly efficient way of conducting a large part of medicine. But I believe it may take away the unique contribution which medicine can bring to our world. People want not only to be kept alive and working properly, they want to be cheered, they want some sort of stimulus, some sort of contact, they want, in fact, a leader. Here we have to resolve an extremely delicate and very difficult balance between what scientific medicine requires and what the personal relation between physician and patient also requires.

I do not begin to know the answer. This is a matter for medical persons who know all the real facts and all the real possibilities of scientific medicine and all the real resources of computerized know-ledge. But I am sure there is a problem and I am perfectly clear that if the personal side is left out we shall be desperately at fault. Let me remind you of a popular television programme called 'Dr. Finlay's Casebook', which is enshrined very deeply in the hearts of people; it shows something which people need—not only want, but need—a real friend, in a society which is constantly getting further from any kind of personal relationship. This we must not lose, and this is what doctors can uniquely give.

Frank Buckland—Medical Naturalist

WILLIAM E. SNELL

MD, FRCP

5 October 1966

An enthusiasm for the instruction and improvement of the poor and for the diffusion of useful knowledge, culminating in the Great Exhibition of 1851, was, as we know, characteristic of the earlier years of the reign of Victoria.

Natural history was one subject exciting interest, and by his numerous lectures and books, Frank Buckland, a medical truant, did much at that time to popularize a knowledge of the animal kingdom. He was impelled to do so by his own consuming interest in nature and also, as he said himself, to trace the power of the Creator in all his works.

Frank Trevelyan Buckland, eldest son of the Rev. Canon William Buckland, was born on 17 December 1826, at Christchurch, Oxford. He was one of 8 children, 4 of whom died young. As a small child he had a remarkable memory and, no doubt encouraged by his father, he began collecting natural history specimens at the early age of 4, and at this date, when shown some fossil bones by a visitor to the house, he instantly identified them as the vertebræ of an ichthyosaurus. At the age of 7 he began his journal, in which one of the earliest recorded events was the installation of the Duke of Wellington as Chancellor of the University in 1834. As part of the celebrations a dinner was held at Christchurch, and the live turtle destined for the soup was given a swim in the College fountain by the Canon, with young Frank riding on its back, and as a further treat he was allowed to assist the chef at its decapitation.

In August 1835 he was sent to school in Northamptonshire, and after two years there to Laleham School under his uncle the Rev. John Buckland, whose wife was a sister of Dr. Arnold of Rugby. During his holidays at Christchurch he enjoyed playing with the cages of snakes and frogs kept by his father in the dining-room and with the guinea-pigs which freely roamed the table; in the stable yard dwelt an assorted menagerie including ferrets, hawks, owls and other birds, cats, dogs, poultry and a fox.

Canon Buckland was also a keen collector of fossils, which later formed the nucleus of the Geological Museum at Oxford, where he became the first Professor of Geology.

At the age of 12 Frank Buckland was sent to Winchester where his life as a junior seems to have closely resembled that described in 'Tom Brown's Schooldays'. He was not interested in games, nor did he do well at school work, but he spent what time he could in natural history pursuits. He became expert at catching field mice on St Catherine's Hill, as his father had done, which he skinned, roasted and ate on the spot; he also snared trout in the River Itchen with piano wire, practised catching previously liberated rats by their tails and kept a number of ferrets, rabbits and hedgehogs which were subsequently dissected. On one occasion he was discovered dissecting a cat in the dormitory at night; the remains were placed in a box under the bed, but he had to give this up owing to the protests of the other boys.

A school friend described him as a true naturalist and, although a bit eccentric, of an equable and happy temperament and popular with other boys; this seems to be a reasonably accurate assessment of his character throughout his life.

He had now decided to become a surgeon, and on his half holidays he used to visit Winchester Hospital where he removed some gruesome specimens for dissection. He also acquired a lancet and practised bleeding on schoolboy volunteers whom he bribed with sixpences to undergo the experiment.

In October 1844 Buckland entered Christchurch as an undergraduate where he had rooms in Fells buildings (now demolished); in the court between this and the Canon's gardens, where his father was still in residence, he built up a collection of animals which at various times included a bear, monkey, eagle, jackal and smaller fry such as marmots, snakes, frogs and chameleons. During two of the long vacations he visited Germany to work under Liebig, the well-known chemist, who was a close friend of his father.

He became a member of a small undergraduate debating society which usually considered rather abstruse subjects; they were brought down to earth, however, by his first paper on 'Whether rocks are beneficial to the farmer or not'.

His preliminary investigations with mice at Winchester and his father's interest in the subject had stimulated Frank Buckland's desire to widen human dietetic habits and when a panther died at the Surrey

Zoological Gardens he wrote asking the curator for its chops. Although it had been buried for two days these were recovered and sent to Oxford but Buckland reluctantly admitted that 'they did not taste very good'.

His pet bear took part in the proceedings of the British Association at Oxford in 1847, attending a party in the Botanic Gardens in cap and gown, when Lord Houghton, with some difficulty it is said, succeeded in mesmerizing it into a senseless condition. There is another version of this story in Cecil Woodham Smith's *Life of Florence Nightingale* where it is stated that she visited this party and that it was she who mesmerized the bear. It was apparently only 3 months old and very small. The British Association had been founded in 1831 and Canon Buckland was its first President when it met at Oxford in 1832.

In 1845 Canon Buckland became Dean of Westminster and left Christchurch, and he also obtained the living of Islip (a little north of Oxford) which became the family country home from then on.

In May 1848 Frank Buckland entered St. George's Hospital and with the idealism of youth wrote in his journal: 'My object in studying medicine is not to gain a name, money and high practice but to do good to my fellow creatures . . . to be a great benefactor to mankind.'

He remained at the hospital until 1853, qualifying in 1851 and subsequently becoming House Surgeon. At the Westminster Deanery his parents entertained on a large scale and Frank met there many of the distinguished figures of the time including Gladstone, the Duke of Wellington, Sir Gilbert Scott, Sir Robert Peel, Professor Owen, Humphry Davy, Faraday, Hooker the botanist and friend of Darwin, Herschel and Whewell the astronomers, and Brunel and Robert Stephenson the engineers.

The usual menagerie was kept at the Deanery and some of the animals were experimented upon with the recently discovered chloroform, and it is recorded that portions of hedgehogs, tortoises, rats, frogs and snails, and of an ostrich, were at times served at Deanery luncheons—presumably without the guests being aware of the nature of the delicacies.

In August 1849 Buckland went to Paris and finding bodies readily obtainable did much dissecting, and in 1850 he visited Guernsey with another medical student, T. H. Huxley. His first articles on natural history, published in 1852 in *Bentley's Miscellany* (whose editor was then Charles Dickens), and in *Household Words*, dealt mainly with rats. In December 1853 he gave the first of many lectures to a working

men's club—the lecture was called 'The House we Live in' and described the human body. He recorded that his lectures frequently
lasted two hours, which he found exhausting, but that he always
tried to amuse his audiences. At about this time he suffered severe
symptoms caused by skinning a rat which had been killed by a cobra
at the Zoo.

On 14 August 1854, Buckland was gazetted Assistant Surgeon to
the 2nd Life Guards and was stationed for the next four years at
Windsor, Knightsbridge or Albany Street Barracks. We know little
about his Army service except that he was conscientious and a keen
disciplinarian, and it appeared to leave him ample time to continue
his natural history pursuits. In that same year he was elected to the
Athenaeum. In 1856 Canon Buckland died. Frank had a great admiration for him and his own life and interests were clearly modelled
on and influenced by those of his father. He later edited the latter's
two-volume work on *Geology and Mineralogy* which he prefaced with
a 60-page memoir of the Canon's life. This work constituted one of
'The Bridgewater Treatises', so called because the late Earl of Bridgewater had bequeathed £8,000 for the publication of 8 works by
different authors chosen by Trustees; these works were intended to
illustrate the Power, Wisdom and Greatness of God.

In the following year, 1857, his mother died; both his parents were
buried in the churchyard at Islip.

In 1856 Buckland began writing regularly for the *Field* and about
this time started making casts of British fish. In 1857 his *Curiosities of
Natural History* (1st series) was published, to be followed later by three
more volumes. On 16 February his journal records that he went to see
the whale stranded at Whitechapel and on 20 March he 'read much
in the Athenaeum about rats etc.' In 1858 he met Lord Palmerston and
Dr. Livingstone.

He was in the habit of working at the Royal College of Surgeons'
Museum and this and the fact that the centenary of John Hunter's
entry to St. Georges' Hospital had recently been celebrated inspired
in Buckland a great interest and admiration for Hunter, whom he
always considered was 'the greatest of Englishmen'.

Buckland describes how, when he was sitting in the Mess Room of
the 2nd Life Guards at Windsor reading *The Times*, he saw a notice
stating that the coffins in the vaults and catacombs of St. Martin-in-
the-Fields were to be finally removed and the vaults closed; friends and
relatives were informed that they could remove coffins before

1 February 1859. He remembered that John Hunter was reputed to be buried there and resolved to try to rescue his remains. Next morning he went to the church but none of the officials had heard of Hunter; however, after consulting Palmer's *Life of Hunter* and the Register of Burials, he established that Hunter was in fact buried there in vault No. 3.

Buckland relates that with Burstall the vestry surveyor he opened the oak gate of the vault to see a room filled from floor to ceiling with coffins in complete disorder. These coffins were all lead covered, but in the adjoining vault were wooden coffins. He writes that 'the faint and sickly effluvia which emanated from these vaults was truly overpowering and poisonous'.

He and Burstall worked for fifteen days clambering over the diminishing piles of coffins to read the name plates, without success, until finally only three remained out of the original 200 or more in the vault. But one of these did in fact bear the name plate and Arms of John Hunter, and Buckland records that he uttered 'a shriek of joy' when it was discovered. The lead coffin was burst from the decomposition within, and the upper lid loosened. Several members of the Council of the Royal College of Surgeons came to view the coffin but no attempt was made to inspect the contents either by them or by Buckland. The total number of coffins interred in this insanitary manner in the vaults of St. Martin-in-the-Fields was no less than 3,260.

The Council of the Royal College of Surgeons made arrangements with the then Dean of Westminster for the reburial of John Hunter's remains in the Abbey and the ceremony took place on 28 March 1859[1]. The procession was led by the Dean, then by a grand-nephew of Hunter, followed, in order, by the Trustees of the Hunterian Museum, Frank Buckland, Professor Owen, the Presidents of the Colleges of Physicians and Surgeons, the Council of the College of Surgeons, the Censors of the College of Physicians, the Master and Wardens of the Apothecaries Company, the Presidents of the Linnean Society, the Royal Medical and Chirurgical Society and the Medical Society of London, members of the staffs of the London teaching hospitals, and distinguished provincial surgeons. About 600 people attended in all.

---

[1] Miss Jessie Dobson has described how Buckland discovered the remains of Ben Jonson when Hunter's grave was dug in Westminster Abbey when he removed some of his bones. These were discovered in a dealer's shop in 1938 and are still preserved.

G

A sum of £1,173 was later collected by the Royal College of Surgeons for a memorial statue of Hunter, by Weekes from the portrait by Reynolds, and the College presented Buckland with thirteen volumes of handsomely bound catalogues of the museum. The Leeds School of Medicine also presented him with an inscribed silver medal.

Presumably because of his familiarity with the Abbey, Buckland had discovered the autograph of Izaak Walton scratched on the monument of Casaubon in Poet's Corner.

In his last essay in *The Log-Book of a Fisherman and Zoologist* Buckland describes his subsequent exploration of John Hunter's country house at Earls Court, which was then still standing and little changed from Hunter's day. The owner, Dr. Gardiner Hill, allowed Buckland to make a thorough inspection of the house and grounds. The main point of interest to him was the boiler in which Hunter reduced his specimens to skeletons; one of these was the body of the Irish Giant O'Brien or Byrne, who was reputed to be 8 ft. 4 in. tall. Buckland describes how he plunged his arm into the old boiler hoping to find some bones left by Hunter, but only a rusty key remained.

He subsequently had an oak chair made from John Hunter's bed which had been given to him by Professor Owen; the chair is now in the Royal College of Surgeons.

On 14 February 1952, a John Hunter Memorial Service was held at St. Martin-in-the-Fields, when a plaque was unveiled by Sir Henry Dale. This records that the body of John Hunter had rested in the vaults for sixty-six years and commemorates also 'the long and diligent search' for the coffin by Frank Buckland. A sermon was preached by Sir Gordon Gordon-Taylor in which he described the circumstances of the discovery and he spoke at some length of Frank Buckland's other interests and activities.

In 1860 Buckland, with others, was instrumental in forming the Acclimatization Society and he became its Honorary Secretary, the Prince of Wales becoming President a few years later. Its object was to acclimatize animals from overseas to augment home food supplies. At this time he took home portions of a whale stranded at Grays, Essex, to eat, but found it 'too strong even when boiled with charcoal'.

On 12 July 1862, after a delay of two years, the inaugural dinner of the Acclimatization Society was held at Willis's Rooms. The menu was enormous and included Birds Nest Soup, Sea Slug Soup and

Deer Sinew Soup, all of which Buckland described as glue-like in taste. The Kangaroo stew, he wrote, was 'not bad but a little gone off'—various wild pigs, peculiar ducks, geese and leporines were also served and washed down with wines from non-European countries.

Buckland now turned his attention to the native fish supply, a subject hitherto neglected in this country, which occupied him for the rest of his life; his first act was to construct a primitive fish hatchery in his house.

In 1863 he resigned from the Life Guards, partly perhaps because he was not promoted to Senior Surgeon, but mainly to devote himself entirely to natural history, and from then on he abandoned the practice of medicine. He busied himself with practical fish culture, personally collecting trout ova from various rivers in the depths of winter, often wading waist deep, and he developed his fish hatching apparatus which was shown to the Royal Society, the Royal Microscopical Society and, for some odd reason, at the Islington Dog Show, where it proved very popular.

Frank Buckland married Hannah Papes on 11 August 1863, but his biographer provides no information about her appearance, character or antecedents, and she receives only a few lines of attention when she was recorded as nursing a sick monkey. They set up house at 37 Albany Street, Regent's Park, where he spent the rest of his life and inevitably gathered around him the usual collection of strange pets which had the run of the house and garden and sometimes escaped to annoy the neighbours.

This house was only recently demolished to form part of the site of the new College of Physicians so that anyone using the ground floor common room there will be among the ghosts of Frank Buckland and his pets. He was accustomed to visit the Zoo to treat sick animals and to perform post-mortems, and as a result was able to pursue his dietetic experiments, consuming elephant trunk soup, roast giraffe and roast viper. Some ailing porpoises at the Zoo were tenderly nursed by him, unfortunately without success, as he described in a letter to *The Times*, which led Thackeray to write an amusing 'Elegy on the Porpoise' in *Punch*.

For some time Buckland had been Editor of the natural history columns of the *Field* but in 1866 he left this journal and with some friends started *Land and Water*, in which somewhat later he wrote a criticism of the current Royal Academy Exhibition, with particular reference to the inacuracy of the pictures of birds and beasts.

In the same year, just one hundred years ago, he was appointed one of the two of H.M. Inspectors of Fisheries. A few years previously, following the decline of the salmon fisheries due to uncontrolled fishing, pollution, and obstruction of rivers by weirs and factories, a Salmon Fisheries Act had been passed, initiating these appointments. Buckland busied himself inspecting various rivers and erecting numerous salmon ladders, each designed by him to suit local conditions. He visited landowners and talked to fishermen and millers, and his enthusiasm and friendly personal approach often overcame difficulties. His activities in this sphere are described fully in his official annual reports. He continued casting fish for his museum and one day, seeing a sturgeon of 212 lb. weight on the slab of a Bond Street fishmonger, he borrowed it for one night, hauled it up the front steps of 37 Albany Street and with difficulty slid it down the area steps into the front kitchen—his casting room. He organized the first transhipment of salmon and trout ova to Australia and New Zealand, and he continued to visit many parts of the country to wade in streams and build salmon ladders; he records that it was during the long train journeys which this work involved that he did most of his writings on natural history.

Apart from fishery work, various other activities occupied him at this time, of which may be mentioned a dinner party to the original Siamese Twins and Miss Swann the giantess, a dinner of horseflesh at the Langham Hotel which he says 'made him feel seedy', and a busy day spent in assisting the removal of the fish, about 5,000 in all, from the Serpentine in Hyde Park to the Round Pond in Kensington Gardens, when the former was cleaned out.

A rather revealing entry in his diary on 30 December 1868, reads as follows: 'I am now 42 . . . and my mind I feel is now hardening into an adult mind.' In this year, largely through his advice, a Bill for protection of sea birds was passed.

In the years that ensued his life followed the same pattern and he was called upon by the Government to investigate both the sea and inland fisheries of Scotland, the Cromer lobster fishing, the Norfolk Broads and the oyster fisheries amongst others. He tabulated the number of ova in British species of fish, and in 1873 published a *History of British Fishes*. He also interested himself in the Arctic seal fisheries where uncontrolled killing was leading to extermination and, largely as a result, an international close season was established.

He continued his popular lectures on natural history and distributed portions of a pie which was made from a deceased rhinoceros at the Zoo, to an audience at Brighton.

In January 1879, after working in icy water collecting salmon ova, Buckland was attacked by inflammation of the lungs with hæmorrhage and was ill for two months; in November he was caught in a severe snowstorm in Norfolk which caused a recurrence of the illness. His health gradually failed but he continued to work on his fish museum which he intended to present to the Nation, and in 1880 he brought out a new edition of the *Natural History of British Fishes*, and also edited a revised edition of Gilbert White's *Natural History of Selborne*. He now developed dropsy for which he was operated on many times—presumably by insertion of Southey's tubes, recently introduced by Dr. Reginald Southey, Physician to St. Bartholomew's Hospital, nephew of Robert Southey the poet. Frank Buckland died on 19 December 1880, and was buried in Brompton Cemetery where his simple tomb without a headstone may be found on the east side. The inscription on the grave mentions also his only child 'Physie' who had died aged 4½ and this, so far as I can ascertain, is the only mention of any children.

It is perhaps unnecessary to speculate on the cause of death at the comparatively early age of 54, but in a letter to a friend he had once complained of his asthma, which suggests the probability of cor pulmonale with cardiac failure and œdema, and he was known to be a heavy smoker of pipes and cigars. The possibility of pulmonary tuberculosis, then of course a common disease, cannot perhaps be excluded. The death certificate reveals that he died at home, his brother-in-law Bompas being present, and the cause is given as 'Hepatic disease about 2 years and Bronchitis'.

For these facts about the life of Frank Buckland we are mainly dependent upon his own writings, notably *The Curiosities of Natural History* and *The Log-Book of a Fisherman and Zoologist*, and the biography written by his brother-in-law G. C. Bompas. The latter includes extensive excerpts from Buckland's own writings and is therefore largely autobiographical, but deals only with his interests in natural history. We learn nothing of his relations, except his father or his friends, and his wife remains a nebulous figure dismissed in a few lines, and there is no reference in the *Life* to any children. On 2 April 1930, Dr. G. R. Peachey gave a demonstration of 'Frank

Buckland at Home' before this Section[1], but unfortunately no record of the nature of this demonstration has been preserved.

If we try briefly to assess Buckland's contribution to scientific knowledge, we must recognize that he was a man of action rather than of philosophic thought and he did not perhaps greatly contribute to the systematic study of zoology. Clearly his life developed in the same mould as that of his father and a profound belief in the goodness and greatness of the Creator was always present; in the preface of one of his books he wrote: 'It is hardly necessary to say that I am not a disciple of Darwin or the developmental theory: I believe in the doctrine—I am sorry to say now old-fashioned—that the Great Creator made all things in the beginning and that he made them Good.' Incidentally I can find no record that he and Darwin ever met.

No doubt he could be labelled an eccentric because his interest in animals seemed far to exceed that in his fellow humans—but shall we give him the more kindly appellation 'a character' and a man to whom too little recognition has been afforded?

His memorials are his books which did much to popularize natural history at that time and which can be recommended not only for their interesting description of giants, dwarfs and circus freaks, but as shedding light on the social conditions of the poor at that time. His many Annual Reports as Inspector of Fisheries led to the passing of a number of useful Acts, resulting in purer rivers and fish conservation, for which the army of present-day anglers are indebted to him.

By his will he left his fish museum to the nation to be retained at South Kensington, the rest of his property to his widow and on her death £5,000 was to be given to found a lectureship on fish culture. There were then about 400 casts of fish in the museum as well as other relevant objects and later a marble bust of Buckland was added.

The fate of the collection is somewhat obscure and it apparently did not reach the South Kensington Museum until 1909, later going to the Science Museum, since when it has not been exhibited and much deterioration has occurred, so that now only 47 casts remain in store at Knockholt, Kent, and his bust also has disappeared.

Some of these delays may have been due to the legal complexities of Buckland's will, and also to the fact that his widow survived him for no less than forty-three years, dying as recently as 1923, with the

[1] The Section of the History of Medicine.

result that the Buckland Research Association and Lectures could not be founded until 1926.

Finally, Frank Buckland was a pioneer in the preservation of wild life—now a much more urgent matter—and doctors have special cause to thank him for his successful efforts to secure a proper resting place for the body of John Hunter.

Acknowledgements

I should like to express my gratitude for help and information to the following: Mr. N. Asherson, FRCS; Dr. A. D. Morris; Mr. C. L. Pascoe; Superintendent of Brompton Cemetery; Mr. L. M. Payne, Librarian of the Royal College of Physicians; Mr. F. T. K. Pentelow, Trustee of the Buckland foundation; Mr. Alwyne Wheeler of the British Museum (Natural History); and Miss Lawton Cornelius of Colindale Hospital.

REFERENCES

Bompas, G. C. (1886). *Life of Frank Buckland.* 11th ed., London.

Buckland, F. (1875). *Log-Book of a Fisherman and Zoologist.* London

Buckland, F. (1900). *Curiosities of Natural History.* 4th series. London

Buckland, W. (1858). *Geology and Minerology.* With memoir of author by Francis T. Buckland. London.

Dictionary of National Biography (1886) London; **7,** 204.

Dobson, J. (1967) *Proc. roy. Soc. Med.* **60,** 296.

Gordon, E. O. (1894). *Life and Correspondence of William Buckland,* DD, FRS. London.

Gordon-Taylor, G. (1952). *Brit. J. Surg.* **39,** 481.

Macaulay, J. (1889). 'Supper with Frank Buckland,' *Leisure-Hour,* **38,** 255.

Spectator (1895). 'Our Debt to Frank Buckland', **74,** 129.

Spectator (1900) Memories of Frank Buckland, **122,** 79.

Three Great Neurologists

HENRY MILLER

MD, FRCP

2 November 1966

Neurologists are of course great ancestor-worshippers, never happier than when they are insisting on the superiority of the 1892–3 edition of Sir William Gower's *Diseases of the Nervous System* (which all self-respecting neurologists have re-bound by Sangorski & Sutcliffe) to any puny contemporary successor, visiting tombs, or ceremonially unveiling plaques in honour of their distinguished predecessors on Yorkshire farmhouses or in obscure villages in the Midi.

In this paper I shall deal briefly with the lives and work of three great physicians who decorated a School of Neurology that has made Paris and the *Salpêtrière* a Mecca for neurologists no less alluring than the familiar building we know so well in Bloomsbury. They are Jean Martin Charcot (1825–93), Joseph Jules Dejerine (1849–1917), and Josef François Felix Babinski, who was born in 1857 and died as recently as 1932. A moment's consideration of the latter date is a sharp reminder of the surprising fact that we owe the physical sign, without which modern clinical neurology is unthinkable, to one of our own contemporaries.

JEAN MARTIN CHARCOT

Of these three, Charcot was the most remarkable. One of the initiators of modern clinicopathiological correlation, he probably made more contributions to nosology than anyone in the history of medicine before or since, and his claim to be numbered amongst the handful of the world's greatest physicians is jeopardized only by certain well-authenticated personal failings. His apparent lack of feeling for his patients seems to have arisen from an intrinsically cold and haughty personality rather than from the extraordinary circumstances of his clinical practice.

A native Parisian, he was born in 1825, the son of a carriage-builder and of four brothers the only one destined for distinction. At the Lycée he revealed early talent as a draughtsman and caricaturist, and was torn for a time between medicine and painting as a career. Medicine won the day, and in 1848, at the age of 23, he completed his training and became an intern of the *Hôpitaux de Paris* at the *Salpêtrière*. For nine years he worked without respite in general medicine and pathology, writing extensively on a wide range of diseases of the heart, lungs, liver, kidneys and joints.

In 1853 he produced a remarkable thesis for his doctorate, in which he firmly established the distinction between chronic rheumatoid arthritis and gout, and gave a description of the clinical features and natural history of the former disorder so complete and so accurate that the modern observer can add little to it. To this day the disease is often referred to as 'Charcot's rheumatism' in continental Europe. In 1853 also he was appointed *chef de clinique* and began private practice. In 1856 he was elected *médecin des Hôpitaux de Paris*, and in 1860 *Professeur agrégé*, submitting an excellent thesis on the chronic pneumonias. In 1856 he contributed the first French account of exophthalmic goitre, and in 1858 demonstrated the pathogenesis of intermittent claudication in an obstructive lesion of the common iliac artery.

La Salpêtrière

These were, however, no more than preliminaries for his life's work as the founder of modern neurology, which began with his appointment in 1862, at the age of 37, as medical superintendent of the *Hospice de la Salpêtrière*, where he had formerly interned. It was this important appointment and the peculiar clinical opportunities it afforded that determined the direction of his career. The next decade especially was enormously productive. In 1872 he succeeded his friend Vulpian as professor of pathological anatomy and ten years later his establishment of clinical neurology as an autonomous discipline was signalized by his appointment to the first Chair of Diseases of the Nervous System, established for him by a special edict of the Council of Ministers. The *Salpêtrière* remained his spiritual home until his sudden death from pulmonary œdema in 1893, at the age of 68 and about three years after his first symptoms of myocardial disease.

There is no British parallel to the *Salpêtrière*, an astonishing institution that exhales the essence of Parisian medicine today as it did when Charcot took over its direction a little more than a century ago. This seventeenth-century hospital owes its name to its origin as Louis XIII's gunpowder store, but in 1650 it was amalgamated with a general hospital in an attempt to clear the streets of Paris of its beggars, prostitutes, incurable invalids, lunatics, criminals and psychopaths. By the time Charcot arrived, a mixed and fluctuating population of between five and eight thousand such inmates had already furnished the material for the psychiatric observations and innovations of Pinel and Esquirol and their successors. However, its wealth of physical disease was as yet untapped—a vivid but confused museum of chronic pathology that needed only his genius for acute observation, clear recording, and brilliant exposition to convert it into pabulum for the textbooks of the succeeding century.

Charcot saw this wonderful opportunity and seized it with avidity. Invoking the assistance of his colleague and fellow-student Vulpian, he set to work to bring order out of chaos, and to establish the nomen-clature and classification of modern neurology. He introduced two innovations. Patients were examined not in bed but in Charcot's own room, where records of their gait and spontaneous movements were incorporated for the first time in the routine clinical protocol. Secondly, he established a microscopical laboratory, where the relative novelty of histopathological study augmented macroscopic morbid anatomy as a firm basis for the definition of the new clinical entities he described.

Before he succeeded his friend Vulpian as professor of pathological anatomy in 1872 he had already clarified a number of major clinical and pathological entities.

Important Researches

In 1865 Vulpian's Genevois assistant Prévost noted atrophy of the anterior horns in poliomyelitis with disappearance of the ganglion cells: four years later Charcot and Joffroy elaborated his description, and speculated on the nature of this sudden and massive but highly selective lesion. They also observed the focal inflammatory changes typical of acute paralytic cases, and understandably (though incorrectly) regarded them as secondary to neuronal damage.

Disseminated sclerosis was described pathologically in the 1830s by Cruveilhier in Paris and Carswell in London, but clinical accounts were sketchy. It was known only to the *cognoscenti* and regarded as a great rarity. Charcot was the first to diagnose the disease during life, and from 1863 onwards Charcot and Vulpian, and later Charcot writing alone, firmly established it as an entity showing a spectrum of severity and chronicity, and formulated valid diagnostic criteria for its clinical recognition. Before Charcot it had been confused with parkinsonism, and it was chiefly from his close study of a personal housemaid that this percipient observer recognized the difference between the intention tremor of the one and the static tremor of the other. Characteristically he retained the services of the girl until her condition demanded admission to the *Salpêtrière*—where he was at last able to confirm his clinical diagnosis of her disseminated sclerosis at autopsy.

In 1862 Charcot and Vulpian first described ankle clonus, and in 1866 a very successful special course of instruction on the diseases of old age furnished the first hint of the future development of geriatrics.

With his pupil, Charles Bouchard, Charcot described in 1868 the military aneurysms which he believed to be the cause of intracerebral hæmorrhage—an attribution subsequently criticized and of course more recently re-established.

In 1869 he established amyotrophic lateral sclerosis as a clinical and pathological entity, and recognized the dependence of the components of progressive muscular atrophy and spastic paraplegia on lesions of the anterior horns and corticospinal tracts respectively: this disease also became eponymous. In the same year he described tabetic arthropathy: curiously enough it is only in Britain that this condition is still known as Charcot's joint. He and his pupil Joffroy regarded the joint changes as a result of lesions of a trophic centre in the anterior horns, and seem to have overlooked the contributions of trauma and insensibility stressed in an almost exactly contemporaneous account by Volkmann in Germany. Charcot's lectures on arthropathy in London attracted much attention, and his gifts of pathological specimens to the Royal College of Surgeons and St. Thomas's Hospital cemented his excellent relations with his English contemporaries.

In 1880 he published a major work on localization of function in the brain and spinal cord, based on the pathological experiments of nature. In this remarkable work he clarified the sites of origin of motor hemiplegia, though the role of the thalamus in hemianæsthetic syndromes had to await the work of Dejerine. Charcot's study, however, also established the occurrence of ascending and descending degenerations in the spinal cord as well as the previously unrecognized functions of its grey matter.

His last major contribution to orthodox neurology came in 1886 when he and his pupil Pierre Marie described peroneal muscular atrophy in the same year as Tooth—and, incidentally, two years after Schultze in Germany and Ormerod in England.

Teaching and Private Life

Throughout the whole of this period, Charcot was continuously active in teaching as well as in research and the conduct of an enormous practice. Every Friday morning '*le patron*' lectured on inpatients and every Tuesday afternoon he demonstrated more informally the most intriguing of the day's new outpatients. Both were enlivened by a wealth of illustration and often by his dramatic mimicry of a gait or paralysis. The new art of photography was for the first time extensively employed in clinical teaching. The evenings he devoted to writing or painting, except for Tuesday, when he entertained cosmopolitan visitors from the worlds of literature, art, and politics. The works of Alphonse Daudet, the Goncourt brothers, Zola, de Maupassant and Paul Bourget all bear witness to his personal influence. His home was palatial, neo-Gothic, and dimly lit by stained-glass windows. It was replete with the best of classical art: in all his tastes he preferred the classical and severe to the romantic and diffuse: he loved Beethoven and detested Wagner. However, it is interesting to learn that although he disliked the impressionists he made a special collection of *objets d'art* connected with demoniac possession and neurological and psychiatric disorders, on the subject of which he published an important monograph.

Charcot employed a technique of consultation foreign to our tradition but still not unknown in France, and all his private as well as his hospital patients were first examined by an assistant. Nevertheless, he enjoyed the most distinguished as well as the largest of international neurological practices, replete with crowned heads, Prime Ministers and a cohort of Russian Grand Dukes. The list of his pupils is an almanac of European neurology, and includes Babinski, Bechterev, Bourneville, Brissaud, Janet, Marie, Marinesco, Parinaud Souques, and Gilles de la Tourette amongst many others—to say nothing of Sigmund Freud and the Americans Allen Starr and Bernard Sachs.

Strange things happen to neurologists in later life. The more orthodox become absorbed in the study of speech and its problems, which lends itself excellently to interminable and inconclusive ratiocination. Those more adventurous embark on daunting voyages into the study of perception and consciousness—a pursuit that must be carefully dis-

tinguished from the study of the *un*conscious, the exploration of
which has usually been the preserve of what would more accurately
be described as renegade neurologists. Charcot was no exception, nor
is it far-fetched to regard his later incursions into the sphere of neuro-
psychiatry as responsible for the genesis of that contemporary hydra
psychoanalysis.

Hysteria

By the late 1860s Charcot had systematized to his own and largely to
history's satisfaction the diseases of most of the chronic neurological
invalids in the *Salpêtrière*, and from this time onwards he devoted his
great energies and talents chiefly to those for whose complaints he
was unable to find any physical basis whatever, either clinically or
pathologically. Until this time such patients had usually been regarded
as malingerers or described by the term 'hysteric', employed in a
pejorative sense. Charcot approached these patients exactly as he did
those suffering from the structural nervous diseases whom they so
closely resembled, using the meticulous and elaborate techniques of
neurological examination that had proved so rewarding in the field of
organic disease. In these circumstances and with these methods it is
hardly surprising that he elicited or induced the bizarre symptoms and
signs that came to characterize the hysteria of the *Salpêtrière*, and lent
his great prestige and authority to the view that these patients were
not cheats and liars, but were suffering from a specific disease of the
brain, functional rather than structural in its basis. Although his
writings show a lively awareness of the relation of hysteria to emotional
disturbance and even to financial compensation, he never regarded
the condition as psychogenic but as an hereditary dynamic 'physical'
lesion localized in the brain, involving for example the cortex in
monoplegia and the internal capsule in hemiplegia. It is fair to say that
Charcot's work in this field greatly contributed to his fame outside
the profession, and gave rise to the claim that he should be regarded
as the father of psychopathology. To one school of thought his
endowment of hypnotism with respectability, and his seminal
contribution to the work of Freud and Janet, represent Charcot at his
greatest.

Even before Charcot, fragmentary attempts had been made to
exorcise the aura of demoniac possession earlier associated with the
dramatic loss of sensation, paralyses and convulsions of the unhappy
and unstable women who both exploited and expiated their emotional

instability as witches. Charcot's contribution consisted in recognizing that hysteria was not limited to women; in appreciating the parts played by imitation, suggestion, and simulation in the genesis of hysterical syndromes; and in developing clinical methods for distinguishing functional from organic lesions. His writings also showed a vivid awareness of the insubstantial nature of the hysterical concept, but like many who came later he found himself fascinated by a disorder whose very existence he was also often impelled to deny. On the debit side too much weight should not be attached to the very small number of actual cases of chronic hysteria studied—and repeatedly reported—by Charcot and his pupils, nor to the fact that today some of them would undoubtedly be regarded as suffering from organic brain disease or temporal lobe epilepsy, and others probably from catatonic schizophrenia. On the other hand Charcot seems to have been genuinely unaware how much the elaborate clinical phenomena, to which he devoted such detailed study, owed to iatrogenic suggestion; and although he sometimes recognized malingering, he dismissed it as a peccadillo of the mentally ill rather than as the financially induced performance it often was.

Hypnotism

Charcot's later excursions into hypnotism led him into even more dubious fields. By this time the 'Cæsar of the *Salpêtrière*' was so eminent as to be widely regarded as almost infallible. He had an army of admiring assistants who prepared his demonstrations, coached the patients, and undertook the actual hypnotic procedure—Charcot himself never hypnotized anybody. He opened his demonstrations to the public, and patients and volunteers appeared before an audience that included actresses, journalists, and lawyers as well as physicians and students. It is intriguing and not entirely irrelevant to remember that this meretricious performance so impressed Sigmund Freud that it became the *fons et origo* of psychoanalysis.

Small wonder that he failed to carry some of his more critical disciples along with him, Pierre Marie especially. What his psychopathological successors regard as his greatest contribution was charitably described by the rest as 'a slight failing' on the part of the master, and it is interesting to learn that towards the end of his days he had second thoughts and set to work on a radical revision of his studies on hysteria. Unfortunately he died before this could be undertaken.

JULES DEJERINE

Youth and Early Life

Born when Charcot was already a 24-year-old intern, Dejerine originated in Savoy and grew up in the then provincial atmosphere of Geneva, where his father was a carriage-proprietor—though travel as a courier had made him a rather unusually polyglot and sophisticated one. Young Dejerine had a powerful physique. At the Lycée Calvin he was better known for his swimming and boxing than for his devotion to study, and spent much of his time sailing and fishing on Lake Leman. Nevertheless he did well at school, and, from 1868 to 1870, at the *Académie de Genève*, where his determination to study medicine was strengthened by a growing interest in biology and comparative anatomy. Overcoming initial family resistance to his departure to conduct his clinical studies in the capital, and after further delay caused by the Franco-Prussian War (during which he helped with the wounded in a Geneva hospital), he left for Paris in the spring of 1871 in a third-class railway carriage and with nothing more substantial than an introduction from Prévost to Vulpian. He was destined to become the latter's most distinguished pupil.

Already the unruly youth had become a serious and dedicated student. Fired by a determination to demonstrate his provincial prowess, and convinced that Paris was open to anyone with talent and enthusiam and without influence, he threw himself into the clinical life of the city, at that time disorganized by the troubles of the Commune. His letters to his mother show that in this connexion he was torn between sympathy for the circumstances of the workers and a love of order—together with an inherent suspicion of Utopianism. These views finally crystallized into the patriotic conservatism that characterized Dejerine's later outlook.

He greatly admired Vulpian and followed him in a wide general interest in all aspects of clinical medicine. In 1875 he became an intern, and in the same year published his first neurological paper, on the appearances of the spinal cord in a case of club foot. Later that year he went to work with Cruveilhier, who had first recognized the pathological appearance of multiple sclerosis forty years before. During the next few years he published important studies of diphtheritic polyneuritis and pulmonary fat embolism, and his achievements were recognized in 1879 when he was appointed *chef de clinique* to Professor Hardy at the *Hospice de la Charité*. A year later he met a charming young American medical student from a famous San Francisco family—Augusta Klumpke, whom he was to marry eight years later and who in 1887 was the first woman ever to be elected an *interne des hôpitaux*. From the time of their marriage she shared his clinical and research activities, and carried on with both after his death in 1917.

Later Years

From 1887 to 1894 Dejerine worked at the *Bicêtre* and from the latter date until 1911 at the *Salpêtrière* where for the six years before his death he held the Chair of Diseases of the Nervous System initiated by Charcot. At the *Bicêtre* he organized a pathological laboratory, and over a period of many years he also continued to carry out experimental studies in Vulpian's laboratories. Amongst his pupils were Bernheim, Roussy, André-Thomas, and Alajouanine. He was a great teacher, always realistic, and as expert in the demonstration of functional disorders of the nervous sytem as in the organic neurology for which he is better known.

For many years his studies were particularly directed to the peripheral nervous system and its diseases. Amongst his first essays several were devoted to the clinical distinction between sensory disturbances of peripheral and those of central origin, but in 1883 the first of a succession of classical papers described the symptomatology of peripheral neuritis and especially of the syndrome which he christened 'peripheral pseudotabes'. In 1886 he published his thesis on the role of heredity in the causation of nervous disease, and it is no coincidence that in the same year he and Landouzy completed their account of the form of progressive muscular dystrophy ever since referred to under their names.

With André-Thomas he defined the syndrome of Friedreich's disease in 1907, and the same colleague shared in the first account of the rare progressive hypertrophic interstitial neuritis always to be associated with the names of Dejerine and Sottas, as well as in the clarification of olivopontocerebellar atrophy.

Dejerine's preocupation with the physiology and pathophysiology of sensation continued throughout his professional life, and although the massive study of cerebral localization which occupied him from 1890 until shortly before his death is usually regarded as his major contribution to systematic neurology, he is of course best known for his classic description of the thalamic syndrome that formed the basis

H

of Roussy's thesis and was jointly reported by them in the *Revue Neurologique* in 1906, in terms which are still reproduced almost exactly by successive writers of neurological textbooks.

Psychiatric Interests

Like all French neurologists of his period and many since, Dejerine had a lively interest in psychiatry, and this was stimulated by his lifelong friendship with Dubois of Berne, with whom he spent a great deal of time during the long summer vacations he so much enjoyed in his native countryside. His method of psychiatric management was simple but extraordinarily successful. It was characterized by sympathy, reassurance and vigorous persuasion—methods that owed little to theory and contributed little to speculative formulations, but which have stood the test of time in many hands before and since. During the long period of his professional maturity Dejerine's achievement owed much to the collaboration of his wife, who was a brilliant as well as a charming woman, and their intellectual partnership has often been compared with those of the Curies and the Vogts.

During the dark days of the First World War Dejerine's patriotism asserted itself in a highly practical manner and he died in 1917 after exhausting hours of overwork in the neurological wards of a military hospital.

In retrospect the pattern of his work shows a remarkable consistency. It began with his early interest in the pathophysiology of sensation, which led him to his studies of degeneration in peripheral nerves, nerve roots and the posterior columns of the spinal cord by the method of examining thin serial sections of tissue which he had perfected in Vulpian's laboratory. His study of sensation led him to the thalamus, and his fascination with microscopic morbid anatomy into the wider fields of cerebral localization involving the study of the central connexions of the pathways concerned with hearing, speech and vision. In turn his investigations of thalamic function stimulated interests in psychotherapy.

JOSEF BABINSKI

The name Babinski so instantly evokes the image of the cutaneous plantar reflex that it is easy to forget that he made many other important contributions to neurology, and that we pay unwitting homage to him every time we examine the nervous system. He was undoubtedly one of the greatest clinical neurologists of all time. I stress the adjective, because although he also made classical contributions to histopathology and experimental neurology, his uniqueness lay in his elucidation of the mysteries of nervous disease by evolving and refining the methods of physical examination. He was familiar with the technical and laboratory aids to diagnosis that were already beginning to dominate and devalue clinical method during the later years of his long and brilliant carrer, but he remained unexcited by them.

Origins and Career

The facts of his life are simple. The cataclysmic European events of 1848 seem to have left Charcot undisturbed—this was the year he began his internship at the *Salpêtrière*—but they violently uprooted Babinski's parents from Poland, where his father was active in the abortive rising against Russian domination. Like many Polish exiles before and since, they settled in Paris, and here their first son Henri was born in 1855, and our hero Josef in 1857. Brought up in modest circumstances in Montparnasse, he attended a Polish school and then became a medical student, being appointed an intern at the *Hôpitaux de Paris* in 1879. After a period as *chef de clinique* to Charcot at the *Salpêtrière* he failed in the highly competitive examination for the title of *Professeur agrégé*, being what one of his contemporaries characteristically described as 'the victim of a regrettable manœuvre', and served instead from 1890 to 1927 as head of the neurological clinic at the nearby *Pitié*. This was a blessing in disguise, since for nearly forty years he was spared the chore of systematic teaching, and was free to devote his mornings to clinical practice and research at the *Pitié*, while his afternoons were similarly occupied in his private consulting room.

Although he was widely regarded as the lineal successor of Charcot, whose chair he never achieved, the two men were very different. Babinski was tall, massive, and strikingly handsome, and his slow and quiet manner contrasted with his senior's panache. However, we have it on Sir Arthur Hurst's authority that Babinski's clinical demonstrations yielded nothing in quality of drama to those of his master. But Babinski's mind was sceptical and doggedly logical, and his work informed by what one of his colleagues aptly described as 'constructive doubts'. Never satisfied, he worried continually at a series of discrete and definable neurological problems for the solution of which he devised increasingly acute and refined clinical methods. His writings were brief and factual: the plantar response was described in a contribution of 28 lines, and he would return again and again to a teasing problem without repetition and with speculations that were always closely tied to hard fact.

Early Studies

Although he obtained his Doctorate in 1884 with a meticulous and substantial thesis on disseminated sclerosis (a subject suggested by Vulpian) he was a distinguished general physician before he became a neurologist, and the conditions of his clinical practice ensured that he remained one all his life. He made important contributions to the study of typhoid fever and aortic aneurysm, as well as of aural vertigo. In 1900 he preceded Fröhlich in a succinct and accurate account of the adiposogenital syndrome and its relation to pituitary-hypothalamic disorder.

In the laboratory, Babinski conducted early and accurate studies of the histopathological differentiation between neuropathic and myopathic muscle lesions, recognized the muscle-spindle as a normal structure, and was intrigued to account for the selective vulnerability of certain groups of muscles that is a hallmark of the genetically determined muscular dystrophies. To pursue the question he embarked on the microscopic study of the musculature of the human foetus, relating pathological susceptibility to evolutionary development in a hypothesis as novel as it was daring. But this was by no means the limit of his pathological contribution. In the field of demyelinating disease he clarified the topography of the multiple sclerotic plaque by making ingenious longitudinal sections of the spinal cord as well as the orthodox transverse preparations, and stressed the relative escape of the axon as well as the presence of an inflammatory element. He drew attention to the hemiplegic form of multiple sclerosis, and was the first to report the necrotic type of transverse myelitis. In 1899, with Charpentier, he described loss of the pupillary response to light in cerebral syphilis.

In 1913 he published his classical study of the symptomatology of the cerebellum and its differentiation from that of vestibular disease: the criteria he formulated remain part of our routine of clinical evaluation and his terminology (asynergia, adiadochokinesis) stands today.

The Techniques of Clinical Examination

However, it is to Babinski's sustained and massive contribution to the development of methods of clinical examination of the nervous system that we pay special tribute, and it is no exaggeration to say that the routine neurological examination of today was largely his creation. Babinski's preoccupation with physical examination sprang from distaste for the play-acting and sham healing in which he was reluctantly and sceptically involved by Charcot's displays of hysteria, and we owe the discovery of the plantar response to his firm determination to evolve reliable methods of distinguishing real from bogus illness. He studied intensively the possible fallacies of reflex elicitation, and the behaviour of the malingerer was the object of his attention no less intensive than the patient delineation of reflexogenic zones and the segmental implications of reflex changes: his patients were invariably examined stark naked. He devoted great attention to the postures best suited to the elicitation of the reflexes, and we acknowledge his contribution every time we ask a patient to facilitate a difficult ankle-jerk by kneeling before us—or, incidentally, when we diagnose sciatica, tabes dorsalis or polyneuritis on the basis of the ankle-jerk's disappearance.

The plantar reflex had been observed earlier by Remak and Strümpell as well as Vulpian, but it was Babinski's brief and historic account of 22 February 1896, that defined the response and established its relation to organic nervous disease and to spastic paresis of central origin. His subsequent contributions, characteristically brief and systematic, stressed the absence of the extensor response in hysteria, its presence in infancy, and its transient appearance in epilepsy and strychnine poisoning. Finally in 1903 he described the associated fanning of the toes subsequently referred to as the *signe de l'éventail*.

Hysteria

Babinski's tacit resistance to Charcot's later excesses has already been mentioned. Babinski clarified the clinical differentiation of hysterical from organic symptomatology, especially by study of the reflexes. He rejected both Charcot's view of hysteria as an organic disease, and the reality of such concepts as hysterical hæmoptysis and hæmaturia, stressing the role of suggestion, and especially of medical suggestion, in provoking hysterical symptoms, and also their reversibility by authoritative persuasion. He abandoned his senior's concept of 'hysteria' in favour of 'pithiatism' (curable by persuasion), a now discarded term that enjoyed a certain vogue for a number of years. In this connexion he noted the disappearance of the symptomatology of Charcot's hysteria even from the *Salpêtrière* after Charcot's death, and stressed the fact that although he himself considered many hysterics to be 'genuine', their disabilities were invariably of a kind that could be simulated, and he had to admit the absence of any reliable method for distinguishing malingering from hysteria, recognizing that their differentiation depended on nothing more substantial than the observer's subjective assessment of the patient's honesty. He appreciated also that this raised insurmountable problems in the field of medicolegal assessment.

No doubt it is due to Charcot's example that French neurologists have paid so much attention to hysteria. During the First World War Babinski wrote extensively with Froment on 'reflex paralysis', which they distinguished from hysteria because of its severity, the association of vascular and trophic changes, and its intractable nature. More long-term observations have demonstrated that its intractability was relative, and related to the military situation: they have also served to increase neurological scepticism about those impassioned discussions on the 'genuineness' of hysteria which so occupied the attention of Babinski and his great contemporaries.

Surgical Neurology

A few days before he died, Babinski said that he regarded his work in surgical neurology and especially his studies in spinal cord compression (which began in the 1890s) as his most important contribution to neurology, since they pointed the way to neurosurgery. He must certainly be regarded as the father of this subject in his own country, encouraging its initiation by his pupils de Martel and Clovis Vincent, and localizing in 1911 the first spinal cord tumour to be successfully removed in France.

Personal Life

Though shy and reserved, Babinski was an enthusiastic attender at the clinical meetings of the *Société de Neurologie de Paris*, which he helped to found in 1899, and while he said little and preferred to let the facts speak for themselves, his gentle scepticism and especially his meticulous personal re-examination of the cases demonstrated were both admired and feared.

He was devoted to the theatre and especially to opera and ballet. Another abiding interest was gastronomy. The story that he broke off his ward-round to speed home in his carriage when the ward sister whispered a telephone message that the soufflé was nearing perfection may be apocryphal—though it was told to me by one of his greatest living pupils. What is certain is that his elder brother, a distinguished engineer who also acted as his housekeeper and amanuensis, was a famous cook whose recipe book, published under the pseudonym *Ali-Bab*, was known to *tout Paris*—and that an invitation to their table was keenly sought after. The brothers were deeply attached to one another: Josef had long been handicapped by parkinsonism and did not long survive Henri's death in 1931.

REFERENCES

André-Thomas (1922). *Madame Dejerine*. Paris.

Beeson, B. B. (1928). *Ann. Med. Hist.* **10,** 126.

Fulton, J. (1933). *Arch. Neurol. Psych., Chicago,* **29,** 168.

Gauckler, E. (1922). *Le Professeur J. Dejerine 1849–1917*. Paris.

Guillain, G. (1959). *J. M. Charcot, his Life and Work*. Trans. Pearce Bailey. New York.

Guillain, G. & Mathieu, P. (1825). La Saltpêtrière. Paris.

Haymaker, W. (1953). *Founders of Neurology*. Springfield, Ill.

The Fruits of Error and False Assumption

THE RT HON. LORD COHEN OF BIRKENHEAD
MD

29 November 1966

It would be sheer affectation if I were to hide my deep appreciation of the honour of being invited to deliver the Nuffield Lecture. My distinguished predecessors have chosen to speak on general themes and I intend to follow their example and to discuss the role that error and false assumption may play in scientific discovery.

The Method of Discovery in Science

The method of scientific discovery has for many centuries been the subject of much discussion and speculation by philosophers. The Greeks, astir with their triumphs in mathematics, had sought to interpret Nature by the syllogistic methods of Aristotle. The outcome was in large measure sterile because they imposed patterns on Nature rather than derived them from her.

It was Francis Bacon in perhaps the greatest of his writings, *Novum Organum Scientiarum*, published in 1620, who first formalized how Nature should be questioned so that her secrets could be extracted from her and her actions controlled. He announced what he regarded as a new method of scientific discovery, which he held to be the only true road to knowledge.

Bacon urged that this, the only true road to knowledge, is through observation and experiment; the facts thus revealed shall be analysed, 'taken to pieces, and by a due process of exclusion and rejection lead to an inevitable conclusion'. Bacon further claimed that the method of induction which he propounded—the orderly arrangement of data which leads inevitably to the valid and tenable hypothesis—was infallible and mechanical, and reduced all minds to the same level in the art of obtaining knowledge. But Bacon overlooked that hypotheses and theories are not *derived* from observed facts but are invented to try and account for them.

Following Bacon, many of the world's most distinguished philosophers have continued critically to examine theories of scientific method. It would not I think be misleading to formulate a typical contemporary view as follows.

First, on the basis of previously established knowledge or observation of novel significant facts, a hypothesis is formulated (induction). Secondly, from this hypothesis are drawn logical conclusions and consequential predictions (deduction) which can be checked by further observation and experiment (including the controlled experiment). Thirdly, if this initial hypothesis is thus confirmed it may be regarded as valid within the limits of known experience. (It is necessary to emphasize that confirmatory tests, however extensive and exacting, cannot provide *conclusive* proof of a hypothesis or theory, but only stronger support). And fourthly, if checking refutes the initial hypothesis, then a fresh hypothesis must be formulated and similarly checked, and this process is repeated until a hypothesis is found which is consistent with all known experience and can be experientially tested.

But any such formal presentation of scientific method fails adequately to explain why one man makes an outstanding discovery which reveals new vistas of knowledge and increases immeasurably our control over Nature, whilst another adds but a brick or two, or if more fortunate a corner stone, to an already existing building. It overlooks disparities in experimental skills and differences in the range of a man's knowledge not only within but outside his special field, for discoveries are commonly made on overlapping frontiers. It takes too little account of the 'hunches' of the great scientist—his flashes of intuition and imaginative insight, and his power to perceive where others are blind; in short it tends to ignore the scientist as a creative artist. Such hunches or 'happy guesses' require a rare gift of ingenuity, especially if they involve a radical departure from current modes of scientific thinking. As Butterfield (1949) has observed:

Of all forms of mental activity the most difficult to induce . . . is the art of handling the same bundle of data as before, but placing them in a new system of relations with one another, by giving them a different framework, all of which virtually means putting on a different kind of thinking-cap for the moment.

The truth is that the methodology of science admits of no rigid formula, for the mind of man—the most important, the most delicate, the most pliant, versatile and adaptable of all the instruments of scientific discovery—cannot be 'cabin'd, cribb'd, confin'd'. Discoveries may result from planned experiment and reason; from intuition, imagination or hunch; from chance or erroneous observation; and all may play their part though in varying measure.

Reason and Design

Reason and design, for example, tend to prevail in the discoveries of mathematics and theoretical physics. The discovery of the planets Uranus, Neptune and Pluto are striking examples of the successful application of rigorous and systematic observation following methodical and diligent calculations based on the general principles of celestial mechanics. In the field of medicine, Semmelweis's demonstration of the main cause of childbed fever, John Snow's epidemiological studies which revealed how cholera spread, and Lister's antisepsis were essentially the outcome of a rational interpretation of observations. But on how tenuous a thread the outcome of reason might hang is shown by Evarts Graham's description of the origins of cholecystography (1931).

Abel and Rowntree had shown that chlorinated phenolphthaleins are excreted almost entirely in the bile. It occurred to Mills and Graham that by substituting for chlorine atoms others opaque to X-rays, it might be possible to obtain a shadow of the gall-bladder. Graham obtained the free acid of tetraiodophenolphthalein and, after converting it to the sodium salt, Warren Cole injected it intravenously into 6 dogs and repeatedly X-rayed them after the injection. In 5 dogs no shadow was obtained, but the sixth showed a faint shadow probably because accidentally he was given no food whilst the others had been fed, thus preventing the injected dye staying in the gall-bladder long enough to be concentrated and cast a shadow. Graham writes: 'If we had failed to get a shadow in all of these animals, we probably should have abandoned the whole idea as a fruitless one.'

The Chance Observation (Serendipity)

Bacon, despite his proposing a mechanistic scientific method that would 'kindle a light in nature', tells us that: 'Men are rather beholden . . . generally to chance, or anything else, than to logic, for the invention of arts and science.' Had not Columbus, nearly a century earlier, set sail for India and discovered America?

The role of the chance observation in scientific discovery has been the theme of many publications, and has attracted to itself the word 'serendipity', first coined in 1754 by Horace Walpole after he had read a fairy tale entitled *The Three Princes of Serendip* (the ancient name of Ceylon). Writing to his friend, Horace Mann, Walpole suggested that 'serendipity' might be added to our language because 'as their highnesses travelled they were always making discoveries, by accident or sagacity, of things they were not in quest of'. Science has been vastly enriched by the chance observation; Luigi Galvani's discovery of current electricity when he noticed twitching of the calf muscles of a frog hanging from an iron balustrade, when an electric spark was produced in the neighbourhood; Malus's discovery of the polarization of light; Oersted's demonstration of the relationship between electricity and magnetism when he observed the deviation of a magnetic needle in an electric field, an observation which led to Pasteur's classic comment that: 'In the field of observation, chance favours only the prepared mind'. And chance led to Pasteur's own discovery of the principle of immunization with attenuated pathogens, and to Richet's recognition of anaphylaxis. In this category too are found Mering and Minkowski's pancreatectomized dogs with resulting diabetes mellitus, Röntgen's X-rays and Becquerel's radioactivity, to which I shall later refer in some detail.

We recall the Dutch physicist Kamelingh-Onnes and his collaborators at the Cryogenic Laboratory of Leyden who in their attempts to liquefy helium chanced upon the major discovery of supraconductivity. And, as dramatic as any, Fleming's discovery of penicillin. Innumerable additional examples could be given of the role of chance in scientific discovery. But chance alone does not suffice. She is indeed a fickle mistress, and favours only those who possess other riches with which to court her. And like a mistress she can delude or lead the unwary astray.

Die Weltwoche, of 4 March 1966, records that recently at Harvard Dr. Karel Slàma was a guest professor. He had brought with him from Prague 1,500 eggs of the fire bug, *Phyrrhocoris apterus*, which had in Prague developed normally through larvæ to adult life. But in Cambridge, Massachusetts, their development ceased at the last larval stage, in which they died.

With his colleague, Professor Carroll M. Williams, Dr. Slàma investigated the ways in which the American experimental details differed from the original and found but one, namely, the strip of newspaper on which the larvæ were laid. In the U.S.A. it was the *Boston Globe* with a political commentary by that controversial and outspoken columnist—Walter Lippman. But he was not the culprit.

Not only the *Boston Globe*, but the *New York Times*, *Wall Street Journal*, *Science*, *Scientific American* and other American papers inhibited maturation of the imported larvæ but not of the indigenous; whereas English papers, e.g. *The Times* and *Nature*, and Japanese papers did not delay maturation of the native larvæ.

Analysis of the American paper showed the presence of an inhibitory substance, which derived from wood-pulp made from yew tree, larch, balsam and hemlock spruce. The significance of this is another story, but had it not been for the detective instinct it might never have been told.

Nor should we forget that Fleming's was not the only element of chance in the story of penicillin. There were at least two others of critical significance. The solid extract of penicillin prepared by the Oxford team in 1940 was thought to be nearly pure. In fact, only 1% was penicillin. If the impurities had been toxic, the beneficial effects of penicillin might well have been masked and further investigation stayed. Again, if penicillin had been tested on guinea-pigs—commonly used in the assessment of drugs—the results would have been most discouraging for penicillin is toxic to guinea-pigs. Fortunately, mice were chosen for the experimental tests.

Intuition and Creative Imagination

The role of intuition and creative imagination—the sudden illuminating flash or *Geistesblitz*—is evident in many of the revolutionary advances in knowledge. Even if the stories of Archimedes' bath and Newton's apple are legendary, as I suspect they are, the famous principles of hydrostatics and gravitation which each enunciated were bold guesses born of intuition. And so, too, with Darwin on evolution by natural selection, and Mendel, the priest who provided the key to the mechanism of evolution, and a thousand others who advanced knowledge by 'some boldness and licence in guessing'. True it is that these guesses are made on the basis of long study, but the role of intuition is paramount and can be illustrated by solutions to problems which have appeared during sleep or immediately on waking. Two examples must suffice.

Otto Loewi (1953) had doubted the view that the electrical excitation produced by stimulation of a nerve, and propagated within the nerve, itself initiates or modifies the function of its effector organ, such as muscle. During the night of Easter Sunday, 1921, he awoke with the design of the crucial experiment which was to test his doubts clearly in his mind. He jotted the details down on a scrap of paper by his bedside and fell asleep. Next morning he failed to decipher the scrawl, so he spent the day in his laboratory trying in vain to recall the design. But that night he awoke again with the design of the experiment once more revealed. He went forthwith to his laboratory and performed the classical crossed circulation experiment which was to establish the chemical mediation of nerve impulses.

The German chemist, Kekulé (Schutz, 1890), conceived similarly the idea of the benzene ring which revolutionized organic chemistry, when writing his textbook. He tells the story. All was not going well so he sat in a chair by the fireside and 'sank into a half-sleep'. He continues:

The atoms flitted before my eyes. Long rows, variously, more closely, united; all in a movement wriggling and turning like snakes . . . one of the snakes seized its own tail and the image whirled scornfully before my eyes. As though from a flash of lightning I awoke; I occupied the rest of the night in working out the consequences of the hypothesis . . . Let us learn to dream, gentlemen.

There are many additional examples which could be quoted in which problems, studied intensively during waking hours without reaching a solution, find it during sleep and sometimes revealed in dreams. Some of the most striking are found in mathematical discovery as related in Henri Poincaré's *Science and Method* (1914).

Error and False Assumption

But there is yet another source of seminal ideas in discovery and this is my major theme. At first glance it seems paradoxical that error and false assumption can have thus played an essential part; yet there are innumerable supporting examples.

May I quote two personal observations before turning to much weightier evidence. The first is the view, which I elaborated in my Harveian Lecture (Cohen 1950), which suggests that Harvey's concept of the circulation of the blood stemmed from an inaccurate observation. After he repeated Galen's experiment of cutting open an artery, which proved that the arteries contain blood and not air as Erasistratus had maintained in naming them, Harvey in like manner incised veins and concluded 'that *the arteries contain the same blood as the veins, and nothing but the same blood*'. This must surely have suggested that the arteries and veins communicate or are in continuity, and leaves little doubt that this error of observation started the train of reasoning in

Harvey's mind which led to the further observations and experiments recorded in *De Motu Cordis*.

The second story begins forty-five years ago, and illustrates the fruits of false assumption. I should explain that I am not referring to those early hypotheses based on inadequate data which are the first approximations in a continuous process leading to discovery but to an assumption based on supposedly established facts for which confirmation is sought by a different route or method. In 1910 Mott had claimed that in degenerative disorders of the nervous system, choline, normally absent, appears in the cerebrospinal fluid from the breakdown of lecithins (Fig. 1). On hydrolysis lecithins yield 2 molecules of fatty acid (R = palmitic, stearic, oleic, &c.), 1 molecule of glycerol, 1 molecule of

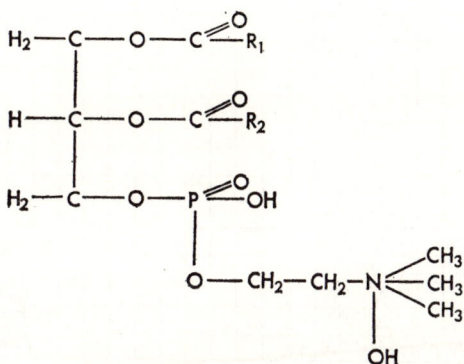

Fig. 1. *Chemical formula of lecithins*

phosphoric acid, and 1 molecule of choline. Thus if choline is present in the CSF in degenerative nervous diseases, the amount of phosphate in the CSF might be expected to rise also.

Since accurate micromethods for the estimation of phosphate were available in the early 1920s, and as there was then an epidemic of acute encephalitis, perhaps the most favourable opportunity for further study, I estimated the phosphate of the blood and CSF in a wide variety of nervous diseases (Cohen, 1924). There was found to be no rise in CSF phosphate in acute or chronic disease of the central nervous system, with the striking exception of meningitis (Fig. 2). Further studies originating from this false assumption led to the general law that, owing to the increased permeability of the blood-CSF barrier in meningitis, the CSF in meningitis tends to approximate in chemical composition to the blood plasma (Cohen, 1927, Table 1).

Sir Henry Dale in his now classical paper on 'Accident and Opportunism in Medical Research' (1948) relates three instances where error through ignorance or inadvertence was to provide the chance observation from which major discoveries were to flow.

He tells how one of Gowland Hopkins' students in biochemistry at Cambridge—John Mellanby, who was later to succeed Sherrington in the Wayneflete Chair of Physiology at Oxford—was the only member of the class who was unable to obtain the Adamkiewicz' colour reaction

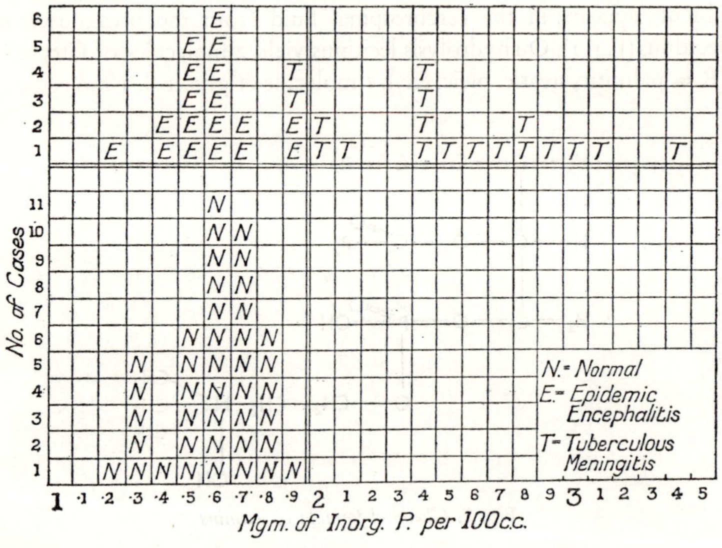

Fig. 2. *Inorganic phosphate content of CSF in normal (N), in encephalitis (E), and in tuberculous meningitis (T). Reproduced from Cohen, 1924, by kind permission)*

for protein. Hopkins confirmed that Mellanby's bottle of acetic acid did not give the reaction whilst the others gave it promptly. This induced Hopkins and Cole to investigate the problem and demonstrate that the reaction is due to glyoxylic acid, which is present as an impurity in most specimens of acetic acid. From this came the identification of tryptophan, which was shown to be a *necessary* constituent of diet.

His second example tells how Ringer's solution was first prepared as an isotonic solution of sodium chloride in *distilled* water. One day the solution was found to be much more effective in maintaining the beat of the frog's heart, because, as Ringer discovered, the laboratory assistant, who saw no reason why he should waste time on distilling water, had used tap water instead in preparing the solution. Ringer soon realized that the greater efficiency of the solution was due to the

Table 1. Chemistry of blood plasma and CSF in meningitis

| | Normal | | Meningitis |
	Blood plasma	CSF	CSF
Group I (substances normally present in greater quantity in the plasma than in the fluid)			
Protein	6–7 g/100 ml	Trace	Increase
Inorganic phosphorus	2–4 mg/100 ml	1·25–2 mg/100 ml	Increase
Uric acid	2–4 mg/100 ml	Trace	Increase
Cholesterol	150 mg/100 ml	Trace	Increase
Calcium	10 mg/100 ml	5–6 mg/100 ml	Increase
Sulphates	4 mg/100 ml	1 mg/100 ml	Increase
Glucose	100 mg/100 ml	50–80 mg/100 ml	Increase in early stage; decreased later
Group II (substances normally present in greater quantity in the fluid than in the plasma)			
Chlorine (as NaCl)	560–620 mg/100 ml	725–750 mg/100 ml	Decrease
Group III (substances which either naturally or after injection are present in the plasma, but normally do not pass into the fluid in any but the most minute traces)			
Fibrinogen Iodides Salicylates Nitrates Sodium fluorescein uranin) Agglutins (meningococcal Bile pigments Organic arsenic, &c.		All these have been shown to pass into the cerebrospinal fluid in meningitis	

Reproduced from Cohen, 1927, by kind permission

calcium ions in the tap water, and he was later led to add an appropriate small amount of potassium which further improved a solution which, with slight modification, is still one of the indispensable fluids in biological laboratories.

The third example derives from Dale's own work. He relates how

I

he was studying the reaction which occurred when fresh blood serum is applied to a strip of involuntary muscle taken from a dead guinea-pig when, he writes:

I suddenly encountered a strip of this tissue from one particular guinea-pig which responded with a contraction of peculiar violence when it was treated with a mere trace of horse serum, though it behaved quite normally in the presence of blood serum from other animals—cat, dog, rabbit, sheep or man. And it occurred to me that many guinea-pigs in that laboratory were used for testing the strength of antitoxic horse serum, and that an economically minded colleague might have provided me with a survivor from such a test. The verification of that suspicion gave us a new idea about the meaning of the anaphylactic or allergic condition.

An example less well known, since it was not published by C. H. Andrewes but communicated personally to W. I. B. Beveridge, relates to the use of ferrets in influenza virus research. It was planned to include ferrets amongst the animals to be infected with influenza virus to determine their susceptibility; however, before their turn came, for they were a long way down the list, it was reported that a colony of ferrets were suffering from an illness which resembled human influenza. Ferrets were, therefore, tried forthwith and found susceptible to influenza. But the disease in the ferret colony was later proved to be distemper and not influenza!

We owe two laboratory methods in daily use to mistakes. Gram's stain came from Gram inadvertently pouring Lugol's iodine solution on to a smear which he had stained with gentian violet. He tried to wash out the stain with alcohol but failed and found that many of the bacteria had been stained a deep purple colour. And the acid-fast method of staining tubercle bacilli stems from Paul Ehrlich having left some preparations on a stove which was later inadvertently lighted. This heat was exactly what was needed to soften the waxy coat of the bacterium and prepare it to take the stain.

But Dale makes it clear that:

Accidents ... do not happen to the merely fanciful speculator who waits on chance to provide him with inspiration. They come rather to him who, whilst continuously busy with the work of research, does not close his attention from matters outside this principal aim and immediate objective but keeps it alert to what unexpected observation may have to offer.

Therapeutic Measures

Many major therapeutic agents also stem from error and false assumption. The seeds of chemotherapy were sown in 1891 by Guttmann and

Ehrlich when they administered methylene blue to two patients suffering from malaria. In both 'the attacks of fever ceased in the course of the first few days and the plasmodia disappeared from the blood after a week at the latest'. The treatment was based on the assumption that the dye in staining the parasites would kill them but would not injure the host. Lack of clinical cases prevented Guttmann and Ehrlich from extending their findings. In 1904, after the discovery of trypanosomes in African 'sleeping sickness', Ehrlich returned to the search started in 1891. With Shiga, he demonstrated that a benzidine dye, trypan-red, had a curative action on rodents infected with trypanosomes though it failed to cure human trypanosomiasis.

Roehl, one of Ehrlich's pupils, was later to discover a complex colourless, or faintly cream-coloured, substance (Bayer 205) which under the name suramin (Antrypol) is still used in trypanosomiasis. This was merely the beginning. Thirty years later Gerhard Domagk, influenced by Ehrlich's early work and seeking for an agent against bacterial infections, tried the effects of a great number of azo-dyes. In 1932 he demonstrated that the red-dye, prontosil, was effective against streptococci in mice and in 1935 published the evidence of its efficacy in humans. But Trefouël was to show that the action was due to the colourless part of the molecule, sulphanilamide.

Thus Ehrlich's false assumption led to discoveries which transformed the face of antibacterial therapy until the advent of penicillin.

We owe Novasurol, the first potent mercurial diuretic, which Willius & Dry (1948) regarded as a discovery which 'has completely revolutionized the treatment of congestive heart failure', to Alfred Vogl (1950), a third-year medical student who was acting as clinical clerk to Dr. Paul Saxl in the Wenckebach Clinic in Vienna.

In his charge in October 1919 was a young patient, Johanna ——, with classical congenital syphilis and juvenile tabes. Vogl was instructed to treat her with 1 c.c. of salicylate of mercury parenterally on alternate days. He wrote out a prescription for 'a 10% solution of mercury salicylate in water for hypodermic injection'. When after a few days the prescription had not been dispensed, he learned that this mercury compound is insoluble in water, so he had to repeat the prescription for a solution in oil, which entailed further delay. During this period, however, a visiting doctor produced a sample which he had received in the mail that morning and suggested that Vogl might try this new mercurial antisyphilitic—Novasurol. Vogl did so, injecting it every other day.

The nurses at the clinic took great pride in their charts, recording the usual clinical measurements in coloured columns; urine output was indicated in blue. Vogl noted that tall blue columns appeared after each injection, and thought perhaps that Novasurol was benefiting the syphilitic kidney. There was another syphilitic patient in the ward at the time—a cab driver with syphilitic heart disease and advanced congestive failure. The usual diuretics had no effect, but 2 c.c. Novasurol resulted in 10 litres of urine being passed in twenty-four hours. Other forms of injectable mercury had no such effect. This led Vogl to doubt whether the drug was acting on a syphilitic kidney. A little later a water-logged boy with a huge rheumatic heart and passing practically no urine was given an injection of Novasurol, and although he died next day, he had passed 3 litres of urine before death. At autopsy there was no sign of syphilis.

The value of Novasurol (and its hazards!) were established by its almost universal use later as a potent diuretic, and it remained in general use until the advent of the benzothiadiazine derivatives.

Here then, error and coincidence, a diligent nurse, and an observant medical student, must all be credited with a notable discovery.

An oft-repeated assertion is that the use of iodine in the treatment of Graves' disease was discovered by the distinguished French physician, Trousseau, when he prescribed in error tincture of iodine to a patient for whom he had intended to prescribe tincture of digitalis.

This is, however, inaccurate. Iodine had long been used both internally and externally in the treatment of goitres of all varieties. It is true that Trousseau (1868) prescribed iodine in mistake for digitalis in a case of Graves' disease, but in general his view was that 'although in the great majority of cases, iodine exerts a bad influence on the exophthalmic neuroses, it seems occasionally to produce temporary improvement of the patient's condition'. He then records the case in which the error occurred:

In the course of October 1863, I was consulted by a young married lady, who habitually resides in Paris. She was suffering from a subacute exophthalmic goitre. The bronchocele was of great size. When I examined her for the first time, although I had let her rest for a long while, and although I repeated the examination several times, and at sufficiently distant intervals, so as to make sure that she was no longer under the influence of emotion, I still found that her heart beat at the rate of 140 to 150 times in the minute. I recommended hydropathy, and I wished to administer at the same time tincture of digitalis, but, preoccupied with the idea that there would be some danger in giving iodine, I wrote iodine instead of digitalis, so that the patient took from 15 to 20 drops of tincture of iodine a day for a fortnight. When she then came back to me, her pulse was only 90. I found out my mistake, and I substituted tincture of digitalis for that of iodine, but, after another fortnight, the pulse had again gone up to 150, so that I at once returned to the iodine.

Yet he continues: 'Notwithstanding these exceptional cases, bear in mind that iodine generally does harm in Graves' disease.'

A false assumption was to lead to the clues which yielded drugs of great value in certain tropical diseases. For over a quarter of a century before 1935 it had been known that in the absence of glucose trypanosomes died, and that in their metabolism they consumed relatively large quantities of glucose. It was, therefore, suggested that if a continuous hypoglycæmia could be maintained, trypanosomes would succumb, and to this end Jancsó & Jancsó (1935) used Synthalin to induce hypoglycæmia in rats infected with *T. equinum* and found that it had a pronounced therapeutic effect. Though they regarded the hypoglycæmia as the chief factor in this they thought that Synthalin might also have a direct toxic action on the parasites. That this latter was indeed the effective cause was clearly demonstrated by Lourie & Yorke (1937) who showed, first, that Synthalin in a concentration of 1/200,000,000 will destroy practically all the trypanosomes in a suspension of nutrient media within twenty-four hours at 37°C; secondly, that Synthalin produces hypoglycæmia only in a dosage which causes liver damage; and thirdly, that insulin exerts no trypanocidal effect *in vitro* or *in vivo*.

Synthalin (a guanidine derivative)[1] is chemically essentially different from the other known trypanocidal drugs such as arsenicals and suramin to which I earlier referred. But it is very toxic, so a large number of similar guanidine compounds were prepared by King and tested by Lourie and Yorke (King *et al.* 1937, 1938). Some of these showed a powerful trypanocidal action and the most active member of the series was found to be undecane-1 : 11/diamidine. With this drug it was possible to secure permanent cures in approximately 100% of mice and rabbits infected with a laboratory strain of *T. rhodesiense*. Unfortunately, however, the effect of this drug in human trypanosomiasis was less satisfactory, but this work led to the production by Dr. A. J. Ewins of May & Baker of a series of aromatic compounds containing the amidine group, and these included stilbamidine, propamidine and pentamidine, which proved of value in the treatment of

---

[1] Synthalin B is dodecamethylene diguanidine dihydrochloride ($C_{14}H_{32}N_6.2HCl$).

early cases of *T. gambiense* with normal cerebrospinal fluid, but failed to cure late cases. These drugs have now been largely discarded in the treatment of trypanosomiasis but stilbamidine, pentamidine and the most recent preparation, hydroxystilbamidine isethionate—the 2-hydroxy derivative of pentamidine—which is more effective and less toxic than pentamidine, have proved to be a great advance in the treatment of Indian kala-azar even when antimony resistant, though Mediterranean and Sudan leishmaniasis require longer courses of treatment and respond less favourably.

Thus, from the false assumption that continued hypoglycæmia would control trypanosomiasis came drugs of value in other tropical diseases.

Surgery in Parkinsonism

The current surgical contribution to the relief of 'the lingering, imprisoned helplessness that has come to be recognized and resolutely accepted as the usual final stage of parkinsonism' is to aim at a precisely controlled destruction of selected portions of the globus pallidus alone, or together with the ventrolateral nucleus of the thalamus, by chemical agents, such as alcohol or procaine, by electrocoagulation, by freezing, or by ultrasonic radiation.

Irving S. Cooper of New York was a pioneer in this field (1954) and was led to it by an error in operative technique which resulted in the tearing of an anterior choroidal artery. He relates that, in October 1952:

During a craniotomy originally planned as a pedunculotomy in a 39-year-old man incapacitated by right-sided tremor and rigidity, the left anterior choroidal artery was torn and had to be completely occluded. Because of uncertainty as to the possible sequelæ of occlusion of this vessel, the operation was terminated without cutting the peduncle. The post-operative course was notable for virtual disappearance of tremor and rigidity from the right extremities, without any lessening of the motor power in these extremities.

Cooper speculated that the unplanned arterial occlusion had contributed to the alleviation of tremor and rigidity in this case.

The branches of the anterior choroidal artery are end-arteries to the globus pallidus and if fully occluded cause focal infarction therein. Although several successful cases were recorded by independent neurosurgeons the operation carried serious hazards for many patients, especially those suffering from the senile and arteriosclerotic types of parkinsonism, so that these became contraindications to the operation.

Cooper, therefore, searched for safer methods of destroying the injurious areas and his studies led to the present less hazardous and more precisely located lesions, made under careful control, which characterize contemporary methods of stereotaxis.

De Vries Mutation Theory

I turn from medicine to the wider field of science where error and false assumption have led to concepts which have profoundly influenced the advance of knowledge. My first illustration is the *mutation theory*. Charles Darwin's theory of natural selection and the survival of the fittest as the mechanism of organic evolution was based on comparative studies of a wide range of animal and plant life. It was generally believed that it could not be tested by direct observation and much less by experimental investigation. Darwin, of course, knew well that breeding could modify animals and that such sports could be maintained by the breeder, but he held that in Nature new species of animals and plants arise by imperceptible gradations from the old. These occur so slowly and continuously that the life span of man was unlikely to permit him to witness the appearance of any new form.

One of the strongest objections to Darwin's theory arose from

the incompatability of the results concerning the age of life on this earth, as propounded by physicists and astronomers, with the demand made by the theory of descent . . .

The deductions made by Lord Kelvin and others from the central heat of the earth, from the rate of production of the calcareous deposits, from the increase of the amount of salt in the seas, and from various other sources, indicate an age for the inhabitable surface of the earth of some millions of years only. The most probable estimates lie between twenty and forty millions of years. The evolutionists of the gradual line, however, had supposed many thousands of millions of years to be the smallest amount that would account for the whole range of evolution, from the very first beginning until the appearance of mankind. This large discrepancy has always been a source of doubt and a weapon in the hands of the opponents of the evolutionary idea . . . The theory of evolution had to be remoulded.

Thus wrote Hugo de Vries, Professor of Botany at Amsterdam, who in 1900-3 had published his mutation theory. He put forward the view that variations in species are of two forms. The first, suggested by Darwin, is that minute changes continuously occur through long periods of time; those which render the organism best fitted to its existing environment result in survival and ultimately in the development of a new species. The second kind of variation, held de Vries, occurs as a sudden jump and this jump immediately produces a distinctly new type. He believed that these mutations play a significant role in evolution.

De Vries's concept of mutations as sudden changes in hereditary material was based on his studies of Lamarck's evening primrose, *Œnothera lamarckiana*,[1] which he had studied since 1886. For the most part this plant breeds true but many unusual variations occur. Some are very large (*gigas*), others are short (*namella*), and others differ in colour, size and shape of various parts.

But although de Vries' mutation theory was the origin of the concept of modern gene mutations (when de Vries formulated it Mendel's paper had not yet been brought to light by de Vries, Correns and Tschermak) the variations de Vries described were later shown to be, in the main, not of this type but due to several different mechanisms.

Thus the giant mutant (*gigas*) had 28 chromosomes whereas the parental form had 14. It is thus tetraploid and results from doubling of the entire chromosome complement. Some mutants were trisomics, i.e. one chromosome is added to the normal set and thus it has 15 chromosomes. Some of the other mutants described by de Vries have been shown to be due to other chromosomal disturbances, for example, permanent heterozygosity.

Thus de Vries's mutation theory was based in practice on striking alterations of phenotypes, not genotypes, in a very unusual organism whose so-called 'mutations' were a mixture of different types of hereditary change. But de Vries's observations introduced the concept of discontinuity in evolution and, though his interpretations were erroneous, the concept of mutation is basic to the study of modern genetics.

Deuterium

Many striking examples of the fruits of error occur in the physico-chemical sciences. Let me relate one of the most dramatic, which led to the discovery of heavy hydrogen by the American chemist, Harold C. Urey. For this he was awarded the Nobel Prize for Chemistry in 1934. The story begins with J. J. Thomson who, by using the magnetic and electric deflection of positive rays in a discharge tube, was led to suggest that the rare gas, neon, of atomic weight 20·2, consists of a

[1] The plants he studied were later shown to be *O. erythrosepola Borbás* which is probably of spontaneous origin from plants introduced from North America.

mixture of two atoms of atomic mass 20 and 22 which, though differing in atomic mass, are identical in chemical properties. The proof had to await Aston's experiments.

By using a mass spectrograph, the first model of which is in the Science Museum, South Kensington, F. W. Aston showed that the majority of natural elements which he was able to investigate were mixtures of 'isotopes', i.e. chemical elements possessing the same chemical properties but differing in atomic mass and often in radio-activity. For example, the chemical atomic weight of chlorine is 35·5 (O = 16). Aston showed this gas to be a mixture of two isotopes, one of atomic mass 35, and the other of atomic mass 37, and that these occur in such proportions that the average mass is 35·5, that is the 'chemical' atomic weight. He was able to show that the atomic masses of isotopes were whole numbers with the exception of hydrogen for which he arrived at a mass spectrographic atomic mass of 1·00778 (O = 16), whereas chemical methods gave the value of 1·00777, which was an excellent agreement. However, in 1929, Giauque & Johnston of America found that oxygen has isotopes of atomic mass 16, 17 and 18, the last being as frequent as 1 in 630. Thus, the scale of 'chemical' atomic weights in which this mixed oxygen is considered as having an atomic weight of 16 is not the same as Aston's mass-spectrographic scale in which the lightest of the oxygen isotopes (i.e. O^{16} = 16) forms the base. Thus Aston's atomic mass of hydrogen, 1·00778, must be reduced to 1·00756 if we are to compare it with the 'chemical' atomic weight of hydrogen, viz. 1·00777. Birge & Menzel (1931) stated that this discrepancy appears to be outside the limits of experimental error, but could be explained by postulating the existence of an isotope of hydrogen of mass 2 with a ratio of H^2 to H^1 of 1 to 4,500 in the naturally occurring hydrogen.

It was this hypothesis which led Urey, who among others had postulated the existence of H^2 on theoretical grounds, to look for the heavy isotope of hydrogen and he succeeded in concentrating it by distillation of liquid hydrogen. He called the heavy isotope, deuterium, and the light one, protium. Since then a third unstable isotope, tritium, of atomic mass 3, for which Urey could secure no evidence, has been discovered.

But as Urey was himself to observe in an addendum to his Nobel Prize Lecture (1935), since this lecture was written Aston had revised his mass spectrographic atomic mass of hydrogen to 1·0081 instead of 1·0078. Urey continues:

With this mass of hydrogen the argument by Birge and Menzel is invalid. However, I prefer to allow the argument of this paragraph to stand, even though it now appears incorrect, because this prediction was of importance in the discovery of deuterium. Without it, it is probable that we would not have made a search for it and the discovery of deuterium might have been delayed for some time.

When we recall the essential role which deuterium has played in the growth and application of nuclear fusions Aston's original error was, depending on one's viewpoint, a curse or a blessing in disguise.

Mathematics

Pure mathematics might be regarded by many as a field in which reason and logic reign supreme. Yet even in the attempted solution of some of its famous problems, errors have yielded new concepts and new methods.

Take, for example, Fermat's famous Last Theorem published in 1637. There are an infinity of solutions to Diophantus' problem, which is to find whole numbers or fractions x, y, z which satisfy the equation $x^2 + y^2 = z^2$; e.g. $x = 3$, $y = 4$, $z = 5$; or $x = 5$, $y = 12$, $z = 13$. Fermat asserted that *no* whole numbers or fractions can be found such that $x^3 + y^3 = z^3$, or $x^4 + y^4 = z^4$, or, generally, such that $x^n + y^n = z^n$ if n is a whole number greater than 2, and he claimed that he possessed a 'marvellous' proof of this theorem. But he never disclosed it and indeed no proof or refutation has so far been demonstrated. In 1845, Kummer, a famous German mathematician, who preferred mathematics to philosophy because 'mere errors or false views cannot enter mathematics', believed he had solved the problem. In fact, as Dirichlet pointed out, he had done so for an extensive class of numbers but not for all, and his proof embodied an assumption which Kummer had considered self-evident. This led Kummer to study the problem even more deeply and from this he was led to the creation of an entirely new species of numbers, his so-called 'ideal numbers', which were to direct him to the theory of algebraic numbers, which are one of the important tools of modern algebra (Bell, 1937).

Many other false problems in the sciences led to important advances in knowledge, for example, squaring the circle and perpetual motion, and the debts of astronomy to astrology and of chemistry to alchemy, provide ample support for the fecundity of error.

Radioactivity

I close, however, as is appropriate for a clinician, with a case history, and I have chosen X-rays and radioactivity because they exemplify my theme so well.

On Friday evening, 8 November 1895, in his laboratory at Würz-berg, Wilhelm Conrad Röntgen discovered X-rays. He had for long studied the cathode rays emitted in vacuum tubes. Whilst observing the flow of current in a Crookes tube covered with black cardboard he noticed that a few crystals of barium platinocyanide, which were lying on the table, showed fluorescence. Crookes had earlier observed this phenomenon but attached no importance to it, but Röntgen realized that this chance finding might be significant and he was able to prove that rays coming from the tube penetrated the black cardboard which was opaque to light. He found also that these rays could affect, as did light, photographic plates, and produce fluorescence in other sub-stances. He called these 'X-rays' and demonstrated that they could penetrate the hand revealing a 'photograph of the bones of the hand'. This was on 22 December 1895, and a fortnight later the X-ray picture of the hand was shown at the Paris Académie des Sciences. Henri Poincaré, the outstanding mathematical physicist of his time, was present and he emphasized the finding that where cathode rays struck the wall of the Crookes tube not only did X-rays appear but fluorescence also occurred. He, therefore, assumed that these two phenomena were related and urged Henry Becquerel, whose father, Edmund, had earlier studied the striking phosphorescence of uranium compounds, to investigate this.

Becquerel then devised experiments to determine if bodies which fluoresce after exposure to light, emit X-rays. Using crystals of the double phosphate of potassium and uranium he did indeed find, after these had been exposed for four hours to sunlight and then placed on photographic plates covered with thick black sheets of paper, that the crystals smudged the plate. It thus appeared that Poincaré's hypothesis had been verified and Becquerel announced his discovery on 24 Febru-ary 1896. He had, however, perpetrated the cardinal sin of omitting the controlled experiment. Fortune, however, favoured him for within a few days he noticed that uranium sulphate crystals which had not been exposed to light had similarly smudged covered photographic plates which were kept in the same drawer as the crystals. This led him to further experiments, and a week later he was able to announce the discovery of natural radioactivity which was shown later to differ from X-rays.

Then came the systematic, intensive and time-consuming study that led Marie Curie first to the discovery of thorium and then with her husband, Pierre Curie, to the discovery of polonium and radium, by observing that certain compounds of uranium oxide (pitchblende) and the double phosphate of uranium and copper were more intensely radioactive than either uranium or thorium.

Here again we see three of the important elements in scientific method—the chance observation which led to the discovery of X-rays, the initial false assumption which was to lead to the discovery of radioactivity, and the determined, painstaking, laborious and systematic search which was to lead the Curies to the discovery of polonium and radium and other radioactive substances.

With this example of how genius profits from error my lecture must close. Others might well have chosen different and more apposite examples to illustrate the theme, and had time allowed I would myself have wished to draw attention to the knowledge which Nature offers to the curious through her own errors, such as inborn errors of metabolism.

I trust, however, that I have satisfied you that scientific research demands more than unbiased observation and logical inference, more than analysis and classification. Without hypothesis, these are blind. And the most fruitful hypotheses in the history of science have usually been postulated, not by the cold light of reason, but by the creative imagination which the great scientist shares with the great artist. And who will deny that for both error may be the spur.

As Voltaire observed: 'Croyez-moi, l'erreur aussi a son mérite.' (Believe me, there's something to be said for making a mistake.)

REFERENCES

Aston, F. W. (1922). *Isotopes*. London.
Aston, F. W. (1923). *Mass Spectra and Isotopes*. London.
Aston, F. W. (1935). *Nature, Lond.* **135**, 541.
Becquerel, H. (1896). *C. R. Acad. Sci. Paris* **122**, 420, 501, 689, 762, 1086.
Bell, E. T. (1937). *Men of Mathematics*. London.
Bernard, C. (1865). *Introduction à l'Étude de la Médicine Expérimentale*. Paris.
Beveridge, W. I. B. (1950). *The Art of Scientific Investigation*, London.
Birge, R. T. & King, A. S. (1929). *Phys. Rev.* **34**, 376.
Birge, R. T. & Menzel, D. H. (1931). *Phys. Rev.* **37**, 1669.
Butterfield, H. (1949). *The Origins of Modern Science*. London.
Cannon, W. B. (1945). *The Way of an Investigator*. New York.
Cohen, H. (1924). *Quart. J. Med.* **17**, 289.

Cohen, H. (1927). *Brain* **50,** 601.

Cohen, H. (1950). *Brit. med. J.* ii. 1406.

Cooper, I. S. (1954). *Surg. Gynec. Obstet.* **99,** 207.

Dale, H. (1948). *Brit. med. J.* ii, 451

Domagk, G. (1935). *Dtsch. med. Wschr.* **61,** 250.

Ehrlich, P. (1909). *Beiträge zur experimentellen Pathologie und Chemotherapie.* Leipzig.

Giauque, W. F. & Johnston, H. L. (1929). *J. Amer. chem. Soc.* **51,** 1436, 3528.

Graham, E. A. (1931). *Amer. J. Surg.* **12,** 330.

Jancsó, N. von & Jancsó, H. von (1935). *Z. Immun.-Forsch.* **86,** 1.

King, H., Lourie, E. M. & Yorke, W. (1937). *Lancet* ii, 1360.

King, H., Lourie, E. M. & Yorke, W. (1938). *Ann. trop. Med. Parasit.* **32,** 177.

Loewi, O. (1953) *From the Workshop of Discoveries.* Lawrence, Kansas.

Lourie, E. M. & Yorke, W. (1937) *Ann. trop. Med. Parasit.* **31,** 435.

Mott, F. (1910). *Lancet* ii, 80.

Nicolle, C. (1932). *Biologie de l'Invention.* Paris.

Poincaré, H. (1914) *Science and Method.* London.

Röntgen, W. C. (1895). *S. B. phys.-med. Ges. Würzburg* (December) p. 132 (translated in *Nature, Lond.,* 1896, **53,** 274).

Schutz, G. (1890). *Ber. dtsch. chem. Ges.* **23,** 1265.

Trousseau, A. (1868). *Lectures on Clinical Medicine.* London, **1,** 587.

Urey, H. C. (1931). *J. Amer. chem. Soc.* **53,** 2872.

Urey, H. C. (1935). *Some Thermodynamic Properties of Hydrogen and Deuterium* (Les Prix Nobel en 1934). Stockholm.

Urey, H. C., Brickwedde, F. G. & Murphy, G. M. (1932) *Physiol. Rev.* **39,** 164, 864; **40,** 1.

Vogl, A. (1950). *Amer. Heart J.* **39,** 881.

Vries, H. de (1904). *Science* **20,** 398.

Vries, H. de (1911). *The Mutation Theory.* London. (Translation of German Edition, 1900–3).

Weltwoche, Die (1966) No. 1686, Mar 4.

Willius, F. A. & Dry, T. J. (1948) *A History of the Heart and the Circulation.* Philadelphia.

Sanctity of Life

PROFESSOR DAVID DAUBE

DCL, Dr hon.c.Paris

9 *June* 1967

I propose to deal with three topics: euthanasia, abortion and the cost of expensive procedures.

Euthanasia

In normal conditions in modern countries, euthanasia for those hopelessly ill and threatened by unbearable suffering no longer constitutes a genuine problem. There are analgesics; and if the requisite dose is such as to speed death, the general consensus is, or will be shortly, that (except in special circumstances, e.g. where the patient dissents) it should nonetheless be administered.

Here let me say a word about the so-called double effect. Many Roman Catholics adopt a permissive stand on this point because the principal effect intended is the elimination of pain, while the hastening of death is merely a secondary effect regretfully put up with. It is often contended (for instance by Williams 1957) that this construction may encourage hypocrisy; and no doubt the danger does exist, as in many comparable cases of moral distinction. But it may also encourage an enhanced consciousness of the precariousness of the action and, with it, of the limits beyond which you may not go. A doctor who simply asks himself whether it is better to kill the patient or not to kill him is more easily led to overstep them than one who asks himself whether, in the particular situation, it is his duty to relieve the pain even though it will kill the patient.

Admittedly, the very setting of limits is in pursuance of a value judgement, which may be disputed. None the less I regard it as an advantage to occupy a position which excludes, for instance, the despatching of the old who are not otherwise terribly afflicted.

By the way, I agree with the lusty octogenarian lady debater who protested against a fixed drawing up of age groups. I suggest that a young man is one whom a pretty girl can make happy or unhappy; a middle-aged man is one whom a pretty girl can make happy but no longer unhappy; and an old man is one whom a girl can no longer make either happy or unhappy. With women, it is quite otherwise. A woman's declining years are under 25: she rarely declines after.

Psychological and subtle indirect consequences appear to be frequently underestimated by the advocates of a wider application of euthanasia. For example, such a policy would surely undermine the relation of trust between patient and doctor. Admittedly, in an era of mass service and specialization, the old-fashioned personal intimacy is on the way out (except in the intensive units about which we heard this morning) and the majority of sick go to an organization—a firm, a hospital—rather than to an individual. Nonetheless they go there confident that the staff into whose hands they surrender themselves are on their side, which means fundamentally, intent on curing them or helping them as far as possible this side of the grave. Once it got around that euthanasia was extensively practised, with whatever safeguards, people's feelings about the profession would undergo a considerable change. (An Oxford doctor recently told me of a colleague of his who, in the first stage of cancer, extracted from the friend who treated him the promise to give him a fatal injection when things became bad. Things became bad, and the patient, frightened and suspicious, refused to have even the injections which would be ordinarily prescribed.) This aspect has a bearing also on the question of mercy-killing of the insane. Quite apart from other considerations, it would be a sad day when doctors came to be looked on as slayers.

An entirely different result which might follow if we relaxed the rules concerning euthanasia I have never seen mentioned.[1] A person in an incurable and distressing state might well request euthanasia, not because he himself desires it, but from consideration for his family and friends: he would pretend that it was his true wish though in reality preferring life. I knew a great and wonderful man suffering from a terrible form of progressive paralysis. He would have been highminded enough, had law and usage permitted it, to demand that he be killed in order to free those near him; and it would have been a grievous loss to his circle, including his wife and children who had no easy time. A friend to whom I put this replied that, since we expect a soldier in war to lay down his life for others, we may expect the same from one who has become a burden to his fellow-beings. I reject this analogy: war has its own necessity which we should not lightly carry over into a civilized society at peace.

[1] It is discussed in my as yet unpublished Edinburgh Gifford Lectures, 'The Deed and the Doer in the Bible'.

Where the problem of euthanasia can still arise in its extreme form is in the absence of routine amenities and drugs; say, on the battlefield (and nowadays one has to add a bombed city) when medical aid is unavailable and the only way of alleviating intolerable pain of somebody mortally wounded is by shooting him. This is not a dilemma specifically for medical ethics. Anybody may find himself confronted by it, and who will judge him for whichever decision he makes?

There are unfortunately other situations so outside normal experience that it is difficult to adhere to usual standards. A certain West German doctor, who elects to remain anonymous, during the last war, at fearful risk to himself, provided Jewish acquaintances about to be deported to torture and extermination with tablets so they could kill themselves. (He also for a while harboured a Jew and thereby saved him.) To be sure, to furnish the means of suicide is not quite the same as to kill; but suppose he had directly injected a paralysed Jew who was unable to handle the tablets or a small child? It would not detract from the nobility of his conduct.[1]

Abortion

One feature of abortion is that there is no relation of trust between doctor and fœtus. In this respect, the situation is comparable to the treatment of an irretrievably unconscious person, a completely demented person, a baby or, in some countries, a slave. In all these cases, the doctor feels chiefly accountable to whoever is in charge, whose interests need not coincide with those of the immediate object of attention.

There are, of course, countless gradations between absolute non-participation and full status of the object. A child of 7 is more than a non-person. An inmate of an old people's home may enjoy less than unreserved recognition. I remember from my youth, when our maid fell ill and the doctor—our doctor—was called in, he addressed himself to my mother. A reason some students keep away from the College doctor is that they impute to him divided loyalty. At all events, the potential conflict of interests between mother and fœtus is obvious; and the doctor is caught between the two.

It is arguable that the fœtus is part of the mother's body; that any risk, burden and annoyance resulting from it has to be borne by the

---

[1] It may interest readers that the concept of death as a release where a man is in the depths of misery first occurs in the apocryphal Book of Tobit (see Daube, 1962).

K

mother; that the ordinances, legal or ethical, for the safety of the fœtus have been drawn up by men, at the expense of women; and that the mother should be entirely free to go on with or end her pregnancy. Yes, but the fœtus is an embryonic, emerging human being, if not—as is held by some creeds, the Roman Catholic in particular—a human being in the fullest sense. If you take the latter view, it must receive the same protection as any ordinary person; and even on the basis of the former, some measure of protection is warranted, though the precise degree is negotiable.

Roman Catholic teaching condemns abortion even where, without it, the mother perishes. This ruling has come under fire for being more rigorously opposed to the destruction of a fœtus than to that of an ordinary man. A man about to kill another man may be killed himself if there is no alternative mode of preventing the deed; and he may be killed (Roman Catholic doctrine admits) not only if he is morally at fault, but even if, say, he is a lunatic. Yet a fœtus about to kill the mother must not be removed—a glaring illogicality, the critics maintain (see Williams, 1957).

The two cases, however, are not so completely alike. The argument was ventilated as long as sixteen hundred years ago. Jewish law allows or even requires destruction of a fœtus in order to save the mother, up to the moment the child is born, that is to say, when the head is out. From this moment (and only from this moment) the Rabbis assume the existence of a full human being, of equal standing with any other. The question was raised in their ancient academies why, even at this stage, it should not be right to kill the child if otherwise the mother would die, seeing that the law authorizes the killing of a man about to kill another man, and authorizes it even if the attacker is a minor, not strictly answerable for what he does (Babylonian Sanhedrin 72b: see Jakobovits, 1959). This is exactly the modern argument, only they did not find it conclusive. Their answer was that the mother is attacked not by the child but from heaven; in other words, the child's presence is not comparable to an attack even by a minor or lunatic, it involves no doing on the child's part at all, the child is there, fatal to the mother by being there but not by any action—hence not to be sacrificed.

Historically and emotionally, the differences are indeed substantial. Where a man threatens to kill another man, in the vast majority of cases a moral wrong is committed; moreover, the emergency leaves no time for reflection, the instinct to rescue the prospective victim comes into instantaneous play. Against this background, it is small wonder that, if there is no other way out, even a deranged attacker may be killed. By contrast, in the vast majority of pregnancies, there is no danger to the mother's life and certainly no wrong; and where, exceptionally, grave risk does arise, in general a careful examination and weighing up of all factors can be undertaken. One may disagree with the Roman Catholic decision because of its very early dating of a human being (or even with the Rabbinic decision because it acknowledges a human being as soon as the head is through), but the charge of a senseless distinction cannot be upheld. I am hardly entitled to throw out three men from a full life-boat in order to rescue three struggling in the water. The former's presence does spell doom for the latter, but, in the words of the Rabbis, the attack emanates not from them but from heaven.

Where legal abortion is difficult to obtain and even where it is easy but at the price of social disapproval, inevitably the operation will often be performed in secret, in unhygienic conditions. As a result, there is much loss of life or health. A religion or morality which strongly insists on the protection of the unborn child must never lose sight of the very sad indirect consequences which are bound to occur. For a just and historically accurate appraisal of views on abortion, it is well to bear in mind that this dilemma is relatively novel. Prior to the revolutionizing of surgical hygiene in pursuance of Pasteur's and Lister's work, even expert intervention involved a high risk.

It is disgraceful that abortion should constitute a major problem in the second half of the twentieth century. By perfecting methods of birth-control—and even the pill is not yet anywhere near what is needed and possible—and by familiarizing people with them thoroughly and openly, the demand could be reduced to a fraction of what it is. There would remain a hard core of hard cases—unexpected complications imperilling the health of the mother or the soundness of the offspring—but they would be few indeed. No doubt in an ideal world contraception would not be thought of. In the world as it is, it is infinitely preferable to abortion which is largely its substitute.

I had written this paragraph when, by chance, two days ago, in West Germany, a report fell into my hands (*Frankfurter Allgemeine Zeitung*, 7 June 1967, 'Natur und Wissenschaft', p. 1): In the Federal Republic of Germany, in the four years 1963-6, while consumption of the pill and the use of other mechanical means of control went up, expectedly, the birth rate in the very same population also went up, quite unexpectedly. Here you are: contraception produces more babies. The explanation is (according to Professor H. Harmsen, a Hamburg expert who has gone into it) that, as pregnancies can be planned, there is a steep fall in abortion—especially among married couples. I do not suppose it follows that the spread of enlightenment in India or Peru will enhance their fertility: the starting-point in those countries is different. (I would not mind if the paradoxical result did happen since, contrary to prevalent fashion, I feel the more the merrier.) What the development does dramatically confirm is the enormous dependence of abortion on failure of birth-control.

I must add a remark drawing your attention to a recent series of actions on account of wrongful life (see Tedeschi, 1966). They have cropped up in some half-a-dozen Western countries, Italy, North America, though not so far in Britain. A child will claim damages for being born under a handicap. He (or somebody on his behalf) may sue a parent for bringing him into the world illegitimate, or a parent, a doctor or the state for causing or allowing him to be born diseased. Actions of this nature have already succeeded and are bound to become part of modern law. An idea which has been mooted is an action by a deformed child on the ground that pregnancy was not terminated when his mother contracted German measles. If legislatures are not careful in correlating and synchronizing their various measures in this field, we may see one partner of a surgeons' firm fined for illegally operating on a woman with rubella, while the other has to pay up for wrongfully letting a woman with rubella bear a cripple.

Cost of Expensive Procedures

Where the cost of treatment is borne by the patient, the limits are up to him. Even in this case complications arise, say, if he is mentally incapacitated through illness, senility or the like, and some prospective heir is waiting in the wings. Nowadays increasing importance attaches to the case where the cost falls on society. This problem is curiously intertwined with two others, that of commission and omission and that of discrimination.

I have already indicated my view that it cannot be right for a doctor to commit a killing. The idiot or dotard kept by the state in an asylum or almshouse must not be put to death. On the other hand, the omission of life-saving measures where a person would be doomed to endless suffering not willingly borne is a different matter. A visiting professor in this connexion recently cited from *King Lear* the words spoken by

Kent as the old man has at last fainted and young Edgar (Gloucester's son) wishes to call him back. Kent gently rebukes him:

> Vex not his ghost: O, let him pass! he hates him
> That would upon the rack of this rough world
> Stretch him out longer.[1]

It would be interesting to know whether hyper-rationalists who pooh-pooh the distinction between commission and omission would really sympathize to the same extent with a Kent who, the moment the king collapsed into a swoon, got hold of a syringe and finished him off.

There is, of course, omission and omission; in other words, besides the all-important distinction between active commission and passive omission, we have further to differentiate between omission of the usual, routine steps and omission of a far-fetched special intervention. Refraining from feeding an unconscious person comes nearer the action of killing than does refraining from giving him insulin. It is, as so often, a matter of gradation. A gynæcologist told me that a woman gave birth to a monster, two heads or something of the sort. He simply omitted the normal measures and the unfortunate being, whose death would in any case have taken place within a week or so, died almost immediately. The course he took was definitely preferable to giving a fatal injection—if only because once the doctor embarks on this method, his outlook is apt to become less unreservedly constructive, which in turn, as I pointed out earlier on, will affect the attitude of his clients.

The situation which, for a variety of reasons, is at the moment receiving a great deal of attention is where a patient can be kept alive and free from pain, indeed, happy and active, yet only at high cost to the community. Naturally, the community may have to choose between the particular therapy and alternative communally financed objectives: defence, education, free lunches for the poor, or, within medicine, other therapeutic tasks. What is worse for the individual doctor, a choice may have to be made between patients since provision

[1] *King Lear* V, iii (see Louisell, 1966). Professor Louisell is injecting a slight dose of modernism when he introduces these lines as concerned with 'artificial prolongation of life at whatever cost in pain and economic resources'. Economics is hardly in Kent's mind. It is noteworthy, incidentally, that as Lear faints, the exclamation 'Break, heart; I pr'y thee, break!', generally attributed to Kent who strongly feels that death would now be a blessing for his king, is given in the Quartos to Lear himself. Here, therefore, Kent has the king's express authority for his discouragement of resuscitation.

for all is not attainable. This means discrimination—against those who must be rejected.

Clearly, there is no question of killing these latter: it is inherent in the case that all that happens is omission of quite extraordinary manœuvres which would save them. That this is sad, even terrible, cannot be denied. But so long as the selection is based on no outrageous standards, doctors should not worry too much. By all means let them work out guide lines or set up committees if they think there are ways of ensuring a high degree of fairness. They can only do their best, and it would be wrong to make them have a bad conscience for what is ultimately not their doing; on the contrary, they would be the first, if entrusted with drawing up the State budget, to increase the means at the disposal of medicine.

Should a person's usefulness to society be a criterion? I am aware of the vagueness and fluctuating meaning of this term. I find women of greater service than men, but some of my colleagues feel the converse. There is a ship-wrecked party: two Italians and an Italian woman, two Frenchmen and a French woman, two Englishmen and an English woman and two Russians and a Russian woman. These twelve are stranded on a desert island. By the third day the following situation has developed. One of the two Italians has murdered the other and has settled down with the woman. The two Frenchmen have come to an amicable arrangement and have settled down to a *ménage à trois*. The two Englishmen have murdered the woman and have settled down. And the three Russians have drafted a letter to Moscow asking for instructions. Let us be down-to-earth and understand usefulness as the unsophisticated citizen would: a young scientist or housewife with children, over against a retired shoeshine man. It will inevitably be one consideration, though we may well hold that it ought not to be the only one. But it would be hypocritical to pretend that it is not a touchstone constantly applied throughout the world in all areas of private and public commerce, and even where it affects life and death. A plane in which a VIP travels is better serviced than one for common passengers; and I certainly feel much safer when I travel together with Lord Cohen.

This does not mean that a doctor should become an agent of the government, in the sense of subordinating his task as a healer to the interests of the State. It merely means that we allow him to be human. None of us can or should free himself entirely from contemporary ideas as to the public good; and, for instance, a long-continued clamour about overpopulation is bound to have a certain effect—an adverse one—on the valuation of an individual life. To some extent, fortunately, this is counterbalanced by the great novel possibilities of fighting death. Experience shows that techniques develop their own momentum: if a brilliant method of curing cancer is available, doctors want to use it no matter how many people to a square mile.

Incidentally, the danger of a doctor becoming the instrument of an administration is not new. Besides such institutions as compulsory notification of certain diseases, where the patient's wishes may have to be flouted, medical ethics has strangely neglected the province of forensic medicine. One can think of business in this branch directly bearing on the issue of the sanctity of life that I am discussing. What about the doctor employed to certify the death of a criminal executed? Or one who by his expert testimony brings a criminal to the gallows? Or, under our present system, to life-long incarceration? This is a puzzling outgrowth of medical art.[1]

As a layman, it is proper for me to stress the cost of some therapies to the doctor. A few weeks ago I passed through an American city. I had lunch with friends from Classics and Law, and we were joined by the professor of surgery. Excellent, un-American wine was produced. I noticed that the surgeon declined it and as I knew him to be healthy and fond of good food and drink I questioned him. It turned out that there was a baby in his hospital with kidney trouble. He could be kept alive for some six months, within which it was hoped to find a kidney that might be given him. If a suitable kidney offered, the transplantation would have to be performed without delay. So the professor kept in continuous touch with the hospital and radically abstained from alcohol. That man, a twentieth-century version of St. Francis did not pause to enquire into food-production per head of population or the gain or loss to the body politic. The baby needed him.

I conclude with a quotation:

It is doubtful if many doctors who actually care for the sick and the infirm plan their actions on the basis of the predicted effect upon society. Instead, the dominant tradition is for the physician to provide the best care of which he is capable for those who either seek his services or who are assigned to his res-

---

[1] The dilemma of a doctor who, during a war of which he disapproves, has to train students for medical posts in the army is not fundamentally different from that of anyone called on to do a job which furthers the war effort: though, understandably, a doctor may see a greater inconsistency than, say, a tax inspector between his calling and war.

ponsibility; by and large this is done without regard for the conceivably broader issue of whether or not treatment is justifiable on social grounds. His reasons may include pride, altruism, compassion, curiosity, a spirit of competition, even avarice, or a combination of all these things. Whatever the motive, the reflexes which follow are sure, and respond similarly to the needs of the productive members of the community, the insane and feeble-minded, children with incurable birth defects, condemned criminals, or even soldiers who moments before were members of a hostile army.

The foregoing viewpoint is a narrow one, but there is no reason to believe that it should be abandoned in the face of advancing technocracy. It has shielded the ill from the caprices of the moral judgments of other men through centuries of evolving philosophical, religious and legal doctrines. It has placed the concept of the sanctity of human life on a practical foundation, since the responsibility of one person for another could not be more clearly defined than through the doctor-patient relationship, irrespective of the reasons for the contract entered into between the two involved parties.

This quotation is taken not from some poetical Utopia, but from an exposition by one of the great young surgeons of our day, a leader of progress, practising and teaching in a very modern, successful country, the United States (Starzl, 1967).

Accipio omen: I eagerly accept his statement as presaging the future pattern of your noble profession.

REFERENCES

Daube, D. (1962). *Novum Testamentum.* Leiden, **5,** 99.

Jakobovits, I. (1959). *Jewish Medical Ethics.* New York & London, p. 184.

Louisell, D. W. (1966). In: *Ethics in Medical Progress.* Ed. G. E. W. Wolstenholme & M. O'Connor, London. p. 93

Starzl, T. E. (1967). *Ann. intern. Med.* Suppl. 7, p. 32.

Tedeschi, G. (1966). *Israel Law Rev.* **1,** 513

Williams, G. L. (1957). *Sanctity of Life and the Criminal Law.* New York, pp. 182 (note 1), 285.

The author has published the following pieces on allied topics:

(1) 'Transplantation: Acceptability of Procedures and the Required Legal Sanctions', in *Ciba Symposium on Ethics in Medical Progress,* ed. G. E. W. Wolstenholme and M. O'Connor, London, 1966, pp. 188 ff (on p. 196, last line but three, for a socialist read a-socialist).

(2) 'Limitations on Self-Sacrifice in Jewish Law and Tradition', *Theology*, vol. 72, 1969, pp. 291 ff.

(3) 'Organ Transplants: Cannibalism, Consent and Control', *The Colorado Quarterly*, vol. 18, 1969, pp. 134 ff.

(4) 'Legal Problems in Medical Advance', *Israel Law Review*, vol. 6, 1971, pp. 1 ff; published separately as Lionel Cohen Lectures, Sixteenth Series, Jerusalem, 1971 (distributed in Britain, etc. by Oxford University Press).

Crime and the British Penal System

Reflections of a Long-service Magistrate

THE BARONESS WOOTTON OF ABINGER[1]

Hon LHD, LLD, DSc

30 November 1967

I should perhaps preface these reflections with some evidence as to the experience on which they are based. On a rough calculation, in my forty-two years of service as a Justice of the Peace, the Benches of which I have been a member (and over which in the past twenty-five years I have generally presided) must have dealt with about 8,000 juveniles, upwards of 7,000 motorists and some 4,000 cases of other offences ranging from street trading to committals on charges of manslaughter. Of the juveniles, only a minority were civil cases relating to non-attendance at school or the need for care, protection or control; most were the subject of criminal charges. All the juveniles and the great majority of the adults have been (subject only to appeal) conclusively dealt with in the courts in which I have officiated, the exception in the case of the adults being committal proceedings concerning cases to be subsequently tried in the higher courts. Out of this whole collection of nearly 20,000 individuals it may entertain you to learn that one—a boy of 15 then serving in the merchant navy—said to his probation officer: 'I should like to go back and thank the lady'—which he did, very charmingly.

Changes in the Pattern of Crime

During these years there have been many changes in the pattern of offences with which we have to deal. Forty years ago drug charges were unheard of and traffic offences made but a modest contribution to our lists. Today, in London at any rate, scarcely a day passes without one or two charges of possessing dangerous drugs or forging prescriptions in order to obtain them, while motoring offences habitually outnumber all the others put together. Variations in criminal tech-

[1] Requests for reprints should be sent to: High Barn, Abinger Common, Dorking.

nique are also noticeable from time to time: in my early days violence was generally inflicted by the use of a blunt instrument: today sharp ones seem to be preferred.

Some features of the picture, however, remain remarkably stable. Thus it is always the young male who swells the criminal statistics. For many years now the proportion of 14-year-old boys found guilty of indictable offences has exceeded the figure for any other age. Some people regard this as symptomatic of the moral degeneracy of contemporary youth; but it is equally possible to see in it cheerful evidence that the majority of wayward youngsters grow up into solid and law-abiding citizens. The sex difference, on the other hand, is gradually diminishing, as women make their way in the criminal, as in other, worlds; yet even today for every one female found guilty of an indictable offence seven males are convicted; so it is still true to say, as I wrote nearly ten years ago, that 'if men behaved like women and boys behaved like girls, the courts would be idle and the prisons empty'.

Since the end of Hitler's war, the jurisdiction of the magistrates' courts has been both widened and narrowed. It has been widened to include the right to deal with cases of breaking and entering (other than those in which a dwelling house is involved) and by the imposition upon us of the exceedingly tedious task of licensing betting shops; it was narrowed in 1964 by the raising of the age of criminal responsibility from 8 to 10, a change which, greatly to my satisfaction, put about 1,300,000 children out of reach of the criminal law. Also, new restrictions will come into force in 1968 upon our power to refuse bail and to impose sentences of imprisonment that are not suspended pending good behaviour.

Something has also been done to ensure that Justices move with the times. We are not quite as amateurish—or as elderly—as we were in 1948, when a Royal Commission on Justices of the Peace [1] found that over 25% of those on the active list were over 70 years old, and asked no more of Justices than that they should be 'fairminded, of good character, intelligent and fully capable of *following* the proceedings in court' (my italics). Today no one is appointed to the Bench over the age of 60 and the Lord Chancellor is known to be contemplating legislation to reduce the present compulsory retiring age below 75. Moreover, in contrast with the state of naïve and bland ignorance in which I assumed my duties forty-odd years ago, Justices are now required, before taking their seats on the Bench, to undertake a prescribed course of basic training, which includes not only instruction in the law and observation of court procedures, but also visits to penal institutions (though the minimum requirement of two visits is remarkably modest) and discussion of sentencing policy.

It is, however, to potentially more fundamental changes, affecting the basic principles of criminal justice, that I wish particularly to direct your attention. Traditionally it is the business of the courts, first, to determine the issue of guilt or innocence and, second, to punish the guilty as they deserve. The strength of this punitive tradition, which I shall suggest is now threatened from more than one quarter, can hardly be overestimated. Indeed I know few lawyers in whose vocabulary the words 'sentence' and 'punishment' are not still virtually interchangeable. Court procedure itself underlines the point, as, for instance, in cases where the accused has the option of trial either by the magistrates or on indictment in a higher court. If he opts for the former, he is told that 'if the magistrates find you guilty and if, after hearing all about you, they think their powers of punishment are not sufficient, you may be sent to Sessions to be sentenced'. The concepts of guilt and punishment are, in short, inextricably linked and are regarded by long and deep-seated tradition as the keynotes of the whole enterprise. Indeed, traditional legal doctrine (though now breached by large exceptions about which I shall have more to say) holds that, without guilty intention, no conduct can be criminal.

In the discharge of this punitive function, the courts are guided, in the first instance, by the scale of heinousness established by the maximum penalties which Parliament has attached to various offences. Within these maxima (which incidentally are seldom reached) the actual sentence imposed is adjusted, in the light of aggravating or mitigating circumstances, to the court's estimate of the offender's guilt. In this way it is supposed that wickedness earns its due reward and the demands of justice as between one offender and another are said to be satisfied.

The Tariff System of Sentencing

This, which is generally known as the tariff system of sentencing, is open to the obvious objection that different courts apply different tariffs. Is it not odd that the proportion of men aged 21 and over imprisoned for indictable offences over a period of four years should have been found to vary as between one court and another from 3% to 55% [2]? Again, even if too much weight should not be attached to small numbers, why were nearly 17% of the 3,750 adults convicted in

Manchester magistrates' courts in 1966 imprisoned without the option of a fine, when under 10% of the 2,526 convicted in Liverpool were similarly treated [3]? Why, indeed, does the Liverpool rate run consistently year after year below that of Manchester? And can it be the superior virtue of the Scots which accounts for the fact that the proportion of male prisoners sentenced to three years or more in England and Wales is not far short of four times the corresponding figure North of the Border [4]?

In the past few years tariff discrepancies as between one court and another have been the subject of much concern both in the magistrates' courts and among the higher judiciary. 'Sentencing exercises' are now frequently organized by the Magistrates' Association and have certainly revealed to those who take part in them remarkable differences in the standards of different Justices. In relation to motoring offences, the Association has attempted to reduce these discrepancies by circulating confidentially to its members a suggested basic tariff, emphasizing, however, that no set of rigid rules can override the need to take account of the particular circumstances of individual cases. It has also recently been announced that the standardization of tariffs is to be encouraged at a more exalted level, by the issue to Justices from the Lord Chancellor's office of periodical statistics relating to average fines imposed for various offences: 'The computer used for this purpose', Lord Gardiner is reported to have said, 'had chewed and digested its diet of criminal statistics with quiet satisfaction for a little more than a year and then burst into enthusiastic activity' [5]. In the higher courts, also, the present Lord Chief Justice has broken new ground by convening 'sentencing conferences' of High Court Judges and Chairmen of Quarter Sessions—following a pattern that is well established on the other side of the Atlantic.

No amount of tidying up, however, can remove the essential subjectivity of any tariff system. For the plain fact is that guilt is not objectively measurable. Bringing divergent tariffs into closer harmony certainly removes chance variations which are liable to create feelings of gross injustice; but there is nothing to show whether a more standardized tariff is more accurately adjusted to the measure of an offender's guilt than were any of the divergent extremes which it has ironed out. Obviously, from the point of view of those of us who operate the present system, it has the one great attraction that none of us can ever be proved wrong. Our decisions may be faulted on appeal, but even the ethical superiority of the judgements of the higher court to those of the humbler fry below remains unproven and unprovable. And John Gordon's fulminations in the Sunday press are still no more than his personal opinions.

It is this system which itself now seems to be exposed to challenge from more than one quarter. Here I would mention particularly three contemporary trends: first, the changing climate of opinion in an age in which social institutions become increasingly exposed to scientific investigation and at the same time increasingly purposive; second, the devastating influence of psychiatry upon traditional conceptions of guilt; third, the accumulating evidence that in the contemporary world the amount of social damage perpetrated by an offender is less and less consistently related to the wickedness of his intentions.

Effects of Criminological Research

Significant of the first of these trends is the appearance on the scene of a formidable body of criminological research. Along with scientists in every field, social or physical, criminologists interest themselves in causal relations, notably in the results of the various sentences imposed by the courts. Of 163 criminological research projects in progress, recently listed by the Home Office Research Advisory Committee, a substantial proportion is concerned with the response of convicted offenders to various forms of treatment or with their after-careers. In this way light, it is hoped, may eventually be thrown upon the relative effectiveness of various sentences in reducing recidivism. Admittedly, the yield of established results is as yet small; for such is the complexity of these investigations, and the difficulty both of ensuring that like is compared only with like and of eliminating variations due to differences in personality or environment, that the assessment of the results of any medical treatment in illness must, by comparison, rank almost as child's play. But the significance of these researches lies less in what they have actually achieved than in the implicit presumption that it is the *consequences* of penal decisions with which we need to be concerned.

I can see trouble coming here for magistrates (and indeed judges also) in more than one form. Consequences are, potentially at least, demonstrable, and once we are judged by results, we are no longer in the happy position of never being liable to be proved wrong or to be shown up as better or worse than our colleagues on the job. For example: on the assumption that the object of a sentence is to prevent an offender from offending again, it would already be possible to establish (if anyone had the courage to do so) from the comparative frequency of reconvictions in similar cases in different courts that there are degrees of skill in sentencing just as much as in, say, interviewing or personnel selection. Moreover, although the results of follow-up researches are still scanty, they are not negligible. It is already possible by observation of features of an offender's background, history and behaviour to classify both young men in Borstals and older persistent offenders into 'risk classes', the validity of which has been established by subsequent experience. Again, investigations into Scottish experience have demonstrated the generally high reconviction rates that follow short prison sentences, as compared either with fines or with longer terms of imprisonment; while south of the Border it appears, somewhat surprisingly, that thieves respond better to fines while housebreakers, if first offenders, are unusually favourable subjects for probation [6]. Stimulated by these findings one should not, of course, run away with the idea that all thieves ought automatically to be fined and all first-time breakers put on probation, or that all short sentences of imprisonment should be converted into longer terms; but in cases in which the court is hesitating on other grounds between alternative methods of disposal, knowledge of these results may be (and in my case sometimes has been) sufficient to tip the scales.

If, as may reasonably be expected, the fruits of criminological research increase fairly rapidly, the question must soon arise as to how far they can be communicated to, and applied by, an amateur magistracy—and indeed a judiciary whose purely legal training is innocent of any contact with either statistics or penology. (Incidentally, it is still possible, though less likely than formerly, for an Assize Judge to be appointed whose previous experience as a barrister has been virtually confined to the civil courts; and Quarter Sessions are often presided over by County Court Judges whose day-to-day work is entirely civil.) Up till now perhaps, neither judge nor magistrate is greatly handicapped in the performance of his duties by failure to digest the still scanty results of criminological research; but, in the long run, money spent on research will be simply wasted unless two vital conditions are fulfilled: the research must produce results that have practical applications and, secondly, those results must be mastered by the judicial authorities who are in a position to apply them. The days of the judge or magistrate who is frightened by the sight of a statistical table are—or at least ought to be—numbered.

Meanwhile we continue to be gravely handicapped by the virtual impossibility of improving our personal proficiency by critical observation of past performance. Unlike doctors, only rarely are we faced with the results of the treatments which we have prescribed. Although in recent years arrangements have been made to enable judges in the higher courts and, in a limited range of cases, magistrates also to be informed of the subsequent history of persons whom they have sentenced, these are largely ineffective through lack of the long-term systematic recording which they require on the part of those who might use them. The melancholy truth is, therefore, that experience in the courts, although, as elsewhere, apt to command respect, is completely valueless. No one knows—least of all do I know myself—whether in my forty odd years I have done more good than harm or more harm than good, nor how my results compare with those of other colleagues of similar experience. It is a sobering thought.

Problems of Sentencing

Improved selection and a modicum of training may tide us over for a time yet. But the amateur Justice, who has survived for 600 years, can hardly enjoy a similar expectation of further life. Eventually the task of sentencing must be recognized as a highly expert job requiring specialized training—by which I emphatically do not mean that the stipendiary magistrates who now function in London and a number of other large cities should everywhere replace the amateur JP; for these professionals (whose number, by the way, is not increasing outside the London area) are themselves trained only in the law, whether as barristers or solicitors. The evolution of sentencing from art into science calls for a far more radical metamorphosis in the qualifications of its practitioners than the mere substitution of lawyer for layman.

Meanwhile, if we are to be judged by results, what, in fact, are the results at which we should aim? The obvious reply is that we should discourage an offender from repeating his offence and other people from imitating him. Yet experience makes it increasingly plain that the hope that, by a single act, respect for the law can always be simultaneously inculcated, both in an offender and in the public at large, is altogether too naïve. Although these twin objectives may often be compatible, this certainly is not always so. To take only one example, our prisons are always well populated with feeble characters who can keep out of trouble only in an exceptionally favourable environment: but the sight of the guilty enjoying not less, but more, eligible con-

L

ditions than the innocent would hardly be regarded as an encouragement to virtue.

In my experience conflicts between the anticipated effect of a sentence upon an offender and upon his potential imitators can be issues of extreme practical difficulty. Such conflicts cannot be resolved unless and until more is known about the areas in which, and the degree to which, it is fear of the consequences, rather than any other method of social conditioning, which restrains the lawless impulses of the murderer, the thief and the careless driver who lurk in every breast. That the effectiveness of any penalty is closely related to the probability of detection may be taken for granted. No doubt there are, and will be, lessons to be learned here from experience of the breathalyser. The dramatic effect which the new Road Safety Act is said to have had upon drivers' consumption of alcohol is indeed melancholy evidence of the feebleness of any conscientious inhibition against driving 'under the influence'. But what is significant is that the cause of this startling change is not that the penalties for drunk driving have been raised (they have not), but merely that the risk of detection has been increased by the introduction of more sophisticated methods. One may confidently predict that the permanence of would-be drinkers' present abstinence will depend upon how nearly current estimates of the increase of risk prove to be justified.

Equally, I suggest, can we be confident that the internal sanction of social conscience, when operative, is a far more reliable buttress against law-breaking than is the external threat of any likely penalty; but we remain woefully ignorant both as to the limits within which this sanction already operates and, still more, as to the social processes by which its influence might be extended. Admittedly, objective investigation in this field is notoriously difficult; but I would like to recommend for empirical testing the commonsense hypothesis that the generally deterrent effectiveness of penal sanctions tends to be inversely related both to the element of malicious intent in the relevant crime and to the rewards to be reaped from successful criminality. The motorist who is tempted to exceed the speed limit, to park selfishly or even to drive under the influence of drink certainly puts his own interest first; but, unlike the burglar, he does not set out to do, and would probably prefer not to do, any actual damage to another person; nor would it make an enormous difference to him if he drove less fast, parked only where authorized and had a drink or two less. His malicious intent is minimal. All this makes him more, rather than less, sensitive to the penalties which he risks by a breach of the law. If he has already two convictions for speeding within three years, he will be exceptionally careful not to incur the almost certain loss of his licence by acquiring a third. By contrast, to the potential burglar and still more to the professional criminal crime is both an end in itself and a source of immediate and possibly substantial profit—with the result that in his case the risk of penal sanctions is likely to be discounted. For these reasons I doubt if much reliance is to be placed upon the introspections of motorists as a guide to the psychological processes of other criminals. But I would call your attention to the inference that, if these speculations are well founded, it will be in relation to the more serious crimes that the deterrent effect of penal sanctions upon the public at large operates least powerfully or, to put the matter the other way round, I doubt if it is fear of penal consequences which restrains most of us from murder or theft, but I do not dispute that this fear is, in certain circumstances, a powerful inducement to sobriety at the wheel and to moderation of speed.

At this stage I can, therefore, only ask your pity for courts which, in the present state of ignorance on these issues, are expected to kill the criminality of all the birds—the one inside the court and all the others outside—with one stone. Imagine, by way of analogy, the plight of a doctor who was required to check the spread of a disease throughout the community by performing radical and, in his opinion, sometimes injurious, surgery upon patients already suffering from it. Imagine that, and you will appreciate the dilemma in which the courts are all too often trapped.

Psychiatric Influences

I turn now to consider the second of the three trends which appear to be undermining the traditional preoccupation of the criminal courts with the punishment of guilt—namely the complications introduced into the assessment of guilt by psychiatric considerations. It is perhaps worth reminding ourselves how rapid have been developments in this field: all the significant changes have fallen within the period of my own service as a Justice. Apart from the 'moral imbeciles' specified in the Mental Deficiency Act of 1913 (of whom little was heard in practice) it could be said that half a century ago the courts were only concerned with the mental condition of defendants on criminal charges in cases of unfitness to plead or of insanity within the McNaghten rules; and a defence of insanity, involving indefinite detention in what was then known as a criminal lunatic asylum, was normally only raised in cases of murder. Since then we have had, first, Section 4 of the Criminal Justice Act of 1948 which permits a court to write into a probation order a condition requiring the probationer to undergo mental treatment either in hospital or as outpatient; next the Homicide Act of 1957 which introduced into English law the defence (long-established in Scotland) of diminished responsibility, which, if successful, reduces a charge of murder to a conviction for manslaughter; and, third, the Mental Health Act of 1959 with its comprehensive provisions that an offender who is diagnosed as suffering from certain forms of mental disorder may, provided that the offence of which he is convicted could carry a sentence of imprisonment, be detained under a hospital order instead of being sentenced in the ordinary way.

As a result of these measures, the guilt of a number of offenders is now held to be, in varying degrees, modified by mental disorder; and the traditional practice of assessing guilt is correspondingly complicated. Somewhat surprisingly, it is the earliest of these three Acts which is drawn in the widest terms, inasmuch as it does not strictly require any prior diagnosis of mental disorder. All that is necessary is that the court should be satisfied, on appropriate medical evidence, that mental treatment offers the best chance of reformation; and it is of interest that a requirement of mental treatment as a condition of probation (at least in the early days of its history—recent information is not available) has been by no means confined to cases, such as sexual offences, which are commonly thought of as involving a 'mental element', but has also been freely used for probationers convicted of such apparently ordinary crimes as thieving.

Under these provisions, however, the offender, though undergoing mental treatment, is not formally transferred from the ranks of the wicked to those of the mentally disordered. The court, one could argue, has been persuaded, not that he is ill, but that mental treatment will have a beneficial effect upon his wickedness. Perhaps it will; but, should this hope be disappointed, or should the probationer fail to submit to the prescribed treatment, he becomes liable to a penal sentence for breach of his probation. In spite of having become a patient, he still retains his potential status as a criminal.

By contrast, the 1957 Homicide Act looks not to treatment, but to the offender's state of mind, as determining the actual crime of which he is convicted: under Section 2 of that Act the difference between murder and manslaughter turns upon proof of impaired responsibility.

Accordingly, in homicide cases where this defence is raised, the court is under obligation to draw a definite line between the wicked and the weak-minded and, until the abolition of the death penalty, this was in capital cases a life and death matter. The result, as anyone who has studied the relevant cases must be aware, has been to create a state of hopeless confusion. The question whether a condition of diminished responsibility is compatible with careful planning of a crime—even the suggestion that a man may be fully responsible when he seizes a stick from the entrance to a house but has become partially irresponsible by the time he is using it to bash an old gentleman in bed upstairs—all this may be an occasion for the display of forensic brilliance, but can leave no doubt in minds not hopelessly dazzled by these exhibitions that either wickedness must itself be a form of mental disorder or, if the two are distinguishable in theory, in practice no tenable line can be drawn between them. No doubt the psychiatrists who give evidence on these matters have their own views as to which side of the line between wickedness and mental aberration a particular individual should be classified. But the trouble is that these opinions cannot be subjected to empirical validation. Hence the psychiatrist also (as well as the court, irrespective of whether or not it accepts his guidance) is in the (perhaps to him not unfamiliar) position of not being open to be proved wrong.

Confusion is, moreover, still further confounded by the fact that, even when a verdict of diminished responsibility is returned, the offender is not necessarily thereafter treated as a sick man. In the six years since the relevant provisions of the Mental Health Act came into force, the proportion of diminished responsibility cases made subject to hospital orders has ranged from 42% to 60%, the remainder being, with few exceptions, sentenced to terms of imprisonment. It is indeed always open to the Home Secretary, provided that the prisoner's mental disability can be subsumed under any of the forms of mental disorder recognized by the Mental Health Act, subsequently to transfer him from prison to hospital under Section 72 of that Act; but this is by no means always done. Over the past six years only 12 out of a total of 99 offenders found to be suffering from diminished responsibility and sentenced to imprisonment have been thus transferred to hospital [7]. Altogether, the most that can be said is that the practice of making hospital orders in cases of conviction for manslaughter with diminished responsibility is on the increase; and that at least those who are committed to hospital are genuinely transformed from criminal into patient. Their position, in fact, becomes analogous to that of any other mental patient who is detained under compulsion, subject only to the court's power to impose an order restricting discharge without the consent of the Home Secretary.

Quite apart from homicide cases, which are sentenced only by Assize Judges, the 1959 Mental Health Act also empowers courts of Quarter Sessions and even amateur magistrates, in any case in which a sentence of imprisonment might alternatively have been imposed, to substitute a hospital (or guardianship) order, if the offender has been appropriately diagnosed as suffering from a specified form of mental disorder and the court is satisfied that such an order is the most suitable way of dealing with him; and, in cases of the severer forms of mental disorder, magistrates have also the power (though few of them realize it) to make hospital or guardianship orders without recording a conviction.

The result of these enactments is that at every level the courts now have to worry their heads about questions of mental competence and about the boundary between the penal and the medical sphere such as forty years ago could have been cheerfully ignored. If the lower courts are spared the sophisticated forensic battles provoked by Section 2 of the Homicide Act, they too, in their quieter and more decorous way, are from time to time concerned with not dissimilar issues— with the decision when to invoke medical guidance or to abdicate in favour of medical colleagues. True, the 1,448 hospital and guardianship orders made in 1966 look insignificant beside the total of over 30,000 sentences of imprisonment imposed in that year on persons convicted of indictable offences; but the number of hospital orders has been creeping up over the past five years and at a somewhat faster rate than committals to prison. It is likely too, with the increase in the number of drug addicts appearing before the courts, that the demands of the therapeutic, as against the penal, approach will become increasingly clamorous. The number of probation orders with a condition of mental treatment may be swelled by the inclusion of addicts under obligation to attend one of the proposed treatment centres or, alternatively, if the statutory category of mental illness can be stretched to embrace addiction, the number of hospital orders may be similarly increased—a development which would incidentally have the effect of undermining the voluntary nature of the treatment centres for addicts. And, to complete the picture, the Criminal Justice Act of 1967 with its proposal to transfer alcoholics from prison to what is described as 'suitable accommodation for the care and treatment of persons convicted of being drunk and disorderly' contains at least a hint that addiction to alcohol, no less than to currently more fashionable drugs, may soon be regarded as more of a disease than a crime.

Social Damage due to Carelessness

The role of the courts, as instruments for the punishment of wickedness, is thus increasingly complicated, not to say frustrated, both by growing interest in the consequences of penal decisions and by growing uncertainty as to where wickedness merges into weakness of mind. To these disturbing factors must now be added the third member of my potentially revolutionary trio, that is to say, the relative decline in the contribution which deliberate wickedness, as compared with carelessness, negligence or simple lack of consideration, now makes to the total of social damage. For this development we have, of course, to thank the invention of the internal combustion engine even more than the Moloch-like qualities of modern industry. Certainly the 1965 aggregate of 205 convictions for murder, manslaughter and infanticide pales beside the figures of 7,952 road deaths and 1,089 fatal accidents in industry. As for the damage to property caused by thefts, breakings and vandalism on the one hand, and by road accidents on the other, reliable estimates are not readily available; but there seems no doubt that it is the latter for which far the larger sums have to be paid out by insurance companies.

In face of this situation the doctrine that guilty intent is an essential element in any crime (and that the prime purpose of the whole criminal process is to locate and punish the guilty in accordance with their deserts) may be said to be fighting a rearguard action. It is in the field of what may be called traditional crime that the hold of this doctrine is at its strongest. The crime of larceny, for example, involves not only the appropriation of someone else's belongings: there must also be proof of intent permanently to deprive the owner of his property; and, what is more, the intent and the deprivation must coincide in time. If you manage to borrow your neighbour's necklace, without her knowledge, meaning to wear it for one party and then slip it back, but afterwards change your mind and decide to keep it, you have not strictly been guilty of theft. Needless to say, to establish these psychological nuances often demands a degree of insight into another's mind that is not given to many of us. I recall, for example, a juvenile court case of some years back in which an office boy was accused of stealing a book describing the history of the well-known publishing house in which he was employed. For the defence it was contended that it was the boy's intention to return the book after reading it and that therefore he could not be found guilty of theft; and this was accepted by starry-eyed magistrates, impressed by the loyalty of the young employee to his firm. Imagine, however, our dismay, on discovering that the next three cases on the list were also charges of stealing from the same publisher, involving books which on the face of them were much more likely to appeal to the average young male.

Again, as evidence of the law's traditional preoccupation with wickedness rather than with social damage, one may contrast the unstinting expenditure of time and money devoted to the apprehension of a single suspected murderer with the absence of any judicial investigation, other than a coroner's inquest, into the great majority of fatal road accidents. The 7,952 road deaths of 1965, for example, were followed by no more than 569 prosecutions (resulting in 436 convictions) for the offence of causing death by dangerous driving. What happened in the other 7,000 odd cases was held to be the private concern of the parties involved and a matter for the civil courts alone.

Nevertheless, even if the sanctity of the principle that it is the guilty intention that makes the crime is still dominant in the sphere of what may be called traditional crimes, this principle now enjoys scant respect in the case of breaches of the mass of statutory regulations by which all our lives are now governed. In the great majority of traffic offences, as well as those relating to such matters as the sale of food and drugs or the conduct of licensed premises, a conviction must be recorded, regardless of whether the offence was in any sense intentional or deliberate, or even knowingly committed. In some cases, as, for example, careless driving, the very nature of the offence virtually precludes implication of deliberate intent: for who is likely to drive carelessly on purpose? But this condition of what the lawyers call 'absolute liability' is by no means confined to offences of this kind. An honest belief that your vehicle was validly insured is, for instance, no defence to a charge of driving without insurance, although it may properly be regarded as justifying a mitigated penalty on the ground that the offence is unlikely to be repeated. Today, therefore, when traffic offences account for more than 65% of the total of convictions recorded in all courts taken together and, it may be presumed, for an even higher proportion of those dealt with by the magistracy, it is already the exception rather than the rule in the magistrates' courts for a conviction to require proof of guilty intention.

Some rather curious anomalies, however, remain. To drive with defective brakes is in all circumstances a criminal offence—even when the defect is due to a one-in-a-million chance or when the driver is an employee and in any case not responsible for the maintenance of the vehicle. Yet, as already mentioned, the criminal courts take no cognizance of the vast majority of fatal accidents on the road. Thus the man whose brakes endanger life earns a criminal conviction, irrespective of guilty intention or even culpable negligence, but he whose vehicle actually destroys life is liable to conviction only on proof of having driven dangerously. It follows, as an incidental consequence of this paradox (and I have known a case in point) that a driver can be convicted of a traffic offence, such as careless driving or driving without insurance, without the court by which he is sentenced being aware that he has a history of more than one fatal accident. If blameworthiness is the criterion for conviction and it is accepted that the accidents were not his fault, that is fair enough. But how can this be reconciled with recording a conviction against an equally blameless defendant for defective brakes? By what logic can we justify this attempt to have it both ways?

As roads of escape from these anomalies, various proposals have been suggested by those who wish at all costs to preserve the punitive function of the courts. The Law Society, for instance, would make a distinction between what are described as truly criminal acts on the one hand and all offences of 'strict liability' on the other, and would remove the latter from criminal jurisdiction altogether—arguing that the stigma of criminality ought not to be attached to those who intended no wrong. Such a course is, however, open to objection on the ground that, while guilty intention is not a necessary element in a crime of 'strict liability', it is in fact by no means always absent. Thus, to exceed a speed limit is an offence, even if it is the result of a moment of inadvertence; but, in practice, it is, as often as not, a deliberate act. Alternatively, many lawyers hold that the concept of guilty intention should be extended to cover a much wider range of cases of negligence or inadvertence—so that, for example, a conviction for driving without insurance might be recorded only if the accused had omitted to take such steps as he might reasonably have been expected to take in order to ascertain the facts relating to his insurance—but not, as at present, in circumstances in which he could not have known, or was the innocent victim of deception as to, the true position. In my view, however, such proposals, if only on grounds of the litigious accretions already attaching to such words as 'knowingly', 'negligently' or 'inadvertently', deserve no enthusiastic welcome.

I myself would argue that society as a whole, and not merely an injured individual, has an interest in the prevention of social damage, whether or not intentionally caused; and that, therefore, it is entirely right and proper that we should all be liable to be called to account for any serious damage that we do, whether by accident, inadvertence or design, since the consequences of an offence bear no necessary relation to the intentions of its perpetrator. I see no logical reason why guilty intention should be written into the definition of every criminal act nor reason to be dismayed by the contemporary proliferation of offences in which this stipulation is omitted. I see this process as not only a necessary, but indeed a welcome adaptation to a world in which the careless and the indifferent do more harm than the wicked.

This development is moreover closely interwoven with the other trends to which I have called your attention. Indeed this lecture might well have carried the subtitle: 'The Decline and Fall of the Concept of Wickedness in British Criminal Procedure'. For not only is wicked intention no longer a necessary ingredient in the definition of every criminal offence: the assessment of culpability has itself, thanks to the influence of psychiatry, become a vastly more complex and uncertain exercise; and in consequence, the tariff system of sentencing, which purports to deal with each according to his deserts, is seen to be less and less compatible with psychological reality. Emphasis, therefore, shifts from the past to the future; and evidence as to an offender's state of mind finds its place, not in the evaluation of his guilt, but as predictive of his probable future behaviour and response to treatment. Prognosis rather than condemnation becomes the password.

I envisage, therefore, a slow—very slow—evolution of the criminal courts from the purely punitive institutions of yesterday, blind to their own social consequences, into social agencies, preventive and remedial, rather than retributive in character, concerned with the future rather than the past. That this implies an increasingly close approximation of penal practice to the practice of medicine, in which each is judged by its skill in combating the mischief which is its own peculiar concern, will not, I think, have escaped your notice.

REFERENCES

[1] Royal Commission on Justices of the Peace (1948). Report (Cmnd 7463). HMSO, London; para. 84.

[2] Hood, R. (1962). *Sentencing in Magistrates' Courts*. London; p. 12.

[3] Home Office (1966). *Supplementary Criminal Statistics*. HMSO, London.

[4] Home Office (1965). *Report on the Work of the Prison Department, Statistical Tables* (Cmnd 3304); Scottish Home and Health Department: *Prisons in Scotland. Report for 1965* (Cmnd 3036). HMSO, London.

[5] *The Times* (1967). 14 October.

[6] Home Office (1964). *The Sentence of the Court*. HMSO, London.

[7] *Hansard* (House of Lords) (1967) 26 October, col. 1809.

The Control of Drugs and Therapeutic Freedom

SIR DERRICK DUNLOP

MD, FRCP

24 May 1968

The modern drug problem—I prefer to call it the medicines problem because the word 'drug' like the word 'love' has undertones as well as overtones—is in miniature that of the modern, complicated democracy which seeks the ideal of ordered freedom within the law, with the force of sanctions far in the background—in which authority and freedom are blended in due proportion and in which the state and the citizen are complementary to each other—a sort of age of Pericles.

Democracy, however, is a very difficult form of government. I do not know why we should expect underdeveloped countries to adopt so easily what has taken us hundreds of years to evolve. It requires constant guarding from slipping in one direction into chaotic licence, possibly due to the relaxation of laws on such things as capital and corporal punishment, gambling, pornography, Sunday observance, homosexuality, abortion and divorce, or in the other into bureaucratic tyranny due to the gradual erosion of certain individual liberties by government action. For example, the law of supply and demand and the devil take the hindmost—the economic rule of the jungle, beloved of Victorian ironmasters—is nowadays abhorrent to most of us but, in attempting to mitigate its asperities it is difficult to find another logical alternative short of complete communist state control—the rule of the ant heap—which most of us do not like very much either. Between these extremes, reforms and revolutions, no matter how salutary, are bound to be hurtful to some and may sometimes create further problems more formidable than the abuses they have sought to remedy. Thus, the drunken motorcar driver had become such a menace that additional measures were required to deal with him but their imposition has interfered with our freedom to enjoy with any peace of mind a bottle of wine with a friend at dinner before driving soberly home. In the same way, largely due to a very few doctors who have prescribed potent narcotics and hallucinogenic agents so injudiciously (I do not use a stronger term), addiction to them in Britain—at one time so minimal as to be a matter of almost incredulous envy in other countries—has suddenly assumed serious proportions. In consequence, under the 1968 Dangerous Drugs Regulations the legal right to prescribe heroin and cocaine to addicts—though not, curiously enough, morphine—has been taken away from us ordinary doctors and confined to those working in special clinics.

Further, the Safety of Drugs Committee has restricted the supply of LSD to the very few psychiatrists who continue to regard that rather sinister drug as a valuable agent in diagnosis and therapeutics. These are perhaps necessary measures but are possibly the thin edge of the bureaucratic wedge to professional medical freedom. The trouble is that, though we nearly all maintain that freedom is good and restriction bad, when someone else's freedom of action becomes inconvenient we usually clamour for its restriction—a restriction which then seems essential in the public interest and based on the purest of motives. 'The Government must do something about it', we say. Such restrictions may be particularly undesirable when imposed hysterically to meet some crisis. We saw recently in Kenya an example of how unrepresented people might have their liberties invaded when our parliamentary machine lacked the opportunity for reflection and worked under pressure of time.

Modern medicines are such potent weapons—like atomic energy, powerful for good but also powerful for evil—that the responsibility for their safe production and use can no longer be left *entirely* to the manufacturer and prescriber. Yet it is difficult to know how far government should attempt to control their manufacture and use without undue interference with the advance of therapeutics, the wellbeing of the pharmaceutical industry and the cherished freedom of the doctor to prescribe anything he likes for his patient, though it is a little doubtful whether the responsibility we have shown in the use of modern medicines entirely justifies that freedom.

Any health service which hopes to win the consent of doctors must allay the fear that bureaucratic interference will affect professional freedom and come between the doctor and his patient. There is no alternative to self-government by the medical profession in all matters affecting the content of its academic life. It is for the community to provide the apparatus of medicine for the doctor. It is for him to use it freely in accordance with the standards of the profession and the requirements of his oath.

Who do you think said that? Rather surprisingly it was that remarkable man, Aneurin Bevan.

Attempts at the control of medicines have gone on for a very long time. The earliest efforts were the catalogues of medicines or herbals providing detailed descriptions of poppies and mandragora, of mercury and antimony, of eyes of newts and toes of frogs to help physicians to recognize and use these agents. Though his head might be cut off if the consequences of their administration were dire, the physician was not then summoned under the provisions of any Act. From these early herbals grew the London and Edinburgh Pharmacopœias—essentially herbals themselves but given authority through their respective Royal Colleges. Then came the *British Pharmacopæia* of 1864 with its numerous subsequent editions and now there is an *International Pharmacopæia*.

We have come a long way since 1864 in laying down standards to try to ensure the purity and strength of medicines; subsequent Food and Drugs and Therapeutic Substances Acts have provided further legal protection for the public in these respects. There has also been a progressive widening in such control so that nowadays a patient can have at least some confidence that he will be supplied with the same agent whether he purchases it in London, New York, Paris or Tokyo. In more spacious days it sufficed if he always bought his infusion of digitalis leaves from Mistress Ford rather than from her rival, Mistress Page down the street, whose brews might differ from each other like the strength of a cup of tea in different homes.

In addition, as the result of the Cancer and Venereal Disease Acts it is no longer possible for charlatans to delude the public by advertising quack nostrums for the treatment of serious disorders. Lastly, various Acts to control the risk of addiction to potent narcotics and to prevent the counter-sale of certain medicines without a medical prescription have been essential measures.

This mass of legislation on medicines undertaken in the last hundred years has been almost entirely salutary. The present responsibilities of government, however, in attempting to ensure their safe and efficacious use are much more complex and difficult.

Though we had been well aware for many years of the toxic nature of many of the medicines we were using, we had been somewhat complacent and ostrich-like regarding them and it took the emotional reaction to the thalidomide disaster to galvanize us out of our somewhat *laissez-faire* attitude. Following it the Ministers of Health, on the advice of a sub-committee under Lord Cohen of Birkenhead of the Standing Medical Advisory Committee, established the Safety of Drugs Committee in 1963 as an interim measure until the comprehensive legislation on medicines now before Parliament could be enacted. It was odd that, in the somewhat bureaucratic welfare state that Britain had become, the Ministers gave the Committee almost complete independence with its own offices, its own staff and with its own records, kept entirely separate from other official papers; but perhaps not so odd when it is remembered that the Minister of Health at the time was Mr. Enoch Powell. The Committee itself consists of eleven part-time scientists and physicians with a permanent staff, paid as civil servants, of six doctors—four of them recruited from industry, on the principle of turning a poacher into a gamekeeper—and two pharmacists.

The Committee does not itself undertake pharmacological tests or clinical trials of medicines: the responsibility for these remains firmly with the manufacturer. The Committee simply weighs the manufacturers' submissions on their tests and lays down certain standards for them. Its remit does not impose upon it responsibility to consider the efficacy or comparative efficacy of medicines except in so far as their safety is concerned. Thus, a high degree of toxicity might well be acceptable in one which stayed the progress of cancer whereas one used for a trivial condition would have to be relatively innocuous. Therefore, the clearance of a medicine for marketing does not imply the Committee's recommendation of it as a therapeutic remedy but only its reasonable safety for its intended purpose.

The Association of the British Pharmaceutical Industry and the Proprietary Association of Great Britain, despite the absence of legal sanctions, promised before the Committee started to function on 1 January 1964, that their members would not submit a new drug for clinical trial or market a new drug against the advice of the Committee. They have loyally observed these agreements.

If there are no legal sanctions there are, of course, some unofficial ones; the Minister, for instance, reports to all practising doctors in the Health Service should a new medicine be marketed without the Committee's approval and doctors would draw their own conclusions. Further, if a medicine which had not been cleared by the Committee gave rise to toxic reactions, neither its manufacturer nor its prescriber would stand in a very favourable position in a Court of Law. These are very formidable sanctions. Nevertheless, I like to think in my ingenuous way that the close co-operation of industry with the Committee has had a more altruistic basis than those to which I have adverted.

A committee with freedom of action, relatively untrammelled by legal niceties, which is not bound by tight procedural rules can often conduct business more expeditiously than official organizations since there is a minimum of paper work. For instance, much of the contact with the applicants—the requests for amplification or clarification—takes place in robust but usually good-humoured encounters over the telephone or in informal discussions rather than in official communications. Manufacturers seem to have appreciated this informal, elastic approach which perhaps has done something to ease the introduction of controls, previously unfamiliar in this country. Most submissions of really new medicines are cleared within three months of their receipt: there are an average of only about 60 of these in a year but their submissions may run into thousands of pages. Submissions of reformulations of established medicines which do not usually require full toxicity data or clinical trials, are very numerous but are usually cleared within a month of their submission.

Out of approximately 3,360 submissions received since 1 January 1964 (about 300 new drugs and the rest reformulations) only 94 have been rejected though some 324 have not been proceeded with by the manufacturer. Doubtless in the case of some of these latter the manufacturer has been unable to produce the evidence required and has retired from the contest. The small number of rejections might suggest that the somewhat elephantine gestation of the primigravid Committee had only produced a mouse. In practice, however, the rejection of medicines which might otherwise have reached the market is a comparatively minor part of the Committee's function: more important is the persuasion of manufacturers to alter their intentions or to modify their promotional claims and to issue early warnings to doctors when the Committee's adverse-reactions-register shows a medicine to be developing undue or unexpected toxic effects. In addition, the mere existence of the Committee may have tightened up standards. As far as possible it has attempted to solve its problems by voluntary compliance and mutual agreement and this seems to have worked fairly well. It may, therefore, be asked why the Government should seek to effect through legislation what is being accomplished reasonably satisfactorily through the Committee's voluntary arrangements with the pharmaceutical industry. There are, however, many

M

reasons for the new legislation which seeks to encompass far more than the limited functions of the Committee:

(1) Probably the least important of these reasons is to give the Committee legal power, the lack of which has not proved an embarrassment in the past, and the danger is probably slight of the Committee's decisions being flouted by industry in the future.

(2) There is a real need for legislation designed to provide an inspection and licensing system to ensure the best conditions for the manufacture, storage and distribution of medicines. At present there is nothing to prevent a small business being set up in a back street, the products of which may not conform to the specifications filed with the applications or be free from hazards which might be detected by a more competent staff. These hazards comprise not only toxicological risks from the active ingredients, but also their diminished effectiveness due to physical or chemical changes during their defective manufacture or subsequent storage.

(3) There is at present remarkably little effective machinery for the enforcement of the quality control of preparations purporting to comply with British Pharmacopœia specifications. Now that many 16-year-old patents are expiring on a vast number of branded products introduced in the 1950s, numerous 'standard' preparations of potent, potentially hazardous medicines are coming on the market, often from abroad; new legislation is necessary to ensure their quality control, which is at present lacking.

(4) Many believe that before licensing a medicine consideration must be given to its efficacy as well as to its safety and that the present remit of the Committee to consider efficacy only in its relationship to a medicine's safety does not go far enough: efficacy and safety, they say, are inseparable.

(5) The licence of a medicine must not only involve its proper manufacture, safety and efficacy but adequate standards for its advertisement and promotion.

(6) Not only human medicines have to be considered but veterinary ones and medicated animal feeding stuffs as well and, in addition, medical devices such as dressings, needles, implants and so forth.

Regulations to control all this and more already operate in America. It is odd that in that freedom-loving country, the home of big business, they have been much more bureaucratic than we have been in their control of medicines. The 1962 Kefauver–Harris Amendments to the

1938 Federal Food, Drug and Cosmetic Act authorized the Food and Drug Authority (the FDA) to establish by regulation standards for good manufacturing practices and, for the first time, to license new medicines not only for their safety but also for their efficacy. Further, the Amendments called for a *retrospective* evaluation of all medicines marketed from 1938 onwards. Lastly, the advertising provisions of the Amendments are designed to ensure that promotional literature on medicines tells the whole truth and nothing but the truth. For its colossal task of inspecting and licensing throughout America the manufacture of foods, cosmetics and pesticides, as well as human and veterinary medicines, and for evaluating retrospectively some 3,500 medicines and the validity of the claims made for them, the FDA employs at its headquarters in Washington and 18 district offices a vast secretarial and professional staff.

The energetic and forcible Commissioner[1] of the FDA believes it to be completely irrational to attempt to separate the safety from the efficacy of medicines for no medicine is safe, he says, if it fails to cure a disease for which a cure is available. Thus, it is the duty of the FDA to prevent as far as possible the needless suffering and protraction of illness resulting from the use of ineffective medicines and the squandering of money on unnecessary, even if relatively innocuous, remedies such, for example, as multivitamin preparations. He is frank in maintaining that it *is* the duty of the FDA to interfere to some extent with medical practice. Doctors must, of course, have the right, once medicines have been cleared for marketing, to prescribe what they think best for their patients but whether a medicine is sufficiently safe and efficacious to be marketed must be decided by Government acting on the advice of experts who are less often wrong than non-experts. It is obvious that among the nearly 8,000 preparations now available there are many that are of limited value, useless, undesirable or even actually harmful. Most doctors see insufficient patients with any one disease to evaluate critically the medicines employed for it and, if the doctor is honest, he must admit that he can only gather impressions about the one he uses. These impressions are largely conditioned by the advertisements of the pharmaceutical industry and the claims of its detail men which are not infreqently so loud, incessant and brash as to jam the channels of communication. Thus, the bewildered physician prescribes by suggestion and seldom from information: it is, therefore, the duty of the FDA to help him by strict supervision of the efficacy as well as the

[1] At the time, Dr. James Goddard.

safety of new and old medicines and their accompanying promotional literature.

The Commissioner pours scorn on the suggestion that a gradual process of medical education in these matters may produce in the long run sounder results than the more immediate effect of legal edicts. He says, in so many words, that when the house is on fire a lecture on how to prevent incendiarism is inopportune; what is needed is to put out the fire and only then is it appropriate to give lessons as to how to prevent more fires in the future.

There is a great deal requiring to be done in this country which the FDA already does, often very well, in America. In doing it, however, it is to be hoped that we will avoid the dangers to professional freedom inherent in such agencies as the FDA. Our freedom in this country did not drop down on us like manna from heaven; it is the result of centuries of resistance to the power of the executive.

The drawbacks to the FDA are first, that it is, of course, entirely composed of civil servants and it is questionable whether a professional bureaucracy, not always attracting the best talent, should dogmatize to the medical profession on the safety, efficacy, dosage, indications, contraindications and dangers of therapeutic agents. It may be argued that the pronouncements of the FDA on package inserts and pharmaceutical advertisements are only guide lines and not official directions, just as we have guide lines in our therapeutic publications. Nevertheless, doctors in America are subject to civil actions by patients much more often than they are here and such actions are also far more frequently successful. Consequently they are becoming extremely chary of deviating in their practice from the package inserts of the FDA which are thus tending to have the effect, if not the actuality, of regulations. Secondly, for reasons which I have no time to develop, delay is almost inseparable from the methods adopted by the FDA in licensing medicines for the market. It must be admitted that its notorious procrastination saved America from the consequences of the thalidomide disaster but it can have a detrimental effect on therapeutic research and is most frustrating to the pharmaceutical industry. It is insufficiently appreciated too, that excessive delay in clearing a valuable medicine for the market may have results as unfortunate as those arising from the clearance of one which is undesirably toxic. Consider, for example, the number of people who would have died from pneumococcal pneumonia had a delay of two or three years been imposed on the introduction of sulphapyridine (M & B 693).

The British alternative to the FDA is now proposed in the Bill before Parliament. In the White Paper introducing it the Minister of Health gave an assurance that his aim would be to maintain the flexibility and the exercise of professional responsibility which the experience of the Safety of Drugs Committee had shown to be necessary. Nevertheless, it is not easy to introduce flexibility and informality into an Act of Parliament and Ministers of the future may not always have the benign aspirations of Mr. Robinson. The intentions of the White Paper were

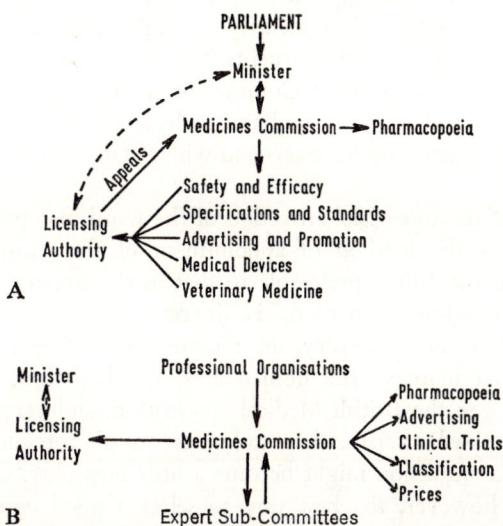

Fig. 1. *Diagrammatic representation of, A, the provisions of the Medicines Bill, and B, the recommendations of the Sainsbury Committee's Report*

admirable: their interpretation into practice will be the touchstone on which they will be judged; for what is now being laid before Parliament could possibly remove certain essential freedoms in medical care and will certainly increase to some extent the growth of bureaucracy.

The Medicines Bill and the Report of the Sainsbury Committee, established by Government to inquire into certain aspects of the pharmaceutical industry, both recommend a Government Licensing Authority to secure the safety and efficacy of medicines and the best conditions for their manufacture, storage, distribution and dispensing. The provisions of the Bill and the recommendations of the Report, however, differ from one another in certain important respects (see Fig. 1).

Though only a very limited number of doctors will have read the Report and still fewer the Bill, I do not expect that this will prevent them from expressing themselves forcibly on the respective merits of the two documents. The Bill and the Report both recommend the setting up of a Medicines Commission to advise, among many other duties, the Government Licensing Authority. In the Bill it is recommended that the Commission should be appointed by the Ministers after consultation with interested organizations and that the staff which the Commission might appoint should be taken into the permanent civil service to protect their security of employment and to ensure their adequate superannuation benefits. The Report, on the other hand, recommends an independent Commission with powers defined by Statute, with members nominated directly by a variety of organizations without intervention by Ministers and with a staff who should not be civil servants.

In spite of the superficial attraction of the word 'independent' it is probable that the method of appointment of the Commission as envisaged in the Bill is preferable to that in the Report. When the numerous organizations that would claim representation are considered —the pharmaceutical industry, the Pharmaceutical Society, the dentists, the veterinarians, the homeopaths, the herbalists, the seven Royal Colleges, the British Medical Association, and very likely the pathologists, pædiatricians, dermatologists, anæsthetists and psychiatrists—the Commission might become a little unwieldy. Quite apart from that, however, the best way to select a good committee or commission is to ascertain, after full consultation, who are the best men in the country for the required purpose, rather than to concentrate on the organizations to be represented.

The Committee on Safety of Drugs was perhaps a Lilliputian forerunner of the Medicines Commission. Its members were certainly appointed by the Ministers—presumably after taking advice—but none of us feel in consequence that we have become the creatures of the Ministers who incidentally have been invariably helpful and never directive. If they had tried to push us around against our wishes it would have been easy to resign for we are not career civil servants as in the FDA. Again, though our Committee is assisted by a small professional staff of civil servants they remain most valued servants but not, I think, our masters.

It is doubtless salutary that our profession should always regard Ministers with a healthy suspicion, yet this can surely be carried to extremes and a degree of mutual confidence is essential if the National Health Service is to achieve its full potential. I was still a boy when, what seems to most of us now that most necessary measure, the National Insurance Bill of 1911 was introduced, but I can well remember that Lloyd George had a far more bitter struggle with the doctors before the First World War than Aneurin Bevan ever had with us after the second one. The Northcliffe Press then told us that the insurance card with its stamps—now so familiar—was the end of freedom; that the Chancellor of the Exchequer was doing what the worst English Kings had failed to accomplish and what our forefathers would have died to prevent; that mistresses would have inspectors invading their drawingrooms to see if their servants' cards were properly stamped and that servants would immediately be dismissed whenever they became sick. Outside and inside the Albert Hall 20,000 women shrieked 'We won't pay' and 'Taffy was a Welshman, Taffy was a thief'. In the same way we could be unnecessarily apprehensive of the present Medicines Bill.

The Bill envisages a Commission to advise the Minister on broad aspects of policy in regard to medicines and on the setting up of expert committees to prepare the British Pharmacopœia and to report directly to the Licensing Authority on the subjects with which they are concerned, such, for example, as safety and efficacy, specifications and standards, advertising and promotion, medical devices, veterinary medicines and so forth. The Commission would also act as an appeal tribunal should an appeal be made against any implementation of the Licensing Authority on the advice of an expert committee. The Bill, therefore, regards the Commission not as the ordinary direct source of advice but as an overall planning and appeals body. As such it would probably not have to sit more often than about three or four times a year.

The Report's recommendations, concerned with the licensing of products, in principle follow similar lines to those in the Bill. Nevertheless, it recommends that the Commission itself should tender advice to the Licensing Authority; the expert committees would thus be subcommittees whose advice would be channelled to the Authority through the Commission and subject to its review and modification in the process. Thus, the Report recommends investing the Commission with wide responsibilities and powers. Its broad functions, determined by statute within which it would be free to extend and develop its operations, would include advice on licensing, the direction of the work of its sub-committees, the preparation of the pharmacopœia, the detailed control of advertising, the regulation of clinical trials, the classification of medicines and an examination of prices.

It is apparent that the Bill gives ultimate power to the Minister acting on professional advice, whereas the Report gives it to the accredited representatives of professional organizations. On the other hand, the Minister is responsible to Parliament and subject to the sanctions of the hustings. As far as I can see the Commission of the Report is responsible to no one and its decisions would not be subject to appeal, and 'Power without responsibility', as Stanley Baldwin once rather surprisingly said, 'is the prerogative of the harlot throughout the ages.'

Finally, and perhaps most importantly, the question arises as to whether any single body could effectively undertake the functions of the Commission as recommended by the Sainsbury Committee or secure the confidence and support of the many organizations affected by its activities. When I recall how often, with the relatively few responsibilities of the Safety of Drugs Committee, one has to travel to London, it is difficult to believe that the commitments suggested for the Commission in the Report could be successfully accomplished save by a number of retired men living in London in practically continuous session. It is also questionable whether they would be able to secure first-class experts for their sub-committees to work in circumstances in which their advice was always subject to review and modification before it reached the Licensing Authority. Such a Commission might well become authoritarian and in due course could profoundly influence or even determine the practice of therapeutics in this country; and medical establishments—Aristotle and Galen for example—have not always been in the van of progress. Perhaps the Minister, properly advised, might only chastise us with little whips, whereas the superannuated sodality which I have perhaps dreamed up of cockney medical, pharmaceutical, veterinary and dental Solons might chastise us with scorpions.

I sometimes envy these people with strong principles and convictions who, confronted by any controversial problem, immediately seem to know what is right and what is wrong. They are the people who do most good in the world—and the most harm. I am not one of them for, as I get older, I seem to find the answer to most controversial questions more and more difficult: there always seems to be so much to be said on both sides. Nevertheless, a proper understanding of the problems involved is the first stage to their intelligent solution.

A Legal Look at Transplants

THE RT HON. LORD JUSTICE EDMUND DAVIES

PC, LLD

5 May 1969

Introduction

Medicine and Law serve the community best when they walk in step. If they proceed at different speeds, trouble is apt to arise. Unfortunately, law is often a laggard, and at times medicine gains the lead by long and rapid strides. Doctors are then startled to learn that their projects may land them in Court for breaking what they condemn as myopic and arthritic laws. The reason is not far to seek. 'Law', it has been said, 'does not *search out* as do science and medicine; it reacts to social needs and demands. . . . The problem must arise . . . before the law reacts to provide a solution. Here is where science and law differ' [1].

The transplantation of organs affords a prime illustration. Consider the remarkable record. It was but fifteen years ago that the first success-ful *kidney* transplant was performed between identical twins and ten years ago that the first of such transplants took place between non-twins. It was on 3 December 1967, that the world's first *heart* transplant took place in South Africa. Last year in Cambridge the *liver* of a 4-year-old boy was transplanted to a woman of 44. Last February the first transplant of a *larynx* was successfully carried out in Belgium. And in March the second *lung* transplant in Britain (and the seventh in the world) was carried out on a man in his fifties.

Doctors are by no means the only people who have been stirred by these achievements. On the contrary, organ transplantation is a subject about which the community rightly feels deeply. The public fascina-tion is similar to the wide interest shown when the eighteenth-century anatomists dismembered bodies in search of the seat of the soul and believed they had located it in the pineal gland. An American Law Journal recently told of a 'sick-humour' cartoon depicting a sleeping hospital patient partly covered by a large sign which warned: 'Patient asleep—*NOT* a heart donor'; of the car-sticker reading, 'Drive carefully—Dr. Barnard may be watching'; and of the Gallup Poll revelation that seven Americans out of ten are willing to donate vital organs at their deaths [2]. And the BBC almost nonchalantly announced last February that a deceased's family had consented to the removal of his heart, liver, kidneys and both eyes for transplant purposes. Some would castigate this as consenting to virtual cannibalization. But lawyers, whatever their attitude towards the ethical problems created by transplants, are also concerned about their *legality*. The considerations involved fall naturally into two groups, depending upon whether the transplant is from a living donor or from a cadaver.

Living Donors

I believe that in France the law still is that organ transplants from living donors are illegal. Under English law we begin with the proposition that no man may lawfully consent to his body being maimed. Accordingly, in 1604, a 'young, strong and lustie rogue, to make himselfe impotent', had his left hand cut off by another so that he might make his living as a beggar, and both men were convicted of a criminal offence [3]. In 1934 it was decided that the consent of the girl involved afforded a man no defence to charges of indecent and common assault by blows intended to cause her bodily harm delivered to gratify his perversion [4]. And where a man had himself sterilized to spite his wife, Lord Denning said in 1954 that the operation was plainly illegal even though performed at his request, since it was without just cause or excuse [5].

English law has hitherto recognized only two cases where consent affords a defence to a charge of unlawfully causing bodily harm: (*a*) blows given in the course of friendly athletic contests; and (*b*) blows given in the course of rough, but innocent horseplay [6]. As far as a transplant *donee* is concerned, the position seems straightforward, for as the operation is designed for his benefit it is difficult to see how he could possibly be said to be 'maimed' as a result. Nevertheless, if he is of full age and in fit condition to give his written consent, it would be wise to obtain it. As to children, I respectfully adopt the view expressed by the Medical Research Council in 1964 that '. . . it is clearly within the competence of the parents or guardian of a child to give permission for procedure intended to benefit that child. . . .' But what of the living *donor*? In the surgical sense, his anatomy is undoubtedly 'maimed' if a healthy organ is removed. Does what lawyers would regard as a *prima-facie* case of 'maiming' cease to be one if its object is to transplant the removed organ in another who might otherwise die? English law gives no clear answer to the question. But Lord Kilbrandon regards the 'maiming' doctrine as 'intended to strike at actions which are socially wrong, or at least inexpedient, such as brutal sports, the gratification of lust, or the evasion of public duties' [7].

For my part (and, of course, I here speak entirely extra-judicially) I should be surprised if a surgeon were successfully sued for trespass to the person or convicted of causing bodily harm to one of full age and intelligence who freely consented to act as donor—always provided that the operation did not present unreasonable risk to that donor's life or health. That proviso is essential. A man may declare himself ready to die for another, but the surgeon must not take him at his word. As Lord Devlin has said, 'The Good Samaritan is a character unesteemed in English law' [8].

So the surgeon must act delicately, since few transplant operations are entirely without some risk to the donor. Thus, although I can survive even though I sacrifice a kidney, I have been depleted of my reserve and would be in a sad plight were my remaining kidney to give trouble. It is true that (certainly in America) I can still have my life insured at standard rates if I am otherwise healthy, so low do insurance companies rate the risk that I may lose my remaining kidney through disease or injury. But the position is by no means the same for all transplants, and consent (no matter how clearly given) confers no absolution on the surgeon who foresees that the operation may seriously endanger the donor's health. Furthermore, as Professor Daube has said, '. . . the plight of the prospective recipient must emerge as heavily outweighing the danger and loss to be incurred by the donor' [9]. So again the surgeon must not operate if, on balance, the risk involved to the donor cannot reasonably be regarded as justified in the public interest by the good likely to enure to the donee.

While that problem must remain inescapable, the surgeon has quite enough on his hands without having to consider the *legality* of his procedure. It is admittedly unlikely that the existing law keeps many transplant teams awake at night. Nevertheless, at present they are undoubtedly exposed to an irritant and at theoretical risk of forensic indignity to which they ought not to be subjected. I would therefore advocate legislation making it clear that an operation for transplant purposes will not *per se* give rise to either civil or criminal liability, while still leaving unaffected the surgeon's duty of proper care in deciding whether the risk involved to the *donor* is so great as to render the operation inadvisable. That degree of protection the surgeon and his team may properly ask for, and it should be speedily provided.

But all this is, of course, contingent upon the consent of the donor being both free and informed. How can this be ensured? Professor Hamburger of the Paris Faculty of Medicine has laid down certain conditions which the lawyer, as well as the scientist, would do well to consider carefully. Here they are:

(*a*) The donor must be made fully aware of the exact dangers he is running.

(*b*) He must have a reasonable motive for wishing to donate part of his body. The Professor adds: 'At Paris . . . we have adopted the habit of considering a volunteer acceptable if he is a relative of the patient to be saved, and unacceptable if he is not'.

(*c*) Adequate steps must be taken to verify whether there has been pressure from the family or elsewhere.

(*d*) There should be a psychological (if not a psychiatric) examination to verify that the volunteer is in full possession of his mental faculties. The Professor concludes: 'This psychological examination seems to us to be *mandatory*' [10].

By such salutary safeguards French surgeons hope to keep out of the Law Courts, even though they break their legal prohibition against operating save for the benefit of the specific patient.

So far, we have assumed that the living donor is of mature years and sensibility. If mentally debilitated, his consent is worthless. Then should prisoners be permitted to act as donors? It seems wrong to deny them this opportunity to manifest an enduring sense of responsibility towards the community from which they are physically set apart, and for some time penal volunteers were accepted in Colorado hospitals. But prisoners are subject to influences inimical to complete freedom of choice, and the risk of their undertaking the role of donor without bringing a balanced judgement to bear on the matter is so great that their acceptance was discontinued in Colorado early in 1966. There are arguments both ways, but, all things considered, that may be regarded as a wise decision.

The consent of a minor to act as donor ought not to be accepted. Nor can a parent or guardian lawfully consent to his child so acting. I venture to express that view notwithstanding that in 1956 the Massachusetts Supreme Judicial Court declared it lawful to transplant a kidney from a healthy boy of 14 to his identical twin dying from renal disease. Accepting the psychiatric evidence that, if the operation were not performed and the sick twin died, there would be 'a grave emotional impact' on the survivor, the Court held the transplant necessary for the continued good health of the *donor* and that the operation would accordingly benefit *both* him and the donee. But no surgeon should assume that the issue would necessarily be decided in the same way under English law.

I trust that the comity of nations will not be seriously undermined if I express a similar view about another American case [11], where a 15-year-old boy consented at his aunt's request to act as donor in a skin graft for the benefit of his cousin. His mother's views were never sought, and, holding the surgeon liable for operating, the Appeals Court said:

Here we have a case of a surgical operation not for the benefit of the person operated upon, but for another, and one so involved in its technique as to require a mature mind to understand precisely what the donor was offering.... The Court below should . . . have instructed that the consent of the *parent* was necessary.

Such reasoning implies that, had the mother consented, all would have been well. I believe that under our English law not even a thousand mothers could have regularized the operation. We would surely adopt the view expressed by the United States Supreme Court in another case [12] that: 'Parents may be free to become martyrs themselves. But it does not follow that they are free . . . to make martyrs of their children. . . .'

In the very nature of things, more time is generally available to ascertain the wishes of the donor than those of the donee, whose condition may well render his consent unobtainable. Adequate means of ensuring that the donor's consent was validly obtained are by no means beyond devising. Take Italy, for instance. Article 5 of its 1940 Civil Code forbade the removal of any part of the living human body if its loss permanently impaired physical integrity. But public opinion changed as advances were made in kidney transplantation, and in 1967 a new law was promulgated which permits transplants from living donors, *provided* (*a*) that they have given written consent, and (*b*) that judicial approval of the transplant is first obtained. Under the recent South African Anatomical Donations and Post-Mortem Examinations Bill, *two* doctors must sanction the removal of tissue from a living person, and that seems a prudent course. But anything in the nature of formal legal procedure is undesirable. I personally favour the suggestion advanced in Canada that the donor's written consent should be given before a magistrate who, while carefully reducing to the minimum all signs of legal technicality, could yet ensure that the donor is a genuine volunteer.

Before we move from the living, consider for a moment the increasingly large number of people who dwell for long periods in a twilight state of life merging almost imperceptibly into death. May tests be conducted on a dying patient without his knowledge or acceptable consent, simply in order to determine the suitability of his organs for transplant purposes after death? Many would regard the very idea as unthinkable had we not been recently alerted by the public complaint of a radiographer that she had been instructed to conduct tests for that very purpose. For my part, I think that the jurist would, if pressed, be forced to say that technically such tests amount to assaults, and that neither the consent of the patient's family nor the ultimate good aimed at would serve to cure the illegality. But I believe that some take the view that, however greatly it may offend susceptibilities, there is nothing illegal in examining terminal patients (even without their consent or that of their relatives) with a view to 'typing' them as potential donors, in the same way as potential *donees* are already regularly typed. In the light of these conflicting views, I can do no more than diffidently indicate that I regard the former view as the correct one.

Cadavers

Cadavers are, for obvious reasons, the more likely source of transplants. But the available time is extremely limited if irreversible organic damage is to be avoided, and the clinical need to act quickly builds up all sorts of pressures operating powerfully upon the surgeon. Unfortunately, the existing law greatly increases his difficulties. Our Common Law presents a curious paradox. No man has any rights in his body after his death [13], and his directions as to its disposal can be ignored. In America, on the other hand, the great Justice Cardozo said that: 'Every human being of adult years and sound mind has a right to determine what shall be done with his own body' [14]. Here a man's direction that upon his death his body should be used for transplant purposes would protect no one. This distinguished audience is familiar with the steps by which that Common Law rule has been modified by Statute—firstly by the Corneal Grafting Act, 1952, and then far more extensively by the Human Tissue Act, 1961. They borrowed their basic pattern from the Anatomy Act of 1832. That Act dealt, firstly, with the granting of permission for the anatomical examination of a corpse by the person legally in possession of it, and, secondly, with the case where the deceased had 'during the illness whereof he died' directed such anatomical examination. But the Act required that the body be decently interred after dissection and it therefore had nothing to do with the *retention* of tissue or organs for *any* purpose. Nevertheless, the grafting of the cornea from the dead to the living had become a frequently performed operation for several years before the 1952 Act for the first time clothed it with legality. There are times when the bold medico makes the cautious lawyer gasp.

Allow me to remind you that Sec. 1(1) of the 1961 Act provides that:

> If any person, either in writing at any time or orally in the presence of two or more witnesses during his last illness, has expressed a *request* that his body or any specified part of his body be used after his death for therapeutic purposes or for purposes of medical education or research, the person lawfully in possession of his body after his death *may, unless* he has reason to believe that the request was subsequently withdrawn, authorize the removal from the body of any part . . . for use in accordance with the request.

It is, perhaps, not always realized that this provision in the Act is *paramount* and that what immediately follows is expressed to be 'without prejudice' to its effectiveness. The Act naturally goes on to prohibit any such removal 'except by a fully registered medical practitioner who must have satisfied himself by personal examination of the body that life is extinct'. The ascertainment of death is a clinical and not a legal problem and I gladly turn from it, especially when I learn that, in the view of an experienced American surgeon: 'The question of deciding death transcends the problem of transplantation'. All I would say in this context is that modern resuscitative methods demand rethinking about the legal dictionary statement that: 'Death does not occur until the heart stops beating and respiration ends. Death is not a continuous event, but an event that takes place at a precise time' [15]. But however it be defined, proper steps are essential to ensure that the event has indeed occurred before any part is removed. To allay what I feel sure is a real fear that this may not always be so, it is an elementary requirement that the doctor pronouncing the donor's death must always be wholly independent of the transplant team. As one MP succinctly put it in last year's Parliamentary debate on renal transplantation: 'We must not have one doctor in the terrible position

of deciding which of two patients should have priority' [16]. Indeed,
the Minister of Health announced last year that a Conference chaired
by Sir Hector MacLennan had gone further and recommended that:

... vital organs should not be removed until spontaneous vital functions had
ceased and *two* doctors, each independent of the transplantation team and one
of them being at least 5 years qualified, had certified that this condition was
irreversible.

Whatever other modifications in the law may be adopted, I venture
to hope that this one will certainly be. And were euthanasia to become
legalized, the need for such independence would become even more
imperative. Indeed, the call becomes strident when one learns that,
according to one eminent surgeon, hopeless respirator cases throughout the world are being subject to organ removal *before* (as well as
after) the respirator has been switched off [17]. The lawyer is not the
only person likely to do some hard thinking over the further observation of the same surgeon that: 'The rights of the dying donor have
been a cause of anxiety in the past, but, accepting that the donor is a
hopeless case, we must now consider the rights of the prospective
recipient.'

The time may come when vital organs can be stored until required.
But, although one reads of miniature machines to keep a removed
heart beating long enough for it to be taken from one hospital to
another for transplant surgery, and of plastic hearts for donees, that
time is not yet. Until then, the imminence between removal and
successful transplant creates great difficulties. Consider what the present
law demands, even in the direst emergency. If a person is *known* to have
requested the use of his body for therapeutic purposes, none may
gainsay his wish—provided it was expressed in the manner specified by
Sec. 1(1) of the 1961 Act. But such cases are rare, and, where no such
request is known to have been made, the Act enables 'the person
lawfully in possession of the body' to authorize the removal of a part
only

if, *having made such reasonable enquiry as may be practicable*, he has *no* reason to
believe (*a*) that the deceased had expressed an objection to his body being so
dealt with after his death, and had not withdrawn it; or (*b*) that the surviving
spouse or *any* surviving relative of the deceased objects to the body being so
dealt with.

To consider how this requirement works, let us take the actual case
of Mrs. X, the mother of three children, who recently lay waiting

at the National Heart Hospital for nearly six months while a transplant team stood by. Eleven times her heart stopped beating, and eleven times she was resuscitated. Relatives and doctors waited hopefully for another heart to become available. But it never did, and she died two months ago. She was not in a general hospital, and accordingly there were no patients who (though otherwise fit) were dying from, for example, motor-crash injuries. And there is understandable reluctance to rush dying donors to the donee's hospital.

But put aside that last complication. Assume that as Mrs. X lay in hospital a crash victim was brought in and soon died. What would there be to prevent an immediate heart transplant? A great deal, says the 1961 Act. The victim may well be unknown at the hospital. The odds are even greater against his being *known* to have requested that his body be used for therapeutic purposes. In those circumstances, may the hospital, as 'the person lawfully in possession of the body' [18], proceed with the transplant? Certainly not. It can do nothing unless and until, 'having made such reasonable enquiry as may be practicable', it has no reason to believe *either* that the deceased had expressed an objection *or* that his 'surviving spouse or *any* surviving relative' objects.

At present the admirable suggestion that people should carry with them a document indicating their consent is insufficiently ventilated, for I think that the vast majority would accept it. In its absence, what of the surviving spouse and relatives? They may be all entirely unknown. Even if known, they may be far distant and quick communication impossible. Nevertheless, the Statute does nothing to dispense with the necessity for making reasonable efforts to ascertain their views. It does not enable the hospital to say that, if the emergency is so great that time does not permit of *any* enquiry, none is 'practicable' and therefore none need be attempted. Meanwhile the precious minutes fly all too swiftly past. Furthermore, even if the circumstances are so remarkably propitious that the family are speedily contacted (and leaving aside the great difficulty of seeking their consent at such a time of shock and sorrow), they still have the power of absolute veto in the absence of any express request by the deceased.

The 1961 Act is quite unsuitable to deal with such cases, and its provisions demand the consideration they are now receiving at the hands of a distinguished group. But, whatever the outcome, there will surely be an outcry. No matter which side wins the day, there will be honourable men in the opposite camp to lament their victory. However desirous of serving humanity they may be, many will on religious

N

or other grounds feel a sense of outrage were a body 'mutilated' (as they would probably describe it), even for the sake of saving lives.

On the other hand, if one accepts (as I do) that the removal of organs for transplant purposes from cadavers *ought* to be facilitated, what should be done to remove the powerful brakes imposed by the present law? There is no dearth of suggestions. A Member of Parliament has twice unsuccessfully introduced a Renal Transplantation Bill which many think has much to commend it but which deals with only part of the problem. Lord Kilbrandon has made a more drastic recommendation which has received wide attention and surely has great merit. He would amend the 1961 Act by a simple provision that:

In any designated hospital it shall be lawful to remove from a dead person *any* organ required for medical or scientific purposes *unless* the hospital authorities have reason to believe that the *deceased* in his lifetime had forbidden this to be done, provided that such removal shall not disfigure the dead body.

This is very sweeping. It would dispense with the necessity for making any enquiry as to whether the deceased had expressed any views about transplants, or whether his relatives have any objections. It would also prevent those relatives taking it upon themselves to impose a veto even where the deceased had expressed none.

The *only* barrier would be if there was 'reason to believe that the deceased' had himself forbidden removals. As to this, the Minister of Health said in Parliament last year that

... an effective system should be devised and effectively publicized, under which persons could record *objections* during life, with certainty that these could be ascertained and would be respected.

For my part, I would also like thought given to means whereby people could make known their desire that their bodies *should* be used for transplant and similar purposes. I say this because I believe that many would wish their dead bodies to be so used. How can their wish be realized? In at least one large American hospital *all* patients (whether seriously ill or not) are automatically asked on admission whether they are willing to donate organs in the event of their death. But I have some doubt whether such a fixed procedure would find general acceptance, and we must think again. In this context, those interested might care to look at the Uniform Anatomical Gift Act of 1967, prepared in America by the Commissioners on Uniform State Laws.

Should the Human Tissue Act, 1961, be amended at all? Basically, this is a political question, and the public must soon face up to it.

Many of us feel that it should. If that view prevails, Lord Kilbrandon's suggestion may prove the most acceptable. But some may regard it as concentrating excessively upon the needs of the donee and as ignoring the feelings of the deceased's family. It would enable a transplant to be performed even though his surviving relatives were *known* to be completely opposed, and this may well provoke strong opposition to an otherwise helpful measure. It is therefore worthy of consideration whether a further qualification should be added, to the effect that the operation must *not* be performed if the hospital authorities have reason to believe that the surviving spouse or near relatives object, confining the latter to parents, children, brothers and sisters. It seems unlikely that such a qualification (which would still impose no *duty* of enquiry) would substantially limit the usefulness of the proposed measure, and it does have regard to family feelings. It would, in effect, apply the language of Sec. 1(2) of the Corneal Grafting Act, 1952, to all organs. But I would stress that *nothing* should be done to diminish the overriding authority which the duly expressed *request* of the deceased even now possesses under the 1961 Act.

Conclusion

And there I must leave the matter. Believe me, I did not carelessly choose the title of these discursive and inadequate remarks. A 'look' is a casual affair and by selecting that word I wanted to emphasize that I was undertaking to decide nothing. Indeed it would have been impertinent had I attempted anything of the kind. In the short time available I have simply sought to underline some of the legal issues involved in a complex of great significance to people of many disciplines. In places I have inevitably trodden ground familiar to many of you. My only aim has been to stimulate thought and discussion, for the public interest in organ transplants demands and deserves deep thought and considerable discussion.

In the words of none other than the Professor of Civil Law at Oxford, Dr. Daube [9], at the splendid CIBA Symposium of 1966 (chaired by Lord Kilbrandon) to which I am greatly indebted:

Progress in transplantation is a matter for wonder and dread; and no tribute to the courage and humanity of the pioneers can be too high. The jurists certainly must adapt their rigid, over-conceptualized thinking to the novel conditions; and the doctors in their turn should perhaps acknowledge in increasing measure their accountability outside their closed circle of peers before a wider forum of society, ethics and law . . . we are becoming more and more answerable to a wider and wider public. If we take care to preserve the principal traditional values in the process, we may yet achieve a civilized result.

REFERENCES

[1] Burger, 'Reflections on Law and Experimental Medicine', quoted in an invaluable article by J.-G. Castel, 'Some Legal Aspects of Human Organ Transplantation in Canada, *Canadian Bar Review*, September 1968, p. 347.

[2] *Georgetown Law Journal*, October 1968.

[3] Co. Litt. 127a and 127b; I Hawk P.C. 108.

[4] *R. v. Donovan* (1934 2 K.B. 498).

[5] *Bravery v. Bravery* (1954 3 All E.R. 54).

[6] *R. v. Coney* (1882 8 Q.B.D. 534).

[7] Kilbrandon, Lord (1968). 'The Human Body and the Law'. An address delivered to the University of Aberdeen Law Society, 26 February 1968.

[8] Devlin, Lord (1962). *Samples of Lawmaking*. Oxford, p. 90.

[9] Daube, D. (1966). In: *Ethics in Medical Progress with special reference to Transplantation*. Ciba Foundation Symposium. Ed. G. E. W. Wolsten-holme & M. O'Connor. London, p. 188.

[10] Hamburger, J. (1967). CIOMS Round Table Conference, 7 November 1967, p. 48.

[11] *Bonner v. Moran* (1941—126 F.2d 121—D.C. Cir. 1941).

[12] *Prince v. Massachusetts* (1943 321 U.S. 158, at p. 170).

[13] *Williams v. Williams* (1882 20 Ch.D. 659).

[14] *Schloendorff v. New York Hospital* (1914, 211 N.Y. 125; 105 N.E. 92).

[15] *Black's Law Dictionary* (U.S.A.), quoted in *Thomas v. Anderson* (1950 Cal. App. 2d. 371; 211 P.2d. 478).

[16] *Hansard* 26.6.68, Col. 45

[17] Dempster, W. J. (1968). *Medical Tribune*, May 1968 (reprinted 5 June 1969, p. 4).

[18] See *R. v. Feist* (1858 169 E.R. 1132).

Toulouse-Lautrec—Triumph over Infirmity

SIR TERENCE CAWTHORNE

FRCS

1 *April* 1970

Some years ago I wrote about 'The Influence of Deafness on the Creative Instinct', giving as examples Dean Swift, Goya and Beethoven. More recently I gave a more detailed account of Goya's deafness and the effect it had upon his imaginative paintings. Consequently when I learned that Toulouse-Lautrec became hard of hearing towards the end of his short life I wondered whether this deafness might be connected with the fracture of his thigh bones during adolescence; for it is known that fragile bones and deafness are sometimes associated. I soon concluded that his deafness was a terminal event and played no part in his career or his childhood bone disorder. I believe, however, that his crippled state influenced his artistic output, for dancing and movement played an important part in so many of his pictures. No doubt also his excessive virility accounted for his choice of some of his subjects.

In order to understand better the life and infirmities of Toulouse-Lautrec, we must enquire into his family and his childhood, and glean what we can from his medical history. His mode of life is seen in his pictures. It has been said that they provide a fitting complement to the stories of de Maupassant and Zola. They certainly illustrate vividly the seamier side of Paris in the last decade of the nineteenth century which earned for itself the sobriquet 'The Naughty Nineties'.

Unfortunately, this combination of a crippled aristocrat who used his artistic genius to depict the dance halls, the cafés chantants, the circuses, the cycle tracks, the race courses and even the maisons closes of Paris has provided the journalist, biographer, novelist and film script writer with a wealth of sensational material, much of it inaccurate and exaggerated.

Lautrec himself is not entirely free from fault in this respect for he tended to exaggerate his physical defects both in the sketches he drew of himself and in his everyday conversation. By so doing, he defended himself successfully against pity and he commanded respect and attention by his wit and his intelligence.

Count Henri Marie-Raymond de Toulouse-Lautrec Montfa, to give him his full name and title, was the last of a long line of a noble family whose large estates were in the South of France near Toulouse, their main home being near Albi on the River Tarn. The fortified cathedral gives some indication of the troubled times suffered by the Albigenois in the thirteenth century when it was built.

The Counts of Toulouse and Viscounts of Lautrec claimed descent from Charlemagne and relationship with the English Royal Family through Henri VI, after whom the little Henri was named. His mother Adèle Tapié de Céleyran was the daughter of a neighbouring Count and a big landowner in the Languedoc. The two were first cousins. One of his father's sisters married a brother of Adèle; their fourteen children were all healthy though undistinguished.

There is no history of any congenital bone disease on either side of the family apart from a single instance of dwarfism in a female cousin.

The cousins fell in love and married when she was 21 and he a dashing cavalry officer of 25. She was quiet and shy, quite unlike her husband who was very much an extrovert, eccentric and unpredictable, a great lover of the open air and hunting and shooting, and a noted expert on falconry.

All the men in the Toulouse-Lautrec family had artistic leanings and in the evenings after a day in the open they would pass their time sketching or modelling in clay. Count Alphonse's mother used to say of her sons: 'When they kill a woodcock the bird affords them three pleasures, those of the gun, the pencil and the fork.' Count Alphonse was not a bad man in the light of his day. Erratic and thoughtless, he was not above a casual love affair here and there, but the young parents were temperamentally unsuited to one another and it seems likely that even before Henri was born the eccentric Count Alphonse and his reserved wife were already falling out of love. A year after the marriage, Henri was born during a thunderstorm on the night of 24 November 1864, at the Hôtel du Bosc in Albi; characteristically Count Alphonse was elsewhere. The birth is said to have been prolonged but otherwise normal. However, too much must not be made of this: as he was a first child and would be heir to the title, the birth was no doubt awaited with some impatience.

He was a lively, happy and alert child from the start and before he was 3 a brother (Richard) was born. At the christening ceremony

Henri insisted on adding his signature to the birth certificate, but as he could not write he drew an ox instead. Alas, Richard died before his first birthday.

Henri had a happy childhood, indulged by his parents, uncles and aunts, and grandparents, cared for by an abbé and a governess and a multitude of indoor and outdoor servants. He was lively and gay and spoilt, but because of his cheerful nature his wilfulness was overlooked. Moving from chateau to chateau he had a wonderful childhood and soon there were plenty of cousins to play with, and he was always leader of the group.

Perhaps because he was so active he was inclined to tire easily.

Photographs of him aged 2 and 5 show a normal-looking boy, though his head is a little larger than usual, and when he was 5 it was noted that his fontanelle had not yet closed. His father in a letter to him when he was 7 praised the value of fresh air and exercise in order to build him up into a strong man. Without wanting to read too much into what may be but natural parental concern for an only child I cannot help feeling that already the seeds of future trouble were beginning to sprout. Henri was always drawing, chiefly animals with which the country estates abounded, and he was encouraged in this by his father's younger brother Charles, who was particularly fond of sketching.

Count Alphonse loved his son and encouraged him to learn to ride a horse and the boy spent many of his waking hours in and around the stables. Henri of course adored his father and all his eccentricities and later provided sketches for the book his father was writing on falconry. There can be no doubt that his father's indifference to public opinion and his fondness for dressing up in curious costumes, more often than not oriental, came out in Henri later on.

In 1872 when Paris had settled down after the Franco-Prussian war, its siege and the subsequent uprising of the Commune, the Count decided to live in the city for a while and the family took the ground floor of the Hôtel Pérey near the Rue du Faubourg-Saint-Honoré. Henri, now aged 8, was sent as a day boy to the Lycée Fontanes where Louis Pascal, a cousin on his mother's side, was a pupil. He made very good progress with his studies, and during his second year met Maurice Joyant who was to become a lifelong friend and who in later life was the first conservator at the Musée d'Albi and wrote the definitive biography of Henri. He went most days with his father to the Duphot riding school for lessons in horse-riding. He also joined a small art class under the painter René Princeteau who was noted for his pictures of horses and cavalry scenes. At the end of his second year at the Lycée, though he received many prizes, it was decided to move him back to Albi on grounds of health. There he had private tutors and encouragement from his Uncle Charles in his drawing. Whilst still at the Lycée the margins of his exercise books and textbooks were filled with drawings, mainly of animals. On 22 September 1875 when he was nearly 11 he wrote from Paris to his mother: 'Dr. Vernier was very satisfied with my legs. When you return I hope you will find me well.' This is the first mention of anything being wrong with his legs. A little later his grandmother wrote: 'The humidity doesn't particularly trouble Henri, and now that the weather is so mild he can go for long rides ... with such a high spirited fellow around how could we persist in being gloomy?' This continues to suggest that all was not well with Henri's physique. On his thirteenth birthday he measured 4 feet 11½ inches which was average for his age. Then on 30 May 1878, when he was 13½, the first accident happened in the drawing room at Albi. His grandmother had not been well and was being visited by her doctor. Henri's mother was there and as he got up from a low chair, with the aid of a stick be it noted, he slipped on the polished floor and broke his left thigh bone. The leg was put in plaster and the bone healed. Fifteen months later in August 1879 at Barèges, while walking with his mother, he slipped and fell into a shallow gully, this time breaking his right leg. This fracture took longer to heal and he had two periods, of at least three months each, in bed with the leg immobilized in plaster. Thereafter he grew no more than ¾ inch and by 18 he was ½ inch over 5 feet. Thus though small he was by no means a dwarf. Walking was his greatest disability and he always needed a stick and walked with a waddle suggesting stiff knees or hip-joints. It may also be that walking was painful. During one of his long sojourns in bed he wrote to a friend about a pretty cousin: 'I began to wonder whether Jeanne d'Armagnac will come and sit by my bed. She does come sometimes and I listen to her but lack the courage to look at her, who is so beautiful and tall, and as for myself—I am neither of these.'

He drew and painted no less than 350 subjects in 1880. For three years he visited with his mother various spas in the South of France in the milder weather and spent his winters in Nice. He returned to Paris in July 1881 to take his baccalaureate examination but failed in French composition probably because he spent too much time in Princeteau's art class. He returned to Albi and passed the examination in Toulouse in the autumn of the same year. By this time he had decided to become an artist and his parents agreed that he should try to join the École des Beaux-Arts in Paris. In the spring of 1882 he returned to Paris to study under Princeteau again. René Princeteau was himself but twelve years older than Henri and they became firm friends, partly through their love of art but also they had the common bond of physical deformity, for Princeteau was partly deaf and dumb. Henri's love of horses and the training he received from Princeteau of depicting horses in movement influenced him greatly and they paid many visits to the circus Fernando (later Medrano). Another artist friend, Louis Forain who knew Degas, interested Henri by his talent for sketching the night life of Paris from the wings of the theatre and at the cafés chantants and influenced him in what was to become his lifetime's work. Henri soon realized that he needed a different teacher from Princeteau and so joined the school of Léon Bonnat, a fashionable portrait painter. When Bonnat closed down his pupils moved to the atelier of Fernand Cormon, a free and easy-going painter then aged 37, who attracted many young and lively artists to his school. Henri remained attached to Cormon for some years using his atelier, as so many young artists did, as a sort of club.

He lived with his mother the Countess Adèle in the Hôtel Pérey and she fondly hoped that he would become a society artist. Little did she realize that the life of Montmartre had taken hold of him though, when he was 20, he was allowed to share an apartment with René Grenier and his wife, who had been a model for Degas. By this time (1884) Degas was all the rage and there can be no doubt that Henri paid Degas the great compliment of following his style, but it is only fair to add that Degas remained the master.

By 1886 he had his own studio in the Rue Caulaincourt in Montmartre. At Cormon's studio he met and became friends with van Gogh who was older by ten years and whose portait he painted. It was a curious friendship between the young aristocrat, clever and merry, who chose to depict the night life of Paris with pitiless accuracy and the penniless son of a Dutch pastor with a social conscience whose few portraits often showed the misery of poverty and loneliness. Henri drew and painted with great care and much preparation, while Vincent dashed off a picture in a frenzy attacking his canvas with such vigour that he almost pushed his easel over. Henri had a crippled body but he had the satisfaction of seeing his work recognized. Vincent van Gogh had a crippled mind and was denied that ultimate pleasure of recognition; instead he was laughed to scorn and sold only one picture during his life and that for but a few francs. Vincent put an end to his life quickly with a gun. Henri shortened his life by his affection for the bottle and for Venus.

In 1885, the year Henri reached his majority, Montmartre, the hilly district overlooking Paris from the north, was turning from rural to urban and from picturesque to sordid, where artists worked in their studios by day and where seekers after pleasure, including those artists who could afford it, spent their nights.

Degas and the young Toulouse-Lautrec were the forerunners of a new school of Impressionism that preferred to concentrate on studies of the stage, dance-halls, the intimacies of the feminine toilette and the race track. There can be no doubt that Degas was the master though he never taught Toulouse-Lautrec. Indeed one suspects he was not a little jealous and scornful of his artistic successor though he admitted Toulouse-Lautrec's great talent. Models worked for both artists, in particular one Suzanne Valadon who was to become an artist herself and the mother of Maurice V Utrillo (the V standing for Valadon for there was always some doubt about the identity of his father). She also modelled for Henri, living with him on and off for three years.

Manet, the forerunner of the Impressionist group, had died in 1883 having shocked the artistic world with his 'Déjeuner sur l'Herbe' and his 'Olympia'. Some thirty years after 'Olympia' was painted Toulouse-Lautrec asked a friend to come on a visit with him. On the way Henri bought a bag of sugared almonds and as they reached a tenement house, climbed up to the third floor and knocked on a door. This was opened by a bloated and dishevelled woman to whom Henri presented the sugared almonds with a bow saying to his friend 'Violà Victorine— the model for Manet's *Olympia*'. After Manet, the Impressionist group headed by Camille Pissaro, Sisley and Monet were more interested in open-air studies of light and shade until we return to Degas who preferred the theatre, the concert, the ballet, the racecourse and Montmartre which was rapidly becoming not only the quarter for artists, but also the centre for the less intellectual forms of night life. There were dance halls such as the Élysée-Montmartre, the Moulin de la Galette (so called after Montmartre's only remaining windmill and the Galette cakes which provided the solid part of the evening's refreshment) and the cafés chantants such as the Mirliton presided over by Toulouse-Lautrec's friend Aristide Bruant. For Toulouse-Lautrec these haunts were his workshop and every night he did his rounds, watching and sketching. It was in such surroundings that he developed his taste for drinking and women, which were for him a refreshing contrast to the rural distractions of the aristocratic life, such as hunting, which were denied him; and he felt as out of place in the ballroom as he did in the drawing-room of the country chateaux. His family, not unnaturally, strongly disapproved of his way of life, and his Uncle Charles burnt some of his pictures. His mother always kept as close a watch as she could upon Henri and his father, too, tried to keep a discreet watch upon his son. The women in Toulouse-Lautrec's life came from much less exalted circles; they were artists' models, midinettes, laundresses, and circus and stage artistes who by their beauty, accommodating nature and, more often than not, red hair attracted his attention. By 1888 he broke his liaison with Suzanne Valadon, and unfortunately took up with Rosa la Rouge from whom he soon contracted syphilis.

His mother had her apartment in Paris where there was always a home for him. His father kept a room in Henri's studio ostensibly to store his effects, and a distant relative Dr. Bourges, a medical student, shared a flat with him in 1886. His mother bought a small estate at Malromé near Bordeaux which he was free to visit and which, I conclude, enabled him to be free from the mutual embarrassment of visiting the family estates farther south.

By 1886 Cormon's pupils were splitting up. Bernard and the strange Gauguin went to Britanny, van Gogh to Arles where he was later followed by Gauguin. Toulouse-Lautrec remained faithful to Montmartre and his painting 'Au Moulin de la Galette' was exhibited for the first time in 1889 at the Salon des Indépendants. This year saw the opening of the Moulin Rouge by Oller. It had never been a windmill but the name was designed no doubt to attract customers from the Moulin de la Galette. It was not a success at first but Toulouse-Lautrec's poster 'La Danse au Moulin Rouge' made it famous. Painted in 1890 it was the earliest of Toulouse-Lautrec's posters and it owes much to the cut-out influence of Japanese art which was so popular with the French school at that time. It also made Toulouse-Lautrec famous and was the first of a series of posters. To be successful, the poster had to be arresting, bold, simple in design and with but few colours. Possibly it was not the highest form of art but it had the great merit of wide exhibition, thus bringing the artist to the notice of the public.

In 1889 the artist's cousin Gabriel Tapié de Céleyran, a medical student at Lille, moved to Paris to be his cousin's companion. It would be wrong to think of any of these carefully chosen medically orientated relatives as guardians. Henri was much too much of an egoist to be anything but a leader and his cousin Tapié was his faithful follower. There are many pictures of the faithful Tapié mournfully but faithfully following his cousin through what to him were no doubt unaccustomed haunts. Through Tapié he became friendly with the great surgeon Dr. Péan whose operations Henri attended and some of which he drew. He was fascinated by the surgeon who 'rummaged in stomachs as if he were looking in his pocket for change'. In 1892 he spent less time in the Montmartre cafés and became interested in lithography of which he became the leading exponent. In 1893 he had an exhibition at his friend Joyant's gallery and found a new group of friends centred round the artistic journal, *La Revue Blanche*. The beautiful Misia, wife of the senior Natanson who with his brothers founded the *Revue*, can be seen on one of the covers of the magazine. Wine and women continued to play a prominent part in his life but they were not allowed to influence his work.

The asthenia of his youth had disappeared and he worked much of the day and played half the night, and in 1895 his output was still large. In this year he took up residence in a famous maison close in the Rue des Moulins from which many of the subjects for his paintings were chosen. Asked why he chose such an abode he replied: 'It is the only place I know where they clean your shoes properly.'

In 1895 he visited London and met, among others, Oscar Wilde (this was before the trial), but they had little in common. He revisited England in 1898 for another exhibition of his work, but by this time he was drinking very heavily; he became an embarrassment to his friends, and his output was suffering in quantity, though not as yet in quality.

In February 1899, as the result of an attack of delirium tremens, he was confined for three months in a private asylum in Neuilly, on the outskirts of Paris. By a series of sketches of circus life from memory he was able to convince his doctors that he was sane, but that he should be safe it was insisted that he should have an attendant. The first was soon led astray by Henri and had to go when he was found helplessly drunk, to be replaced by a distant but teetotal relative. Thanks to a hollow walking-stick, Henri was able to keep himself supplied with alcohol, and soon he was drinking heavily again. In order to try to curb him, in 1900 his allowance was cut down ostensibly on the grounds that the phylloxera fungus had destroyed the vines on the family estates. Most of the year he spent away from Paris, returning in May 1901, where he

painted his last picture, of his cousin and intimate, Dr. Tapié de Céleyran being questioned on his medical thesis, and tidied up his studio. He
had a slight seizure and was taken by his mother to Malromé, where a
further seizure or stroke left him helpless and dying. He survived until
the morning of 9 September when, in the presence of his father and
mother, he died, three months before his 37th birthday.

Possibly, because of his disability, he preferred the low life of
Montmartre, where they accepted him as a convivial and generous
companion, to the more respectable life of the elegant 'man about
town' of Paris, or the quieter country life of the landed aristocrat. His
determination to go his own way, first noted in childhood, left his
family no choice but to let him do what he desired.

Now we come to a more detailed consideration of his infirmity;
his ailments, and the cause of his early death.

From his earliest years he was a charming, happy and mischievous
child who could draw before he could write. He was adept at getting
his own way with both the family, who may well have spoiled him a
little, and his cousins and other young friends for whom he invented
games. Until he was 13 his height was average for his age, though he
was regarded as delicate, for he tired easily. His fontanelle remained
open longer than normal, but there is no mention of any broken
bones until the slight accidents which led to a fractured femur, the
left when he was 13½, and the right when he was 14¾. Before the first
fracture he had been in the habit of walking with a stick, and he did
suffer from pains in his legs, but I have not found any record of when
this started—possibly at the age of 11, when he wrote from Paris to his
mother saying that the doctor was pleased with his legs. At the age of
13 he measured 4 feet 11½ inches, but after his accidents further growth
was very slow and at 18 he measured but 5 feet ½ inch. Had he suffered
from fragilitas ossium there would surely have been many more
fractures, especially in childhood, and there is nothing in his appearance
or growth to suggest achondroplasia. I have been greatly helped in
trying to unravel the mystery of his infirmity by the *Atlas of General
Affections of the Skeleton* by my former chief, the late Sir Thomas
Fairbank (1951, Edinburgh & London, p. 31). He describes the condition of osteopetrosis or marble bones in which the medullary spaces
in the long bones are replaced by bone which may at times be soft,
predisposing to fractures. As the blood-forming marrow in the bones
is reduced, anaemia and even leukaemia may supervene. It was first

described by Albers-Schönberg in 1904 as marmorization of bones, osteosclerosis fragilis generalisata. Consanguinity of the parents has been found by Nussey (1938) in 20% of cases. A tendency to fracture has been noted in some, and the facture is likely to be sharp, abrupt and transverse. In Toulouse-Lautrec's case the fractures may well have occurred near the lower end of the femur interfering with further growth at the epiphysis. Åke Ahlberg, the orthopædic surgeon in Malmö, was the first to suggest osteopetrosis in 1965. The other possibility is melorheostosis, a very rare condition where one or two bones may be petrosed. Pain in the affected bones is a prominent feature, and there is limitation of movements in the joints formed by the affected bones. Shortening of the limb has been a feature in some cases, and of the 47 cases reported, 7 had more than one limb affected. In none was there a family history or history of consanguinity, nor has an undue tendency to fracture been reported. One of the four cases reported in this country was by my friend and colleague, Sir Cecil Wakeley.

Another possibility is Albright's syndrome, osteitis fibrosa disseminata, in which many bones, especially long bones, may be affected, fractures or bending of bones being not uncommon; there may be sexual precocity especially in females, and pigmentation of the skin. After growing fast early in life, growth ceases too soon so that permanent height is below average. Parkes Weber coined the phrase 'Infant Hercules' for the rare males of this syndrome, and in view of Henri's behaviour in adult life, this syndrome cannot be ignored. However, there is nothing to suggest that in childhood there was sexual precocity, merely a heightened sexual appetite when fully grown. The differentiation of these various disorders of bone is greatly helped by X-rays which were not discovered until 1895, and by blood examinations which were first reported in 1854 but again were not in general use when Henri was young.

The exact cause of Toulouse-Lautrec's infirmity can only be a matter of conjecture, but in the light of present-day knowledge, his shortness following the femoral fractures and his crippled state which started before the fractures suggests osteopetrosis with some degree of anæmia, though he might equally have had melorheostosis. That he overcame his disabilities as he reached adult life is reasonably certain, because at the height of his powers he could work most of the day and play much of the night, being content with but a few hours' sleep.

He was powerfully attracted to women, though the reverse did not apply—so he sought his pleasures where he could pay for them. His love of night-life led to the habit of drinking regularly and often too much. By 1897 he was drinking by day as well as by night and by 1898 his drunken state became an embarrassment to his friends. A sharp attack of delirium tremens kept him in a private sanatorium between February and May 1899, and thereafter he had a discreet keeper with him. After this, not only the quantity but also the quality of his artistic output altered dramatically, and early in 1901 he had a slight seizure or stroke to be followed in July by a more severe seizure with hemiparesis. This no doubt was the result of the syphilis which he contracted in 1888. His early death, before he was 37, was brought about by the combined effect of syphilis and alcohol.

Despite his deformity, he braved the world, scorned pity and always saw to it that he was the life and soul of any party. From the photographs available it is only with his mother that his defences were down. They never looked at one another, he for the pity he would see in her eyes and she for the wreck he was making of himself and, as she thought, of the shame he was bringing on his family. But, in the course of wrecking his life, he made the name of Toulouse-Lautrec immortal, and in so doing he triumphed over infirmity.

This paper was the last written by Sir Terence Cawthorne before his death in January 1970. It was intended as his Presidential Address to the Section of the History of Medicine and was read by his successor as President of the Section, Dr. K. Bryn Thomas.

Florence Nightingale: New Lamps for Old

G. E. W. WOLSTENHOLME

FRCP

11 *May* 1970

The night nurse should have a reversible lamp, or something that without disturbing the patient, gives her light, brighter than the fire or gaslight properly maintained in the wards at night.

This remark by Florence Nightingale is typical of the detail she went into about all aspects of nursing and about many other matters as well. It was in the hope of obtaining Aladdin's lamp that new lamps were offered for old, and today I want to suggest that we might well give away many of our modern lamps in order to find that lamp which Florence Nightingale used to shed light, not only on nursing but also on many other aspects of personal, national and international welfare. I think it will be seen that she was far ahead of her time, and is still, regrettably, ahead of us today in some respects.

Here was a remarkable woman; some people commonly refer to her as 'that dreadful woman'. She seems to have become known chiefly for imposing discipline on nurses, the suggestion being that this is a particularly herculean task. Florence Nightingale was as formidable and domineering as Queen Victoria, but perhaps more easily amused. Yet there is something morbid, even distasteful, though pathetic, about a woman who for more than fifty years was virtually confined to a couch in her room, choosing to see never more than three or four people a day, one at a time, for not more than about twenty minutes each. She would even write letters to a dear friend who was in the next room.

As an influential invalid, Florence Nightingale was very similar to two other great figures of her age, Charles Darwin and Harriet Martineau. Perhaps in these busy days we have a need for similar people who through illness or inclination have ample time to read, write and meditate—if only they could do so to such effect as Florence Nightingale herself. I want to sketch an outline of this astonishing woman, using many of her own words to indicate her peculiar genius, but first let me remind you of some of the main facts about her life.

She was born just 150 years ago, on 12 May, 1820. Her mother had

o

already called one older daughter by the name of the city in which she was born, Parthenope (using the old name for Naples) and she followed the same custom when her second daughter arrived in Florence. One cannot help wondering what she would have done had she been taken short on the way to Florence, say in Poggibonsi or Pisa. Florence grew up into a lovely young woman. She was described by a contemporary in these words: 'She is tall; very slight and willowy in figure; thick shortish, rich brown hair; very delicate colouring; grey eyes which are generally pensive and drooping, but which when they choose can be the merriest eyes I ever saw; and perfect teeth . . .' When she was 16 she felt she received a personal call to God's service, but without any indication of the form that that service might take. As a result of visiting the sick poor in the villages around her home, she slowly developed a conviction that it was to the care of the sick that God required her complete devotion. This was tremendously strengthened by a most assiduous study of every detail about hospitals and nursing which she could acquire, working in the early hours of the morning and largely unknown to her family. When her parents and sister did become aware of the seriousness of her intentions, they put all possible pressure on her to abandon any such notion, hospital nursing at that time being regarded as fit only for women without respectability or reputation, of no education, often addicted to drink and prostitution. Her sister, Parthe, decided that if Florence had to nurse somebody it might as well be herself and she threw a series of hysterical illnesses to oblige her in this respect. It was only when Florence reached the age of 33 that, with the encouragement of Sir James Clark, she made up her mind to defy her family and accept the charge of the Institution for Sick Gentlewomen in Harley Street. She had received several proposals of marriage and one in particular, from Richard Monckton Milnes, she seems to have turned down in considerable denial of her own affections, but firm in the knowledge that a conventional marriage in those times would make it quite impossible for her to follow her chosen vocation. It could be that this was a major contributory factor towards her subsequent neurosis. As one person put it: 'She stands perfectly alone, halfway between God and his creatures.'

From the beginning in Harley Street, Florence showed a surprising capacity for management. I will mention only one example: she had two committees and she was not above leading both of them to believe that what she was saying had been proposed or already agreed to by the other, in this way protecting herself from attack on grounds of her own inexperience. She was indeed so dramatically successful from the very beginning in the practical management not only of the nursing but also of the administration and finances of the Institution, that soon after the Crimean war broke out she was invited by the Minister at War, her great friend Sir Sidney Herbert, to recruit some forty nurses and take them out to Constantinople. She duly arrived there in November 1854 and remained in this theatre of war until July 1856. The building which the army had acquired for the treatment of the wounded was the Selimiye barracks with a small attached hospital in Scutari on the Asian side of the Bosphorus. It is a vast building, originally constructed fifty to sixty years before Florence Nightingale's arrival, with outer walls of stone and an interior of wood; vast corridors running the whole length of each wing of the building with smaller rooms going off on the outer side. The barracks are now being carefully and extensively repaired for occupation by the Turkish army, the members of which proudly preserve two small rooms, one above the other in one of the corner towers, as a memorial to Florence Nightingale, with some of the simple furniture which she used. There is even a 'Nightingale Week' each year in Turkey when schoolchildren are encouraged to study what she did and to visit these rooms.

In 1854 the small hospital was soon overrun with cases of cholera, and both sick and wounded were laid in the great corridors of the artillery barracks. Much has been said about the dreadful conditions in which the wretched soldiers were received in this building. One side of it had been burned and had not been repaired, but as a whole it was probably as good a place as any available and could accommodate very large numbers of patients lying in the wide corridors, though never the many thousands carried into it in the winter of 1854–5. Its sanitation was, however, abysmal, not only with a terrible lack of the most primitive latrines, but also in regard to the tiny quantity and filthy quality of its water supply, which at one stage was found to pass through the rotting carcase of a horse. However bad things were, they were made infinitely worse by the bureaucratic attitude of the supply officers towards the issue of food, clothing, blankets, medicaments, even when there were tolerable stocks of them. To the horror of these officious minds, Miss Nightingale bought all she needed in the town with her own allowance and money collected by *The Times* in England on her behalf. She also instructed and paid Turkish workmen to repair the plumbing and the wards.

Because of the opposition and prejudice which faced her when she arrived at Scutari, Miss Nightingale waited until the aid of her nurses was actually requested before she would let them near the sick men. Then she left it to the doctors to realize just how useful the skilled aid of such women could be in support of their own overwhelming work. Florence Nightingale's achievements in the provision of this skilled aid and also, very importantly, in a most unfashionable devotion to the human dignity of each individual soldier, gave her in England power on the scale of Queen Victoria's, and a popularity far beyond that of the Queen. For the rest of her life Miss Nightingale used this power to achieve reforms based not only on her searing experiences for twenty months in this crucible of war, but also on a huge correspondence with people in many parts of the world, which gave her an almost unrivalled collection of facts on nursing, hospitals and sanitation, which she studied profoundly, analysed statistically, and marshalled for their utmost effect in government reports and other documents.

Her last years were clouded with mental deterioration and blindness. It is doubtful whether she could appreciate the significance of the award of the Order of Merit. Death, which she had expected if not daily, certainly weekly for over fifty years, occurred on 13 August 1910, sixty years ago. If anyone had ever lived each day of her life as if it were the last, it was Florence Nightingale.

From her sickroom, Florence Nightingale put out a tremendous volume of reports, pamphlets, letters; there are said to be some 150 large volumes of her notes and letters in the British Museum alone. Most of these were concerned with nursing, hospital construction, district nursing, rural hygiene and rural health visitors, the health of the British army and sanitation in India. The books about her include Sir Edward Cook's official biography, Mrs. Cecil Woodham-Smith's enthralling story of her life, Sir Zachary Cope's perceptive observations on her relations with the medical profession, and the biobibliography compiled by the late Mr. W. J. Bishop and by Miss Sue Goldie.

I should like now to give you a number of quotations from Florence Nightingale's own writings. Obviously I must start with nursing, but there was a surprising variety of subjects on which she expressed an opinion—an opinion always based on much study and original thinking.

In 1860 Miss Nightingale was writing:

I use the word Nursing for want of a better. It has been limited to signify little more than the administration of medicines and the applications of poultices. It ought to signify the proper use of fresh air, light, warmth, cleanliness, quiet and the proper selection and administration of diet—all at least expense of vital power to the patient. . . . The art of nursing, as now practised seems to be expressly constituted to unmake what God had made disease to be, viz., a reparative process.

Much later on, in 1890, she was still singing the same song:

Nursing is putting us in the best possible condition for nature to restore or to preserve health. Health is not only to be well, but to be able to use well every power we have to use.

We may compare the expressed aims in 1946 of the World Health Organization—'the complete physical, mental and social well being' of all people.

What kind of person was to do the nursing?

A woman who takes a sentimental view of Nursing (which she calls 'ministering', as if she were an angel) is of course, worse than useless. . . . Those who undertake such work must not be sentimental enthusiasts, but downright lovers of hard work. If there is any work which is simple, stern necessity, it is that of waiting upon sick and wounded . . .

It is a common accusation against this 'dreadful' woman that she so stressed the vocational nature of a nurse's work that even today nurses are still hampered by the Nightingale tradition in obtaining proper pay. In support of this view, something she wrote in a letter to Benjamin Jowett in 1889 is sometimes quoted: 'When very many years ago I planned a future, my one idea was not organising a hospital, but organising a Religion.' In my opinion this was a literal statement, in an historical sense, and does not carry the implication that she intended nursing itself to be a religion. Certainly in 1867 Florence Nightingale was writing: 'I need scarcely add that nurses must be paid the market price for their labour, like any other workers; and that this is yearly rising.' And in 1858, even before any body of military nursing had been established, she was making proposals for the nurses' pensions, possibly to be obtained partly by deductions from pay, which she anticipated would be increased with every five years of service, even if the nurse was not promoted, though she herself would have preferred slow and steady annual increments.

Miss Nightingale is also widely regarded as a redoubtable Victorian dragon, breathing fire and brimstone about nurses' discipline, and still today inspiring some matrons and sisters to breathe hotly down the necks of nurses both on and off duty. It must be remembered that she was laying down rules to ensure, for the first time, the respectability of nurses. Yet it was this 'dragon' who could write in 1858: 'Nurses trusted to do their duty in wards, must be trusted to walk out alone if they choose.' And: 'Ward Sisters must exercise authority without appearing to exercise it . . . no one can trample upon others and govern them.' And: 'No one was ever able to govern who was not able to obey.' Also: 'She who rules best is she who loves best.' Florence Nightingale more than once emphasized that what she wanted from nurses was 'the obedience of intelligence, not the obedience of slavery'.

For very many years Miss Nightingale's opposition to the registration of nurses delayed the great efforts of Mrs. Bedford Fenwick who herself only in 1919 became 'No 1' on that register (Hector 1970). I think it is fair to remember that in resisting state examinations and a register, Florence Nightingale's fear was that nursing would be bound by regulations on paper, before it had shown what it might become. 'Will you have women or will you have words? Which nurse best?' As late as 1893 she was pleading: 'We have scarcely crossed the threshold of uncivilised civilisation in nursing . . . don't let us stereotype mediocrity.'

Florence Nightingale was totally opposed to the very idea that diseases were caused by germs, and retrospectively she may be subject for mockery on this ground. But she was an incomparable believer in facts: 'Give us detailed facts' was her constant cry in letters to her correspondents in many parts of the world. It is hard to believe that she would not have accepted the evidence for bacteria if this could have been properly presented to her, and in fact the measures of hygiene which she advocated so strongly, if fully adopted, could have done much to bridge the gap between Koch's laboratory and the first antibiotics. In 1862 she was urging an international congress in London to recognize that 'the waste of human life, the destruction of human health and happiness have been in all ages, many times greater from disease than from actual encounters in the field'.

In 1863—and for how long afterwards?—Florence Nightingale could write: 'It may seem a strange principle to enunciate as the very first requirement in a hospital that it should do the sick no harm.' She asked why 'mortality is far far greater in lying-in hospitals than among women lying-in at home?'

Her criticisms of the plans for Netley Hospital led her to write of Sixteen Sanitary Defects in the Construction of Hospital Wards in extraordinary detail, for example regarding the composition of walls, ceilings, furniture, &c. She compared the British plans unfavourably, and I imagine unpopularly, with French hospitals in Paris and Vincennes. When the new St. Thomas's was being built a hundred years ago, she had a great deal to say—possibly as much as all the present committees today involved in the same task—on matters such as the structure of beds, materials of bedding, the siting and quality of lavatories and baths, ventilators, cupboard space, employment of ward maids, lifts for food, chutes for soiled linen, &c.

Not long afterwards, she was commenting: 'The time will soon come when the public—including especially "Doctors"—will consider a great hospital as incomplete without its training school for nurses as without its Medical School for students.' This may look like a glimpse of the obvious, but at the time Mr. South, then President of the College of Surgeons and senior consulting surgeon to St. Thomas's, could see no point in 'any special Institution for Training' and rejoiced that, in the enormous list of subscribers to the Nightingale Fund, there were to be found the names of 'only three physicians and one surgeon from one London hospital and one physician from a second', and this at a time when there were ninety-four physicians and seventy-nine surgeons in the seventeen hospitals in London.

Some doctors were very fearful of the professional recognition of nursing: 'FRCP', writing to the *Lancet* in 1897, complained that 'this new profession is taking a very large sum that would otherwise go to the doctors', and the Court of the Society of Apothecaries opposed the registration of nurses for the same pecuniary reason. Incidentally, the same Society, having licensed Elizabeth Garrett to practise medicine in 1865, hurried just a few years later to close this loophole for the practice of medicine by women—a misogyny perhaps influenced by the monastic atmosphere of the halls of the Black Friars and still detectable today.

Miss Nightingale appears to have gone out of her way to avoid provoking antagonism or envy among the doctors, despite the temptations to her caustic tongue and pen. She could write privately: 'Until the British public is enlightened enough to pay the doctors for their knowledge and not for their drugs, the medical profession will be a base and not distinguished one', but publicly she was diplomatic. In her earliest days of responsibility in Harley Street, she made it a rule not to engage any nurse without the doctors' 'approbation'. When she and her group of nurses arrived in Constantinople, she was absolutely adamant about not permitting her women to work in the wards unless and until the army doctors made a request for their services—

to the fury of the women who saw so much unnecessary suffering around them in the first few weeks. She was optimistic enough in her 'Notes on Nursing' to write: 'In the long run a firm, discreet woman, *who is an efficient Nurse*, can get on with any Surgeon, *who has his Sick at heart.*' And she stated clearly: 'Let there be as few women, and these few as efficient and as respectable as can be. Let all that can be done by men be so done.'

Florence Nightingale's whole inspiration, granted her 'call' to God's service, was based on the great surplus of women in England in the middle of the last century, estimated by Josephine Butler at some 2½ million widows and spinsters, many reasonably educated but without an outlet for creative work. As Miss Nightingale wrote: 'A woman cannot live in the light of intellect. Society forbids it. These conventional frivolities, which are called her "duties" forbid it.' As we noted earlier, it took her many years and intense dedication to escape from the social conventions of her age. She asked bitterly: 'Is it better to learn pianoforte than to learn the laws which subserve the preservation of offspring?' She was very conscious of the benefit to the one able to give service, as well as to the recipient: 'If the poor receive good from the living, loving intercourse of the trained and educated woman, she in her turn receives quite as much good from theirs.' She shrewdly observed of her sex: 'Give them plenty to do, and great responsibility— two effectual means of steadying women.' There was no lack of work, in hospitals or in homes: 'Till every mother knows how to *feed*, clothe, wash her children—so as to secure them the best chance of health; till every sick person can have a share of a trained district nurse.'

If Florence Nightingale had a passionate concern for the lives of her fellow women, it was not at the expense of care for the patient. Who indeed ever cared more for every detail of a sick person's needs?

How well a patient will generally bear, e.g., the putting up of a scaffolding close to the house, when he cannot bear the talking, still less the whispering . . . outside his door. . . . Apprehension, uncertainty, waiting, expectation, fear of surprise, do a patient far more harm than any exertion. . . . The shyness of patients is seldom allowed for. . . . Volumes are now written and spoken upon the effect of the mind upon the body . . . I wish a little more was thought of the effect of the body on the mind. You who believe yourselves overwhelmed with anxieties, but are able every day to walk up Regent Street, or out in the country, to take your meals with other groups, etc., you little know how much your anxieties are thereby lightened; you little know how intensified they become to those who have no change.

She was convinced that it mattered greatly that patients could see out of windows, see sunlight, sky and trees, and flowers—she thought red flowers stimulating, blue flowers perhaps depressing; she thought it desirable to change the pictures on the wall from time to time but not so frequently as to be disturbing; she was persuaded of the beneficial qualities of music; she even wrote about the distress to a patient obliged to drink from a cup resting on a saucer in which fluid had been slopped. And was it perhaps Florence Nightingale who created the legend of the 'English cup of tea'? She noted that: 'English men and women who have undergone great fatigue . . . could do it best upon an occasional cup of tea—and nothing else. Let experience, not theory decide upon this as upon all other things.'

The same woman who bothered about tea spilt in saucers was capable of great humanity. As I mentioned earlier, she was remarkable in her recognition of the value of each British soldier. He had been described as 'the scum of the earth', you will remember, by Wellington, whose own mother spoke of him as 'food for powder and nothing more'. In the 1850s the soldier was still treated with utter contempt as little more than an animal by his own officers, but Florence Nightingale could recognize immediately his 'innate dignity, gentleness and chivalry in the lowest sinks of human misery'. She could never, after the Crimean War, get out of her mind 'the handful of men who defended their trenches at Sebastapol . . . and who, when dying of slow torture in hospital, drew their blankets over their heads and died without a word'. She found it necessary to remind an International Congress in London in 1862 that: 'The soldier is a mortal man, subject to all the ills following on wet and cold, want of shelter, bad food, excessive fatigue, bad water, intemperate habits, and foul air.' It must have been startling at the time to read her recommendations in 1864 for Indian Army stations, not only her demand for pure water and good drainage, but also for provision of gymnasia, workshops, games, soldiers' gardens and reading rooms.

Her *Notes on Matters Affecting the Health, Efficiency, and Hospital Administration of the British Army* in 1858 include the following fourteen chapter headings (out of twenty-one) slightly abbreviated:

Deficiencies of Sick Transport
Sanitary Recommendations for Hospitals
First Employment of Female Nurses
Employment of Male Nurses
Necessity of Special Sanitary Functionaries (at home and abroad)

Inaccuracy of Hospital Statistics
Necessity for a Statistical Department
Actual and Proposed Forms for Medical Statistics
Greater Mortality and Morbidity in Certain Corps
Education, Employment and Promotion of Medical Officers
Notes on Pay and Stoppages
Notes on Dieting and Cooking
Soldiers' Wives
Construction of Hospitals

Of her recommendations Henry Hurd of the Johns Hopkins Hospital
commented: 'Had the conclusions which she reached been heeded in the
Civil War in America, or in the Boer War in South Africa, or in the
Spanish-American War, hundred of thousands of lives might have been
saved.' We in our generation can be thankful that such lessons began to
be applied with great effect in the First World War, for example in
regard to inoculations against typhoid, whilst in the Second World
War many of us had reason to be grateful for the remarkable degree of
consultation between the fighting forces and the medical services.

I hope you noted particularly the emphasis on statistics. Florence
Nightingale was a devoted follower of Dr. William Farr, one of the
founders of medical statistics, and she was a pioneer herself in graphic
methods of statistical representation.

Quite as unusual was her care for people of other races. Based wholly
on her voluminous correspondence, she produced a book on life in
India, both native and British, said to be more complete than any other
book then available. She urged the development of a system of railways
and canals, and industry based on water-power. For example:

This great essential work of the regulation of the water in India is perhaps at
this moment, the most important question in the world ... another very
important point, and intimately connected with irrigation in all ways, has to
be taken up; and that is, the subject of manufacturing in India. There are, at
this moment, at least 100,000 horse water power available and made no use
of in the great irrigation canals. The canals will convey the goods to and from
manufactories, the irrigation will set free millions from agricultural labour
for such work ... with cheap labour, cheap power, cheap carriage, and cheap
food, India will have the very highest advantages for manufacture, for civilisation, and also for life, and all that makes life worth living. ... If only
£14,000,000 were spent on irrigation and navigation, we should be saved
from famine expenditure without returns but the sad returns of loss of life;
our revenue would be raised by incalculable increase of produce and we should

be doing our duty to one fifth of the human race—our own fellow country-men and country-women.

Yet she observed sadly: 'We do not care for the people in India. . . . We English have to learn a new language to India.' She cried for legislation to control 'the sharp-witted, highly educated moneylenders, highly educated in the knowledge of fraud' and she urged the use of co-operatives to enable Indian cultivators to rescue themselves from money-lenders. Nearly 100 years ago, long before many of our present international agencies, Florence Nightingale realized that:

A people cannot really be helped except through itself; a people must be *in*formed, *re*formed, *in*spired through itself. A people is its own soil and its own water, others may plant, but it must *grow* its own produce.

At a time when paternalism might have been regarded as an advanced ideal, Miss Nightingale was reminding Queen Victoria herself that she had agreed to 'admit the natives of India to share in the government of that country without distinction of race and creed'. Miss Nightingale was also worried, long before most people, about the harm done to native cultures by the introduction of Western methods, and gathered information from 143 schools in Ceylon, Australia, Natal, West Africa and North America about the effect of European civilization on the disappearance of aboriginal races. Her attitude to excessive and exclusive nationalism is reflected in a sentence which does credit to her doctor friends: 'I can always talk better to a medical man than anyone else. They have not that detestable nationality which makes it so difficult to talk with an Englishman.'

May I give just a few more scattered quotations? On hydrotherapy: 'The water-cure—a highly popular amusement in the last few years amongst athletic invalids who have felt . . . those indefinable diseases which a large income and unbounded leisure are so well calculated to produce.' On life insurance: 'Were they instead of having the person examined by the medical man, to have the houses, conditions, ways of life, of these persons examined, at how much truer results would they arrive!' On work: 'A State . . . must supply for its willing workers the means to work so as to maintain a livelihood—and to its criminals the means to work their way out of prison.' Recently *Nature* (1970, **225,** 116) was deploring the Indian Government's ban on the acceptance by Indian scientists of invitations to attend meetings abroad: in 1891 Florence Nightingale was arguing with the government of India about the importance of sending delegates to the 7th International Congress of Hygiene and Demography. Even on birds she had something to say which might have been quoted recently in *The Times*, or even more relevantly in *Il Tempo*, for she thought that far too little was being done about indiscriminate trapping and destruction of wild birds. In destroying them, man is his worst enemy, for 'the order of nature is upset'.

However much or however little affection we may feel for this genius of a woman, our admiration now, 150 years after her birth and 60 years after her death, would have little meaning or validity if we treated her work and writings only as history. I have mentioned how much her determination owed to her recognition of the despairing lack of opportunities for some 2½ million women. I would suggest that we have a somewhat similar situation with millions of young people of both sexes in many countries today. At the same time we begin to face increasing world shortages of medical manpower, doctors, nurses and all forms of trained ancillary personnel, which we seem unlikely to solve, at least on a world basis, even if the population were to remain stable—and we all know it is almost inevitable, barring a third world war, that the world population will grow within the lifetime of people already born to a figure of at least 12,000 million, compared with the present figure of 3,300 million.

The words 'brain drain' have come to have an almost facetious connotation, but what could be more immoral than that the more privileged countries should attract away from the underprivileged countries those comparatively few doctors and nurses they have. This country is said to benefit at present from the intake of nearly 2,000 doctors a year. According to Dr. Oscar Gish of Sussex University, the 14,000 foreign-born doctors in Britain at the end of 1967 made up over 22% of all the doctors in the country, and at the end of 1969 the Department of Health and Social Security revealed that no less than 48% of the doctors under training in England and Wales had been born overseas. I personally am always acutely conscious of the fact that a country like Ethiopia, with some 25 million inhabitants, has not more than 250 doctors—80% of them from many other countries and nearly all of them in a few main cities, so that some 20 million people are without medical aid of any kind. Such problems could be tackled on the model of the Soviet Union which, in some fifty years, has almost from zero produced an adequate service of medical care by some ½ million doctors, ¾ million nurses, and ¼ million midwives, for a population of around 200 million people. Or there is China's present system under which at any one time up to one-third of the total staff of general hospitals, from senior surgeon and matron down to boilerman, are compulsorily but also willingly providing service in rural areas and at the same time training rural students in basic medicine. These are methods which do meet great human needs and are not to be sneered at, but we must also keep in mind the importance of the preservation and enhancement of excellence in practice and in teaching the next generation, and the vital necessity of continuing research.

Even the most privileged countries, such as our own, are I believe facing a period of comparative starvation in medical care for at least a generation, during which there will be many fewer people engaged in the provision of health services than we would wish to have. The answer seems to lie in a more economic use of those we do have, with a far greater emphasis than we have so far on the use of paramedical personnel; not only of such highly trained people as nurses, pharmacists, radiographers, physiotherapists, laboratory technicians, sanitary engineers, but also of secretaries, receptionists, porters, dressers and drivers.

If I may intrude a personal experience, I was in charge of a Base Transfusion Unit in the Mediterranean during the war, for which during the main part of the war there was no official establishment. The only people I could recruit to help me were those rendered unfit by war service, some admirable conscientious objectors, local labour or the like. They inevitably included some very unpromising recruits, but I can say that in time it did prove possible to find ways in which every single individual could make a notable and valuable contribution to our teamwork as a whole. I am therfore convinced that there is a role in support of medical services for a very large body of initially unskilled labour, on a voluntary or short-term basis, perhaps for one to two years, both national and world-wide in character.

I do not see this as a threat to present professional standards—quite the reverse, since we would demand more and more skill from those trained to apply it. Nor need there be any blurring of professional distinctions, rather a truer recognition of the skill which each section has acquired. I should like to see every doctor and every other member of the medical team trained to ever-rising standards of knowledge and skill; not competing, but consciously co-operating to help the sick and defective and to prevent disease, working together in such teams as are economic in manpower and money and capable of rapid variation according to the circumstances, in hospitals and in communities, in both advanced and developing countries.

It is vital now and must increasingly become so, that no person contributing to medical care should perform tasks which can adequately be carried out by someone of lesser skill and training; however few or many medical staff are working cooperatively together, there will always be a demand for work of an unskilled or less skilled kind in support of their efforts.

One often hears nowadays talk about which is the world's most important problem; population growth, 'have and have-nots', pollution, nationalism, &c. I see no hope of solving any of them unless work is found for the high energy of idealism and humanism among the young which at present is without purpose—a vast store of energy which will otherwise generate enough heat to melt away our civilization.

I cannot now discuss the extent to which youth service of not less than one to two years' duration could be organized and sustained to relieve trained people for their proper purposes, but I am confident that the response would be impressive, satisfying and constructive, not only in supporting health services directly, but in creating a bridge between generations in which both parties would have much to give and much to gain. Experience even at the lowest level of unskilled help could be expected to enrich our whole community from generation to generation.

But if we could think of an *international* organization of medical service, an extension of the admirable work of the World Health Organization and the International Red Cross, to provide a permanent world-wide framework for the use of medical teams, extended by voluntary service of the kind I have suggested, would not doctors appropriately be making a most vital contribution to the whole health of mankind? If the medical profession is not prepared to set an example, where is hope to be found? It is no good waiting for international organizations set up by governmental agreement; we ourselves must first have the wish and the will to provide care for men, women and children wherever they are found.

It may sound hopelessly idealistic and unrealistic, but I believe that doctors and nurses and their colleagues, through their schools, colleges, academies and institutions, could obtain large financial backing from enlightened philanthropists, industrialists and even governments in their programmes of aid without strings, for it seems to me that even in the present bleak economic climate, perhaps just because of it, there is recognition of the need for ways of strengthening networks between peoples of all countries, races and beliefs against the forces of competition, disruption and despair. Perhaps a new 'Nightingale Fund', this time on a global footing, is not beyond all possibility.

It is in the nature of a presidential address to a Section of the Royal Society of Medicine that the lecturer should be a person very conscious of his increasing age, but I hope that there are younger people with energy, determination and compassion who want a fairer, healthier and more co-operative world badly enough to do something about it, possibly on the lines I have suggested.

I should like to close in the words of Florence Nightingale herself: 'It would be a noble beginning to the new order of things to use hygiene as the handmaid of civilisation.'

REFERENCES

Bishop, W. J. & Goldie, S. (1962). *Bibliography of Florence Nightingale*. London.

Cook E. (1913). *The Life of Florence Nightingale*. London.

Cope, Z. (1958). *Florence Nightingale and the Doctors*. London.

Hector, W. E. (1970). M. Phil. Soc. Thesis, City University, London.

Woodham-Smith, C. (1950). *Florence Nightingale*. London.

The Economic and Academic Freedom of Universities

SIR JOHN WOLFENDEN

CBE

13 *May* 1970

I am deeply sensible of the honour which you, Sir, and your Council have done me in inviting me to deliver this year's Jephcott Lecture. I am still more conscious that this honour carries with it a correspondingly great responsibility; and while I appreciate the former to the full I cannot hope to fulfil the latter at all adequately. And that for two reasons. First, I confess that I found the list of the names of my predecessors in this place more than ordinarily daunting; and I should be a fool (or, more accurately, an even bigger fool than I am) if I thought I could compete with or even maintain the standard set by men like Adrian, Florey and Todd. Secondly, the nature of the topic I am going to try to discuss may well seem to you to be hardly appropriate to the intentions of Sir Harry Jephcott's Trust. It, as I understand, was established to advance the cause of education by, *inter alia*, the provision of lectures 'on scientific and/or medical subjects generally, including economics, business management and other subjects with which business and/or trade is directly or indirectly concerned and to which scientific methods have been, are or may be applied'. And yet, on a rather closer look, perhaps this topic is not wholly outwith the terms of the benefaction. I hope, in the course of the next few minutes, to advance the cause of education, my own if not yours; if the topic is not scientific or medical, it is closely concerned with economics and business management, however novel this notion may be to some academics; it is not only indirectly but directly concerned with business and/or trade, if only because if there were no money made by business or trade there would be no money to pay for universities; and, finally, the subject is one to which scientific methods have been slightly, are increasingly, or may be, and, indeed, under the guidance of my distinguished successor at the University Grants Committee, progressively more will be, applied. So if you will bear with me I will see what I can do.

P

To begin with, we must try to look this notion of academic freedom squarely in the eye. This is not as easy as you might think. 'Freedom' is one of those concepts, like 'democracy', 'happiness', 'virtue', or even, in your own line of business, 'health', which are perfectly intelligible to everybody until you come to examine them. Everbody knows what he means by any one of these words. It represents something which he regards as a Good Thing, something which he wishes to possess or enjoy, something which he would have everybody else enjoy. It is, in short, a universally desired good. Splendid: but that does not really tell us very much about it specifically. Democracy does not mean the same to those who live in Britain, France, South Africa, the USA or the USSR—or, indeed, to all of those who live in any one of them. Virtue does not mean the same to Aristotle, Cato, St. Paul, John Knox. or Bertrand Russell. Similarly, freedom varies in its meaning with the circumstances of the individual. Robinson Crusoe was free in one sense, an American Negro in another, you and I in a third. A penniless tramp is free as air—to stay where he is or go somewhere else: a millionaire is free to do as he likes—within the constraints of his responsibilities and of the law. Perhaps we could agree, as a general proposition, that in what we call a civilized society a man is free to do what he wishes on condition that his doing so does not infringe the equal right of everybody else to do what he wishes. This, in dogmatic summary, is what we mean by the rule of law and what distinguishes freedom from anarchy and liberty from licence. The rule of law in a civilized society ensures that a man is (negatively, if you like) free from certain hazards and threats and (more positively) free to do certain things which otherwise persons or forces stronger than himself would prevent him from doing.

Forgive these platitudinous theorizings. They are not as irrelevant as they might seem. At the least, they may be an indication that we have to use our words rather carefully and that there is a danger, even in academic discussions, of using particular words without attaching any precise or accurate meaning to them.

When we prefix the adjective 'academic' to the noun 'freedom' we add complications in a new dimension. We ought to ask, but we have not time to do so, in what respects an academic community differs from any other kind of community, whether there are any specifically academic criteria by which the freedom of such a community is to be judged, and what, if anything, distinguishes the academic freedom of a university from the academic freedom of any other kind of academic community. But our immediate concern is with the academic freedom of universities, and these other attractive by-paths must remain untrodden.

The first distinction I think we must make is between the academic freedom of a university and the separate academic freedoms of the individuals who compose it. I doubt if anybody here present would deny that a university has, or ought to have, as part of its own nature and essence, a form of institutional academic freedom which is distinguishable from what we mean by the words 'academic freedom' as applied to individual professors, lecturers, tutors, researchers and scholars generally. There may well be differences of opinion about the precise nature and limits of that institutional freedom, but for those who have grown up in our tradition something of the kind is almost assumed as part of the definition of a university. In this country a university enjoys the degree of autonomy guaranteed by a Royal Charter and Statutes to a self-governing institution. And that is a very high degree by comparison with universities in some other parts of the world. In matters which can properly be called academic and in matters of internal government the rights, functions, duties, responsibilities, procedures of the university (and of its constituent parts) are laid down in considerable detail in these instruments; and once laid down they are not easily changed. It is true, of course, that not everybody inside each university accepts as coming from Sinai each item which the Charter and Statutes enunciate. In recent years a fair amount of criticism of statutory provisions has come from at any rate one section of the academic community. But these criticisms and the protests which have accompanied them have come from inside the institutions themselves, from members of the institution which is being criticized. They have not come from outside the university world altogether, as attempts to destroy the academic freedom of the university institution from without—except insofar as they are manifestations, inside a particular community, of a violent urge to destroy all institutions of any kind whatever.

But, granted these 'local difficulties', what should we regard as the irreducible minimum of institutional freedom? My guess is that we should put the minimum a good deal higher in this country than the operational minimum elsewhere. Any university in Britain would, I think, insist as an institution on two absolutely fundamental freedoms. It would insist, as an institution and as an academic community, on the right to admit as students any persons whom it chose to admit. And it would insist on the right to choose its own academic staff. Absolute power, within the Charter and Statutes, of admission and appointment are cardinal. Indeed, in the standard form of Royal Charter they are explicitly spelt out. And the rather elaborate provisions made for the appointment of members of the academic staff ensure that there shall be no interference from any external non-academic body, such as the State, a Minister of Education, a Government department or even a Parliament. *O fortunatos nimium, sua si bona norint!*

In some countries, as everybody knows, the free choice of students for admission is not accepted as an axiom. To be eligible in some places your skin has to be of a certain colour; in other places you have to express yourself as loyal to certain political principles. To us any discrimination of this kind would be an intolerable violation of the academic freedom of the university as an institution. Similarly, in some countries professors are not elected and appointed by due academic process inside a university. They are posted from one university to another as civil servants—note 'as', not 'like'. Such external appointments would be regarded here as inadmissible infringements of the university's right to appoint the person who seems, after due advertisement, examination and interview, to be the right person for this particular job at this particular moment. Institutional autonomy in selection of students and appointment of staff is for us the irreducible minimum. Some countries and their universities have never enjoyed either.

Here a word must be said about those constituent elements in the government of a university which are not strictly academic. The contractual employer in most of our universities is the university council; and it includes, besides academics from inside the university, externally-appointed persons affectionately known as 'lay members'. They are, not only often but usually, individuals distinguished in public life, industrialists, public servants, local notables, business men. Their very presence in the essentially academic atmosphere of a university seems to some to pollute it. My own personal experience, limited perhaps but wider than that of most of the protestors, would lead to the conclusion exactly opposite to theirs. In my view the active presence of non-academics on the supreme governing body of a university is a source of real strength rather than of weakness or of divided counsels, so far as academic freedom is concerned. I have never known a split on a university council between the academic and the non-academic members. I have never known an occasion when on an academic matter, concerned, for instance, with curriculum, academic appointments, or degree regulations, the non-academic members of a university council tried to override the judgement of the academic members. On the contrary, by the weight of their outside-world authority, the non-academics have substantially increased the academic freedom of the academics by trusting them and endorsing their specialist academic judgement. I say nothing, at this point, of the experience and worldly wisdom which these lay members can bring to discussion of the nonacademic concerns of a university, in matters of finance, public relations and so on; for our present concern is with academic freedom. They are part of the family of the university and they behave accordingly, as jealous of the university's autonomy against interference from outside as any professor; and university administration in Britain would be the poorer if they were not part of it.

But after this digression we ought perhaps to take a leap from the irreducible minimum to the desired maximum. In an ideal world, if there were no constrictions or restraints of any kind, what would a university see as its ideal of institutional academic freedom? Besides the two fundamental freedoms we have postulated it would, presumably, like to be free to engage in teaching and research in whatever fields it might itself wish to enter. I am assuming, perhaps dangerously but I think justifiably, that there is an 'it', that there is an overall university policy, arrived at by internal constitutional procedures, which directs a university's activities in teaching and research. I am well aware that at each stage there is argument and perhaps compromise. It is not always realized that in a healthy British university academic policy discussions start at the bottom of the organizational hierarchy and move upwards. A bright idea about a curriculum change or a new field of research occurs to a lecturer while he is shaving; he brings it to the next meeting of his faculty board; they adopt it with enthusiasm, as a result of his eloquent advocacy; it becomes part of the faculty board's next report to the senate; the senate approves it, either after discussion or, as the Greeks used to say, 'escaping their own notice doing so'; the senate's recommendations become operative academic practice after the next meeting of the Council. This bright idea, born of the shaving-mirror, is now an accepted and approved part of the university's academic policy. And that policy is composed of such individual inspirations, of the findings of *ad hoc* committees, and of senatorial investigations. What, in total, does it amount to?

First, it must be noted that the origin of these items is normally internal and academic. There are exceptions. The origin of an academic suggestion may be the University Grants Committee, or an industrial firm, or a government department. Any one of these may, for instance, offer money to a university for a particular line of teaching or research. But—and here is the crunch—none of these agencies can compel any university to accept any offer which may be made to it. The freedom to say 'No' is a very precious one, and I have known of many cases in which it has been exercised. This is important, because it means that a university can legitimately say to the UGC or to an enterprising and benevolent industrialist: 'Thank you very much indeed. It is very good of you to offer us money to start a School of Dentistry or a Chair in Precast Concrete Engineering. We entirely appreciate your generous intentions. But we honestly believe that this sort of development is not in line with our own academic plans, so, if you will not think us ungrateful, we would rather not take your money for this particular purpose.' This seems to me to be a significant exercise of academic freedom.

Secondly, in connexion with the shaving-mirror inspiration, it is important that we should not overlook the individual in fixing our attention on the university as an institution. For, as another crashing platitude, the quality of a university's work depends on the quality of the work of the individuals who work in it. Each of them has to live with his irreducible minimum of freedom, the freedom to follow the argument whithersoever it leads, the freedom to search for the truth wherever it may be found, the freedom to transmit the truth as he sees it to those whom he teaches. This is the irreducible minimum; there must be no restraints on speculation, no censorship, no bans on publication. (There may indeed by economic and financial restraints and those I shall mention later; but for the academic such academic freedom as I have outlined is the irreducible minimum.)

He would like, of course, much more than that. He would like the most up-to-date equipment in his laboratory, any book he may happen to wish to read available in his university library, the opportunity to visit his fellow-workers in Moscow or MIT. But he can, at a pinch, do without these or make second-best arrangements in their stead. He would like all he would like—which of us would not? What he cannot do without, if he is to preserve his academic conscience, is academic freedom to think, speak, teach and publish what he believes to be true.

But by now I have more than once teetered on the brink of the economic, as distinct from the academic, freedom of universities and of their members, and the time has come to take the plunge into these chilly waters.

It seems to me that there are three questions in which universities are interested, in this financial area. The first is: How much money is there? The second is: Where does it come from? And the third is: With what conditions or strings does it come? Each of these questions, and the answers to them, demands a little more examination.

So far as the first question goes, it ought to be remembered that, in this country at any rate, the amount of money which is to be provided for the universities in any one year is not determined by some antecedent rules. The process of reaching this quantitative decision is lengthy and laborious. But the essence of it is that it begins inside the universities themselves and not in the office of a civil servant in Whitehall. There are different procedures for capital expenditure and for recurrent expenditure. But in both cases the initiatives come from the universities. On the capital side, universities are requested at regular intervals to submit building programmes which they would like to see carried out. The University Grants Committee, after due examination of these proposals by its own officers, makes a submission to the Government; and that submission is either successful or unsuccessful or partially successful. In this capital area each proposal from each university is a separate item, and when permission has been obtained to carry out a building programme, the money is attached to particular buildings. That is to say, on the capital side funds provided by the Government are earmarked and cannot be switched from one building to another.

On the recurrent side, it is again true that the initiative lies with the universities. Once in five years they are invited, individually and collectively, to submit programmes of developments they would wish to undertake over a period of five years. The University Grants Committee examines in detail the proposals of each university and then submits a composite bid to the Government. A good deal of argument and negotiation follows—in my experience at any rate—and on the basis of the cases submitted by the universities and the UGC a Government decision is announced.

There are two very significant differences between what happens on the capital side and what happens on the recurrent side. First, when a Government announcement is made about the recurrent grant, that announcement includes amounts to be made available over each of the forthcoming five years. As the five-year period proceeds, the number of years in advance for which a university knows its income from the Government is reduced, because there is not yet in operation a 'rolling quinquennium'. But at any rate, even as the quinquennium moves by, there is a guarantee of a known amount of money from the Government for a number of years ahead. This is not so with the capital programme; this is seldom announced for more than two or three years ahead.

The second important difference is crucial. Each item in an approved building programme carries with it, as I have said, an exact sum of money which cannot be transferred to any other project. The essence of the recurrent grant is that it is not ear-marked or specified or attached to particular items of expenditure at all. Although the evidence and arguments on which the recurrent grant is based are detailed and specific in the extreme, the final award is a block grant which is deployed by each university on its own responsibility. We shall have to return to this important point later.

Our original question in this area was: How much money is there? Obviously, there is never enough. Universities, like ordinary individuals, never have as much money as they would like to have; there are those who think that it would be bad for them, as it would for you and me, if they had. Clearly, there are all kinds of things any enterprising university would like to do, which it simply cannot afford. In this country we do not have the rising spiral of competition between universities in the matter of salaries. There are, as I am sure you know, national scales for academic salaries, just as there are for technicians and other university employees. So we are not subject to the inter-university bidding for individuals which occurs elsewhere. But there are, of course, a great many areas where an ambitious university would like to be able to spend more money than its neighbour. The only consolation for each of them is that all the others are subject to the same constraints.

It is perhaps just worth adding that by comparison with their predecessors of even fifty years ago academics in this country might be regarded as hideously spoilt. The great experimentalists of earlier days would not recognize the equipment of scientific laboratories in the universities today—and they would not know how to use it if they did. Team research must be more expensive than individual experiments. And the sensible thing for a university to do is the same as for an individual, to cut coat according to cloth and be thankful for the amount of cloth there is.

The second question was: Where does the money come from? So far as Britain is concerned, the answer is fairly simple. By far the greater part of it comes from the Exchequer. Something like 85% of all recurrent expenditure and something like 90% of all capital expenditure on the part of the universities comes from the Exchequer. Not all of it comes through the University Grants Committee. The Research Councils also make substantial contributions to the funds of universities, on a rather different basis from the procedures of the University Grants Committee. The remainder of a university's income comes from fees, local authority grants, contributions from industry, benefactions or bequests. But it can be said, in broad terms, that the proportion which comes from public funds vastly exceeds the whole of the remainder. The consequences for institutional freedom of this state of affairs we must look at in a minute.

Our third question asked what were the strings or conditions attached to the various forms of a university's income. I have already tried to explain that the recurrent grant which flows to a university through the UGC is a block grant, which the university itself deploys. With very rare exceptions it would be true to say that this recurrent grant has no strings or conditions attached to it at all. There are occasions when the University Grants Committee, with the deliberate intention of encouraging this or that form of teaching or research, may earmark a certain amount of the block grant, but this is so rare that we need not bother about it.

The position about the Research Councils is quite different, and deliberately so. Whereas the block grant is made to the university as an institution, and deployed by it in accordance with the university's total academic strategy, grants from the Research Councils are made to particular departments, indeed, usually to particular individuals, for specific research programmes. So these funds can obviously not be transferred to any other department or used for any purpose except the specific one for which they were made. A Research Council retains the right to follow up and exercise some general supervision of the work which is financed by its grant, and when a capital grant is made the Research Council reserves the formal right to possession of any buildings which may be built. Local authority grants are for the most part not ear-marked but are intended for the general purposes of the university. There have lately been ingenious suggestions about the use of local authority grants for such specific purposes as student housing; but, broadly speaking, money which comes from the pocket of the ratepayer goes into the general coffers of the university. (I am not, of course, here talking about grants made to students. They are not part of our concern, except in the indirect sense that grants made by local authorities to students may in part pass to the university in payment of fees.) The benefactions and bequests are, naturally enough, specific in their intention, and it is plainly the duty of a university to carry out the wishes of a benefactor. Income from industrial sources may be of several kinds. Increasingly, industrial firms are entering into contracts with universities for specific pieces of research which the firm thinks can be more effectively done in a university laboratory than by its own scientific team. Or an industry may corporately endow a professorship of whatever it may be at some university or other. Or there may be a handsome contribution from a big commercial undertaking towards the appeal launched by a university in the neighbourhood. Or there may be arrangements for a particular department in a university to enjoy some facilities, financial or experimental, from a manufacturing firm. Boards of directors are very conscious of their obligations to their shareholders; and it is only reasonable that they should expect to see some benefit, direct or indirect, coming to them from funds which they give to universities. So it is not unreasonable that grants of this kind should have conditions attached to them; if a university does not like the conditions that are proposed it can always decline the offer of money, from whatever source.

The moment has come to try to bring together these unorganized and platitudinous observations, to bring into juxtaposition the two freedoms of our title, academic and economic, and to try to assess the consequences for an academic institution of the pattern of financing I have outlined.

It is with considerable diffidence that I pontificate about the University Grants Committee, for the views of my successor as Chairman of that body may well, and legitimately, differ from mine. What follows is my own personal view, which commits nobody but myself but which, with natural egotism, I should like to feel represented doctrine rather than personal whim.

I believe, and roundly assert, that under the UGC pattern of financial support the universities of this country are both economically better off than they would be under any other system, and academically more free than the universities of any other country.

Let us compare them, under both headings, with the universities of the United States of America. In that country, as you know, there are two broad types of university. There are private universities and there are state universities. The former are academically free. They can set their own standards of admission, lay down their own pattern of what they charmingly call 'offerings', regulate their own requirements for degrees, hire their own staff at whatever salaries they choose to pay, and, generally, exercise full academic freedom. Yes, on one condition, that they can privately raise the money—all the money—which is needed to carry out this libertarian programme. They do it partly, of course, by charging high fees. (It is not always recognized that in British universities the fees charged to a student, whether they are paid by a local education authority or by his father, represent about one-tenth of the actual cost of teaching him.) But high fees alone would not meet the cost of an American student in a private university. So the American university president spends about three-fifths of his time on fund-raising. And where do these funds come from? They come in large part from either alumni or industrial corporations or Government research grants. And it is idle to pretend that funds which come from these sources are without strings. Government research grants, in the North American context, are almost always 'mission-oriented'; that is, they are for specific pusposes, designed to produce results. There are many American university presidents, to my personal knowledge, who fear that acceptance of federal research grants is constricting or distorting the academic programme of their universities. Industrial corporations, there no less than here (perhaps more), expect to see some tangible or applicable results from their investments in the universities. Alumni are not always the most enlightened of benefactors; in some universities they are more ready to subscribe to the building of an ice-rink than to the endowment of a Chair. It is an illusion to suppose that a private university is, by being private, academically independent. And those who contemplate establishing one in Britain should take to heart the experience and advice of their American colleagues before they embark on a will-o'-the-wisp enterprise here.

The other type of American university is wholly State-financed. And here the outward picture is almost the exact opposite of the picture of the private university. Standards and conditions of admission are subject to the State legislature; particular professional needs within the State it is the university's business to meet. Provided that the university fulfils the decisions of the legislature the necessary funds will be voted. In this case the university president spends his time not so much in stumping the country to address alumni dinners as in lobbying the State legislators to try to persuade them to do what he would wish to see done or, more often, in trying to dissuade them from decisions which would erode his institution's academic freedom still further.

In brief, in a private university you can do what you like (that is, you can exercise total academic freedom) if you can find the money to do it: in a State university you can get all the money you want if you will do what the State legislature wants you to do (that is, if you are prepared to surrender your academic freedom).

My submission is that the existence and operations of the University Grants Committee enable us to avoid this antithesis and elude both horns of this dilemma. It is not easy to persuade our American friends of this fact. Their first notion is that, somehow, Oxford and Cambridge are private universities and all the rest State universities. When this misunderstanding has been removed, and when it has been shown that all the universities of Britain derive four-fifths of their recurrent income from the State, the understandable (but erroneous) conclusion is that all our universities are State universities in the American sense. How can it be that this dilemma is evaded?

We have managed to evolve in this country, largely as the result of the good sense of successive Governments, a procedure which on the face of it is illogical, unworkable and theoretically indefensible but which in real life—like so many British institutions deserving the same adjectives—works. In theory the UGC exists to advise the Government of the day about the needs of the universities: in practice it has the executive job of distributing among the universities the money it can persuade the Government to make available to them. And £250m a year is not peanuts. In theory it is absurd that a body which consists largely of university professors should, in handling that amount of money, be able to decide equitably between 44 grant-enjoying institutions: in practice I have only heard of one case where a Vice-Chancellor said that his university had been unfairly treated in comparison with another.

The fundamental reason why the system works is reciprocal confidence between the three partners, the universities, the Government and the UGC. If either the universities or the Government ceased to trust the UGC, and if it reached a point where it could not speak its mind to the other two, then the whole system would collapse overnight.

In my days at the UGC we used to say, inside the office, that we operated on the principle of Equal and Opposite Unpopularity. If we were too popular with the universities, the Government would suspect that we were in the universities' pockets, and *vice versa*. Actually, excessive popularity with either was not, in my experience, a real danger.

All this derives from the traditional view of the UGC as a buffer between the universities, on the one hand, and the Government, on the other. It has been a cardinal principle of relations between the two, in this country, that they never come face to face. Ministers and Secretaries of State, of course, visit individual universities; selected Vice-Chancellors dine from time to time at No. 10 Downing Street; professors fulfil many and varied functions in relation to Government departments. But the Government as such and the universities as a body do not meet to argue about money, still less about the universities' internal affairs; between the two stands the UGC, ready to have its bottom kicked by both.

That is where we start, with the UGC as a buffer or shock-absorber. But that is not where, in this present age, we stop.

Over recent years the UGC has gradually but visibly moved from being a buffer to becoming the strategist. The reasons for this change are complex, but not the least of them is the sheer size, in numbers of human beings and in amounts of money, of the present-day operation. In 1958 the number of university students in Britain was 100,000; in 1968 it was 200,000; today it is 220,000; and I do hear tell of a projected figure of over 400,000 for 1981-2. And the financial contribution from public funds has gone up to match, to a figure, all in, of something like £300m a year—this without taking into account grants made to students. If through these dramatic and rapid changes, the former relationship between Government and the universities was to endure, if, that is, there was not to be allowed to develop a direct control by the Government of the activities of the universities, then the passive buffer must come to life and undertake some positive and planning initiatives. This is what has happened; and the UGC has taken upon itself the task of encouraging, discouraging, fostering, financing or not financing, these or those studies in this or that university.

This is a difficult and delicate undertaking. It is a cardinal principle, you will remember, of the whole arrangement that a university's recurrent grant is a block grant, which the university deploys annually in the exercise of its internal budgetary autonomy. But it is not illegitimate, I think, for the UGC to let a university know which of the elements in the university's original submission have been taken into account in arriving at the grant allocation and which have not. The UGC can see the total university scene in a way that individual universities cannot. When one university puts in its quinquennial bid for funds it cannot be expected to know what all the other universities are asking for. It would not make sense that all 44 universities, or even 22 of them, should simultaneously institute professorships of Chinese literature, or, for that matter, of banking. And when new universities are coming into existence in fairly considerable numbers it is an advantage to each of them that not all of them should try to excel in the same things. It no longer makes sense, if ever it did, that everybody should try to do everything. Nor would it make sense, if in this company I may be allowed to say so, for each of 44 universities to have a medical school.

This is not, in my view at any rate, just a matter of money, though that is obviously important. In parenthesis, a medical student is not, as is commonly thought, the most expensive kind of student there is: the most expensive kind of student is a vet, presumably because his (what we must not call) clinical material is not provided free by the National Health Service. It is more than a matter of money. It is a matter of the most effective distribution and deployment of a very scarce commodity, highly skilled and specialized academic man-power. This is where we get back to something like the generalizations of my first few minutes. Each of us, as a citizen, may legitimately do what he likes provided that his doing so does not impair the freedom of his neighbour to do what he likes on the same conditions. The total, complete and unlimited autonomy of 44 university institutions could well result in the kind of fratricidal anarchy which would prevent any from enjoying that freedom within the law which characterizes a civilized society.

It seems to me not to be shocking, either, that the UGC, and indeed from a different standpoint the Comptroller and Auditor General, should encourage universities to be decently economical in the spending of the public funds which are allocated to them. Once upon a time (and I am old enough to remember it) it was thought to be somehow ungentlemanly and indelicate to try to be efficient in the running of a university or a college; academics were expected to be decently amateur in their dealings with money—it was part of the image. It has now come to be realized that if it is efficiently managed money will, as they say, go further. That is, you can get more of what you want out of the same amount of it. That is, you can do more academic things with your grant if you administer it economically. That is, your freedom to do what you aspire to do academically, as an academic institution, is increased. There are some, still, who shudder at the introduction into the academic environment of such notions as businesslike management and cost-effectiveness. In real life, properly interpreted and applied, these concepts increase the academic freedom of a university institution.

All this applies also to the individual academic. He has not usually got all the money he wants, either on his salary cheque or in his laboratory. But the funds his department enjoys are voted to it by his colleagues inside his own university. There is any amount of professorial in-fighting in any university at the time of annual estimates. But he gets what his colleagues think he deserves. For the rest, he is free— no academic anywhere more free—to follow his own programme of teaching and research within the law as laid down by his own university. If he chooses to undertake research sponsored from outside, with whatever strings attached, he is free to do so: if he does not so choose, that is his affair.

Of course there are dangers. Life is like that. There is the danger that a Government might wish to take over the universities and make them the instrument of some policy or other which might be totally antagonistic to the academic freedom in which we all believe. That has happened elsewhere, and it would be naïve to suppose that it could never happen here. More insidiously, because less obviously, Parliament, acting through a Select Committee, believing itself to be responding to public opinion, might exert pressure on a Government to ensure that the universities 'did what they were told'. And then we should be in the position of the State universities in North America. But, believe me, the UGC are well aware of all this. The majority of the members of the UGC, remember, are practising professors. They know exactly what it is like at the other end. And I do not believe that they will ever sell this pass.

It is time I brought this long ramble to an end. We are in the realm of value-judgements, and who can say that his own private values should prevail? Let me try to summarize. We believe that the ideal of a civilized society is freedom within the law; we believe that academic freedom includes the right of institutions to govern themselves and of individuals to pursue a life of scholarly teaching and research without interference or outside pressures. We believe also that universities have obligations to the society from which they draw their financial life-blood; and the major obligation is that they should behave as academic communities, cherishing and enriching the truly academic virtues. All this needs to be guarded, jealously, zealously and steadfastly, for it would be a terrible thing if the truly academic virtues vanished from our society. We must all be their guardians, governments, parliaments, tax-payers, the University Grants Committee, and, above all, the universities themselves, who must be seen to be worthy of the freedom which is accorded to them.

Nearly two hundred years ago words were spoken which are constantly misquoted, and which may perhaps serve as epitaph to this tedious discourse though not, I hope, to the academic freedom of the universities. As John Philpot Curran said in his speech on the right of election of the Lord Mayor of Dublin (1790):

The condition upon which God hath given liberty to man is eternal vigilance; which condition if he break, servitude is at once the consequence of his crime, and the punishment of his guilt.

The Next Ten Years in Education
LORD JAMES OF RUSHOLME
9 December 1970

I need scarcely say how honoured I feel to be asked to deliver this Lloyd Roberts lecture. It is an honour that I appreciate all the more, though with increasing misgiving, when I look at the list of my predecessors. Had I fully realized that I should find such formidable names as those of my friends Lord Cohen of Birkenhead and the Baroness Wootton, I think that prudence would have led me to decline. My only encouragement is that Lloyd Roberts was a Manchester man, and as I always hope that my sixteen years there made me a kind of honorary Mancunian, I feel that I have some small title to give the lecture that commemorates one who was clearly a remarkable Manchester character. Manchester has always been famous for producing great doctors, and it is an interesting thought that some of those who were my friends there, Fletcher Shaw, John Stopford, and the incomparable Geoffrey Jefferson, must have known Lloyd Roberts.

It encourages me, too, to speak about education that Lloyd Roberts was himself a very broadly educated man. That he should have prepared an edition of the 'Religio Medici' is not, perhaps, surprising since that was written by a remarkable doctor. But that he should have moved so far from his own field as to write about Dante is an example of a breadth of scholarship and a sense of value that is an inspiration to the educator.

There is, perhaps, a further reason why the subject of education is an appropriate one on which to address this body, for medical education as it is at present organized exemplifies, if I may be bold enough to say so, both some of the best and some of the worst educational practices. In the obituaries of Lloyd Roberts one reads of his apprenticeship first to one practitioner and then to another, and this element of apprenticeship which still dominates higher education in medicine, by which the young doctor, if he is fortunate, works with successive masters of his craft, whom he can often come to admire as people, is surely giving him one of the truest educational experiences anyone can have. On the other hand, the sheer amount of memorization, and its divorce from the actual patient, that is still characteristic of some

Q

medical education, is a feature that cannot but cause some questioning in the mind of the modern educator.

But it is not my wish to comment on medical education, were I competent to do so. I have chosen a larger theme in attempting to look at some of the problems and opportunities that face our educational system today. My nominal subject is the next ten years in education, but I am really thinking of a more distant horizon, say that of the year 2000. For it is then that the young people we are teaching will be living and active. It is in the next millenium that many of the teachers we are now producing will still be at the height of their powers, and the kind of skill, knowledge and idealism which they will bring to the problems of that time will depend on the decisions we take now.

Aims of Education

Let me, then, begin with some quite general remarks about the aims of education. It is, in the first place, a process which embodies a number of different, and in some ways contradictory, functions. It is the means by which a society seeks to perpetuate certain values and to make its citizens inheritors of a great tradition. But it is also the means by which new knowledge is discovered and new interpretations put on established ideas. It has both a conservative function (and I use the adjective in the best sense) and a revolutionary one, and I use that word in the best sense too. It must clearly produce people who will serve their society whether as doctors or civil servants or plumbers, but it must also try to produce—or at any rate not to stifle—the urge to question presuppositions. It must to some extent give its parent society what it wants: it must also try to discover what are the right things, and to make that society want them. We must never forget (particularly when one is over 60 and the arteries are hardening) that the two greatest teachers were both killed by their contemporaries because they encouraged this questioning—and indeed one of the two specific charges against Socrates was that he was a teacher, and corrupted the young men. It is the attempt to reconcile these various functions that makes a study of the aims and methods of education a particularly useful bridge between a past embodying, in spite of its errors and its cruelties, incomparable revelations of wisdom and beauty, and a future of which our pupils will be the architects.

At no time in history has it been more important that we should concern ourselves with education, because at no time have the changes through which we are passing been more profound or more rapid.

That platitude could have been, and indeed in various more literary forms has been, uttered during a number of previous epochs, and with truth. The turbulence of ideas in the medieval world can be seen both in the foundation of universities and in the disorders that often affected them. The conflicts of authorities and of classes, coupled with a great tide of new knowledge that occurred in the sixteenth and seventeenth centuries, made educational change a matter of concern to some of the best minds, and produced, for example, on the one hand the Society of Jesus, and on the other the nonconformist academies. The educational writers of the nineteenth century saw themselves, rightly, as living in a time of moral and intellectual flux—and the result was two of the greatest books on education; I mean, of course, Matthew Arnold's *Culture and Anarchy* and Newman's *Idea of a University*. It is true that the actual practice of education often failed society, so that we see the corrupt and inefficient universities of the eighteenth and early nineteenth centuries, and we can read about them in, for example, two of the great autobiographies, those of Gibbon and Mark Pattison. The sense of rapid change was in the minds of intelligent men. Yet as we look back on those revolutionary periods and look forward to our own future we really have some justice for regarding ours as a time more revolutionary in ideas and demanding perhaps greater changes in practice. The year 2000 is merely, of course, a symbol of a future which the figures make comfortably remote and yet will be a year in which, as I have said, our pupils will be at their prime, and when, and this is a still more alarming thought, teachers already well established in the schools will still be teaching. What are the factors which make it so certain that the world for which they will have to prepare their pupils is so radically different from our own, that makes us so certain that we are not simply repeating the cry, whether of hope or despair, when we say that never before has the fact of change made such revolutionary demands on the educational process?

I want to consider some of those factors under three heads. The first is the amount of knowledge; the second the development of technology; and the third, changes in society itself.

The Amount of Knowledge

It is a truism to say that in the last century and particularly in the last thirty years the sheer amount of knowledge that exists has increased with explosive force. Since the new-knowledge industry, called research, came into existence, say, fifty years ago, there has been discovered in sheer bulk more than in the whole of man's previous history. Truism though this is, it cannot be overemphasized. Let me illustrate it by a homely example: my own. I took a degree in chemistry in 1930. If I look at the papers set in chemistry today I obviously cannot do them: I would not expect to. But that is not the point: what is significant is that I never *could* have done them, since at least two-thirds of the questions are concerned with knowledge that simply did not exist when I was a student. And how obvious this is in the field of medicine! What would a Lloyd Roberts, or even an Osler or a Trotter have made of a state of affairs in which every pre-clinical student must understand, or at least memorize, the mysteries of the Krebs cycle? Would they have recognized their own profession when the experience, the flair, the eyes and hands of the diagnostician are supplemented, if, thank God, not yet supplanted, by an array of electronic gadgetry that raises its own moral problems by forcing us to ask how much of it should be devoted to any one patient? And if this knowledge explosion is most obvious, perhaps, in science, it is true in great degree of every subject. It is a phenomenon that obviously has profound educational implications, into all of which I have no time to go. It makes it imperative, for example, that we must create a machinery of in-service training for all professions, not least for teachers, on a scale that we have never contemplated. Into the minds of some people there is creeping a conviction that we must diminish the effort we put into research, or at any rate concentrate on synthesis and reinterpretation rather than on an accumulation of facts, lest the pursuit of knowledge grind to a halt overwhelmed by the sheer bulk of irretrievable and largely insignificant information. But the main conclusion is that we must inevitably become more specialized if we are to have any comprehension of what is now known in our own field.

But there is another side to this problem. If one looks at the curriculum adopted by the greatest of schoolmasters, Thomas Arnold, a hundred years ago, we find that it consisted almost entirely of the classics, with some divinity and ancient history, mitigated by a very little mathematics, taught by a master of inferior status, and an hour or two of French taught by a visiting native. And this manifestly would not do for the year 1900 let alone 2000. How, it may be asked, can one understand a world that has shrunk as ours has, without modern history or geography or economics, or perhaps, above all, natural science? And of course there is always English literature! Further, our concept of education has grown wider as our pupils come from uneducated homes. Have they no eyes that they shall never see Piero even in reproduction: no ears that they never hear the G minor quintet: no hands that they shall never actually make things in wood or clay: no bodies that they shall not have physical education? Therefore, we say, quite clearly we must discard the hopelessly specialized curriculum of Arnold and give a broad general education. We have here one of the crucial paradoxes of education in our time. On the one side we must specialize more intensively to bring some of our pupils to the frontiers of knowledge, to adopt the normal cliché. On the other we must abjure specialization so that our pupils may be fitted to understand the breadth of questions on which a citizen of a twentieth-century democracy should have a view. How can the fashionable demand for 'participation' have any meaning unless it rests on hard knowledge? Yet it is the feeling that we increasingly live in a world too complex to understand and too impersonal to control that leads to some of the obvious strains in our society. The problem of what we mean by general education and how we are to give it, is one of the most intractable of our time and will become ever more acute, and will dominate some of our schools and universities for years to come. The common answer is to add subjects to the curriculum and in a way it is right. It is the answer given, for example, by my friend Professor F. S. Dainton as it was by Milton—who wanted a curriculum including almost everything from Greek to fortification. But it will not solve the problem, for it is ultimately absurd to think, say, that making chemistry a compulsory examination requirement in the sixth form will give anyone a grasp of modern science. I wish I had time to discuss these problems of the curriculum at greater length. All I can do is to say this. I believe that more important than a body of general information is the development of a quality of mind, tough, questioning, anxious to discover the truth and knowing how to set about doing so in at any rate one field. This I believe we can only do by pursuing one or two subjects to the maximum depth the pupil can take. We can surround this core by subjects taught not in depth but with great efficiency useful to him in his work or his life—for example Russian for the scientist. Finally, we must stimulate him to read for himself, to argue rationally and to be aware of some of the great seminal ideas over wider fields of experience even if in a more superficial way. That great American educator, Hutchins, had the idea of a programme based on the reading and discussion of a hundred great books. It is an idea that in a modified form might well be revived. But whatever our answer may be, I am convinced that experiment in the field of general education and hard discussion about what we mean by an educated man in the latter half of the twentieth century are among the most significant growth points of education over the next few decades.

The Development of Technology

The answers which we are able to find to these questions of the content and methods of education will colour our approach to the more general subjects to which I now turn. First, what is the relevance of technological change for education? In a way it is easy to underestimate this. For there are elements in the nature of man which transcend his physical environment and these are among the most important. I have no idea at all what a Cycladic islander was like three thousand years ago, except that his material and intellectual background was totally different from my own. But he was producing works of plastic art that have exactly the same effect on me as those of a Chinaman in the seventh century or an inhabitant of Tuscany in the fifteenth or as Henry Moore has today. A Greek of the fifth century before Christ was writing about some moral problems that are recognizably the same as those, say, of Henry James, a Europeanized American of the nineteenth century. There are elements in human experience that leap across centuries and cultures and make the material environment irrelevant. But admitting these common elements of human experience, which it is one of the greatest tasks of education to reveal to our pupils, there are other important ways in which the real fabric of our thought is being altered by material change, in some ways for the worse. This may well be happening in the field of communication as it began happening in the sixteenth century. If printing had a significant effect on the Reformation, so did the development of the thermionic valve on politics from 1925 onwards, for it made it possible for a Hitler to address tens of thousands of people. What in the long run is going to be the effect of television not only on politics but on thought generally? We do not know. It is easy to be pessimistic about it, but on the credit side one must put its genuine power for adult education, as one of your previous lecturers, the Chancellor of my own university, Lord Clark, has recently shown in a superlative way in his series on Civilization. But one must be honest and say that a medium which encourages even some of its more serious performers to encapsulate a very difficult idea in something under two minutes of speech, and if he oversteps it to cut him off, and which subjects an air-weary politician to making a statement of policy on the tarmac, must lead to a trivialization of great matters. Further, by its very immediacy, its necessity to find some telegenic events, it lends an air of crisis to events which a previous generation would have had time to get into perspective. And by its techniques of interviewing, though some may claim them as triumphs of participatory democracy, others will feel that they are designed to create a distrust of democratic leadership, because not all statesmen can answer the loaded question with the slick smirk of the disc jockey. Here is one particular field in which the quality of life is being quite certainly changed by technological advance. Another obvious example is in the field of sexual morality. The discovery of a completely efficient contraceptive device must inevitably alter society's attitudes to sexual relationships.

There is much to be said on the credit side. The most moral of us have in the past professed a morality which we knew to be disingenuous (and to some extent we still do) because we knew that nothing could save many millions from starvation or from lives of labour little better than those of animals. I have myself just returned from Pakistan and, contemplating the lives of the teeming millions of the Eastern region, I was at times tempted to wonder what I really meant when I talked of the essential dignity and brotherhood of men. But we do now know that, given the will, science is at any rate increasingly giving us the means to make that profession far less of a hypocrisy than it has ever been. Our morality can no longer shelter behind the sheer technical impossibility of making happier the lives of the majority of mankind. Here, both for better and for worse, we have examples, and there are many more (I have resolutely not even mentioned the bomb), where technological change does not alter simply the amenities of life, but the whole climate of possibility in which intellectual and moral decisions can be made. It will become increasingly necessary for the problems raised by this technological revolution to be discussed in our classrooms and lecture rooms at levels appropriate to the various abilities of our pupils.

Changes in Society

We are naturally led by this all-too-superficial reference to social changes arising from technology to the much wider questions that the next thirty years will bring in the relations between education and society. Let us once more look back, to get some perspective in our discussion. Society has nearly always tried to educate a minority of socially useful people. The medieval church was unusually democratic in that it would occasionally identify and educate a boy, even from a poor home, so that he might even become a Pope. The society of the Renaissance with its emphasis on hereditary aristocracy produced a Castiglione with his curriculum for a courtier. The education of the eighteenth century designed to produce a gentleman ignored Locke and produced at its best a common culture of an educated class that was rigidly classical in content. In the early years of the nineteenth century men began for the first time to consider seriously the education of the majority of the population and, with some exceptions, even then in the bare essentials of literacy. The movements of the nineteenth century towards a universal literacy and sometimes to something more, inspired by working-class movements, by the Church, by the economic need for an educated working class, and most important of all by the growth of democratic ideas, led to educational change on a wider scale than ever before in history. The Act of 1870, though it did not itself make elementary education free and compulsory, made this inevitable in a few years. The Act of 1902, moulded by the greatest and too little known of civil servants, Morant, made secondary education of a kind that seemed to him, a Wykehamist, the highest form of secondary education, accessible to an elite of the able. And finally the Act of 1944 opened the doors of secondary education to all. What changes in attitudes towards a democratic society, what modifications in technique, what a revolution in the function of the state have I summarized in those three dates! And now we have opened the way to some kind of tertiary education, whether in university or polytechnic, whether in college of education or adult class, by removing at any rate the most obvious financial barriers. Let me say something about the new world we are entering, in which higher education of some kind is regarded as a right and not a privilege. The expansion of higher education beyond the school stage will, without doubt, be one of the dominant features of the next few decades. It raises a variety of very difficult questions to which answers will have to be found. One, for example, is the kind of institutions appropriate to the increasing number of young people in this tier of education. At present we have established a binary system with autonomous universities on the one hand and on the other colleges of education, of art and a growing number of polytechnics already doing work of degree standard. What we have not decided is what proportion of the population involved should go to one kind of institution rather than another, and why, and this is clearly bound up with very difficult questions as to whether existing universities should expand, some of them very greatly, or whether new ones should be created. That some such expansion should occur I am convinced. That the number of those going to a university, as I would interpret the term, should increase proportionately with the number of those possessing the required paper qualification is something about which I am more doubtful. A university course, with its rigour, its emphasis on independent work, its assumption of a positive love of learning, demands a strength of motive that not all of those technically qualified may possess, and they may well be happier in institutions whose work is more obviously related to the immediate and the concrete.

The very massive developments in the sheer quantity of education over the past century have arisen not simply from economic needs but also from political sentiments. They are natural results of the growth during the nineteenth century of a whole complex of ideas associated with the word 'democracy'. There are two particular aspects of that word, the educational implications of which I want to remind you. The first is that a democratic philosophy involves a belief in liberty and this belief in turn has two different meanings for education. In the first place it has led to changing attitudes in the schools and elsewhere, attitudes which are very loosely associated with the word libertarianism. In the sense that these attitudes have made schools much happier places than they once were, and replaced rigid discipline by attitudes of mutual respect between teacher and pupil, I myself welcome them, believe that they lead actually to greater efficiency and trust that they will continue in spite of what may be written in a Black Paper. In the sense that a misinterpretation of them leads to a distrust of all authority as such, even the authority that comes from manifestly greater knowledge and experience, I believe that they may be harmful. There can be no doubt that the next decades will involve a constant dialogue as to the proper methods of government of schools and colleges, and the proper means by which decisions should be made. What the educator must strive to ensure is that these discussions rest on knowledge and on reason. This dialogue is further complicated by the fact that the growth of democratic sentiment and the magnitude of the whole educational system makes it inevitable that the state should play an ever-increasing part in every kind of education. This is a process that rouses in some profound alarm, particularly in the universities. I myself view this movement with less apprehension than many of my friends. As I see it, one of the main tasks, if the educational system of thirty years hence is to meet its obligations adequately, is to decide exactly what are the areas in which the freedom of academic institutions and individuals is most vital. If they become simply places in which the material and manpower needs of society are met as cheaply as possible then we shall have lost something of priceless value. For in a world where religion has lost its universal authority, places of education, and particularly of higher education, have become the chief custodians and interpreters of value in society, and such a function can only be pursued in an atmosphere of responsible freedom. The responsibility of such places is not only to the state: it is also to a tradition of culture and to the pursuit of truth.

One other very powerful element in the word 'democracy' as we normally use it is the idea of equality. I have, I fear, no time to pursue the very profound implications of this word for education as I would wish. Some of them conflict with the no less democratic belief in liberty. To take an obvious example, one controversy that will be with us for many years is whether it is right that some people should be free to buy an education for their children different from, and in some ways perhaps better than, that provided freely by the state. It is obvious that here the two central ideas of democracy are in conflict. My other fear is lest a humane and in some fields justifiable belief in equality may lead us to undervalue excellence, and lest we create an institutional framework which makes it more rather than less difficult for great natural talents to flourish. It is, indeed, for us the central problem of education in the next twenty or thirty years to attempt to reconcile the demands of an increasingly democratic society for both freedom and equality, and especially to reconcile its equalitarian tendencies with a recognition and fostering of excellence. Thus in my own field of higher education one of the greatest of American educators and scientists, Lee du Bridge, has said:

It is important to the national interest to have many good universities, and it is desirable for every college and university to get a little better. But it is equally important that there be a few institutions of really superb quality. We must for the sake of future generations have a few outstanding leaders, a few institutions that are blazing the trail of the future.

This I believe to be profoundly true. The crucial problem on which the quality of our life will in fact depend is to win acceptance for such heterogeneity, such a recognition of a hierarchy, with the administrative arrangements that go with it, in a society that is nominally committed to egalitarianism.

The reconciliation if it is achieved will lie in giving a greater reality to the conception of equality of opportunity, rather than in attempting to behave as though individual differences of endowment did not exist. And that phrase brings me to my last line of thought. We are coming to realize more and more clearly the fact that we expect too much from education, in the sense that however equal we make educational opportunity, however much we improve our schools, their influence is far from predominant when compared with that of the home and of the subculture in which the child lives. We cannot really talk about equality of opportunity between the child from the good home, with books and music and rational conversation, and that from the overcrowded tenement with feckless or indifferent or incompetent parents, however well-meaning, whose very vocabulary is limited. We can and do and must struggle to redress the balance by widening the activities of our schools. We surprisingly often have our successes with the child of exceptional endowments. But in some ways our task is becoming more difficult by the dis-educative effects of the life and culture of our great cities. We delude ourselves if we believe that education by itself can bring about further immense social progress. It must be seen as but one part of a great movement to enrich the lives of communities. It may be heretical for a teacher to say so, but today I feel that an education act, whatever is in it, will actually do less for education and for the moral and intellectual as well as the physical well-being of our children than, for example, the implementation of the Seebohm Report. We require more fundamental measures than tinkering with school organization, a process that may actually be harmful, if the year 2000 is to see ours a more just society. This is not simply an abdication of responsibility by the teacher: it is a statement of what every teacher knows; that for education to be effective it must be supported by the family and the community and must regard itself as only one of the agencies which seek to support those institutions.

Faced with such problems, we may be forgiven if we despair, as one of the greatest of modern poets, T. S. Eliot, despaired when he wrote:

We can assert with some confidence that our own period is one of decline; that the standards of culture are lower than they were fifty years ago; and that the evidences of this decline are visible in every department of human activity. . . . And we know that whether education can foster and improve culture, it can surely adulterate and degrade it. For there is no doubt that in our headlong rush to educate everybody we are lowering our standards, and more and more abandoning the study of those subjects by which the essentials of our culture are transmitted, destroying our ancient edifices to make ready the ground upon which the barbarian nomads of the future will encamp in their mechanised caravans.

And Eliot may, of course, be right. The kind of society which mass education and scientific technology together create, even if it does not destroy itself physically, may be one in which human values have declined: in which a candyfloss culture, dominated by the standards of an uncritical majority manipulated by the ad-man, has become dominant. In other words education may lose, and if it does it will be towards some kind of Philistine totalitarianism that we shall move.

But though most of us have felt at times as Eliot felt, no teacher can remain a pessimist or he would give up his job. We have got to believe that we can reconcile the idea of a more humane, more just, more materially affluent society with a belief in standards of excellence. What we must never do is to lose our nerve, and believe that matters of judgement in questions of value, whether in æsthetics or morals or truth, can be settled by majority votes. The teacher, of all men, must regard his task as a continuous battle to perceive by self-education the right values more clearly, to proclaim them, and to defend them by rational means even if he seems to have lost.

Let me end by quoting one of my favourite passages written over a century ago by the greatest analyst of the most powerful democracy the world has known:

I am full of apprehension and of hopes. I perceive mighty dangers which it is possible to ward off, mighty evils which may be avoided or alleviated; and I cling with a firmer hold to the belief that for the democratic nations to be virtuous and prosperous they require but to will it. . . . The nations of our time cannot prevent the conditions of man from becoming equal; but it depends upon ourselves whether the principle of equality is to lead them to servitude or freedom, to knowledge or barbarism, to prosperity or wretchedness.

It is in the spirit of that passage from Tocqueville that I, as a teacher, want us to contemplate the past, to judge the present and to approach the future, daunting though it may sometimes seem. It is a sentiment that must appeal to this Society, dedicated as it is both to the advancement of knowledge and to the well-being of mankind.